In grateful memory
of two fathers:
Joseph
and
"George"

LOVE OR HONOR

For Pat McGrady
With all best wishes
and blessings —
Joan Barthel

1

Liz raised her head from the pillow when the alarm buzzed. She groaned, and folded the pillow in half, covering her ear. "Don't forget to comb your hair," she said in a muffled voice.

Chris was out of bed quickly; years of cop's hours had trained him to come instantly awake. When he emerged from the shower, his hair was still wet, flinging drops of water across her pillow as he leaned down to kiss the top of her head. "Comb your hair," Liz murmured. "I will," Chris promised. "See you tonight." Then he remembered that she had a weekend booking at a club in the Catskills. "See you Monday," he said.

In the kitchen, he poured a glass of orange juice, but he didn't bother making coffee. There'd be plenty downtown. Brass or patrolmen, hairbags or rookies, cops survived on coffee.

He stood at the kitchen window, looking down at the quiet courtyard. Three young children, holding hands, were walking along the pathway to the street, with two mothers behind them carrying lunchboxes. An elderly man in white shorts and windbreaker was jogging on the opposite path, taking high, lengthy strides, as though in slow motion.

Watching this peaceful picture, Chris felt peaceful. As he set out from his apartment in Forest Hills to take the subway into Manhattan, he felt settled and comfortable. His second wedding anniversary was coming up; he was happy in his work with the street unit, doing "buy and bust" with drug pushers. After some rocky times in both his personal and his professional life, he felt he'd straightened out. He felt good about himself.

Still, he couldn't help worrying, as the train rumbled through Queens, into the city, about why he had been summoned to a meeting at the Intelligence Division. He hadn't a clue. He'd been working the street when the message had come clattering over the teletype at the station: P O ANASTOS REPORT INTEL DIV 0900 HRS FRI.

All afternoon, cops passing in and out of the station had speculated and gossiped. The teletype directive couldn't mean a simple transfer; that order would have been spelled out on the wire, and wouldn't have involved the Intelligence Division. Anastos wasn't due for a promotion; in his seven years with the New York Police Department, he'd gone quickly, within the first eighteen months, from uniform into plainclothes, and was successfully settled in the anticrime unit. It was too soon for another step up, even for a guy like Anastos. More likely, he was in trouble, some cops thought. Some of them hoped so.

Christian Anastos was thirty-three years old. He had a mop of black curly hair, bright dark eyes, a playful sense of humor and a flaring Mediterranean temper—once, when he was losing a burglar who was escaping over a fence, Chris had smashed the concrete wall below the fence so hard, in frustration and fury, that he'd broken his hand.

That had happened in his early days at the 40th Precinct—the 4-oh—when he'd taken every chase, every case, very personally, when he'd viewed it as his specific mission to save, maybe not the whole world, but this sordid wedge of it in the South Bronx. In that desolate neighborhood above Harlem, where the neighboring 41st Precinct was "Fort Apache," the 4-oh was "The Alamo." The label was not just a romantic flourish; the station house was often besieged, its doors barricaded against invaders, and buckets of water sometimes dumped from a second-floor window on the enemy below. Once, Chris was walking along the sidewalk when a garbage can filled with bricks was rolled off a rooftop, thundering to the pavement only about ten feet in front of him. When Chris and his partner Phil emerged from an apartment building where they'd spent about twenty minutes on a domestic dispute call, they found their radio car ablaze from a Molotov cocktail.

Even in quieter seasons, when the police themselves were not barraged, the South Bronx trembled. Every crime invented by man was practiced there, by experts and amateurs alike; only prostitution was uncommon, the neighborhood being too poor to support such a relatively expensive occupation. Armed robberies, rapes, and murders were abundant; more than once, during Chris's time there, the 4-oh recorded the first homicide of the new year. Cops came to expect that, a minute or two after midnight, somebody would be dead. On a day-to-day basis, people routinely wrapped thick chains around their television sets, then wound the end of the chain around the radiator. But there was not really a crisis of crime in the community. It was worse than that. Violence had passed beyond crisis, to become accepted as part of the tattered fabric of everyday life.

The 4-oh was not a plum assignment, so a guy who had screwed up somewhere else—too much drinking, too many times caught cooping—sleeping on duty—maybe suspected of taking payoffs—was likely to be "dumped," moved from a quiet precinct to a high-crime post. It seemed a curious rationale, considering that such a desperate neighborhood called for the best men, not the misfits; considering that in the barrooms and back alleys, numbers runners and drug dealers were more than willing to cooperate with the police. In such a grievous climate, a man with a drinking problem was likely to find more sorrows he needed to drown. Sometimes, though, a man who was dumped into the 4-oh was indeed shocked into good behavior. One boss was famous for his ritual of bringing out a full bottle of bourbon every morning and setting it on his desk with an emphatic thump. The bottle was taped shut, with wide brown masking tape. For years the lieutenant kept the bottle on his desk to remind himself never to take another drink, and as far as anyone could tell, he never did.

Chris liked the 4-oh. He'd asked to be assigned to either the South Bronx or to Harlem—definitely a quirk, some guys thought—where he'd have real work to do. He wasn't a bleeding heart; he was tough when he had to be, and stubborn when he didn't have to be. But he didn't become hardened, as some cops did, defensively. Where poverty bred despair, and despair nurtured criminals, he considered the plight of people in the neighborhood as a crime in itself. "They're trapped. They're victims," he said. "I really believe that! Maybe one out of a hundred can make it out of here, with some kind of talent, but the others are trapped here forever. If they have jobs at all, they're low-paying jobs, in a factory or in a sweatshop or washing dishes. They have nothing to look forward to. You could stand on a street corner for a year and ask every person who passes, 'Did you see the play, *A Chorus Line?*' and not one of them would say yes."

He was particularly aware of the problems of families, when he saw the long lines of women at bus stops, early in the morning, never any men. The women were more employable as chambermaids, in sweatshops, while the men stayed behind to linger on stoops, nowhere to go. It was destructive to the family, Chris knew, and he was careful never to degrade a Puerto Rican man; if he stopped a guy for speeding and saw a woman and some kids in the car, he called him "Mister." In fact, Chris gave out fewer than ten traffic summonses in seven years, and one of those he paid himself. He'd written a ticket for double-parking, one Christmas Eve; when the man came out of a store, children in tow, his face crumpled in such dismay that Chris took it back. He didn't void it, which would have looked suspiciously like a payoff; he got a money order and mailed it in.

He didn't perceive himself as a social worker, just as a guy who had the authority and sometimes the power to help. He knew how to get heat turned on in a building where families huddled around the gas burners on the kitchen stove for warmth. He knew where to call when a tenement's water pipe burst and the slumlord was not to be found. He was annoyed at cops who refused to do these things, who pointed out that it wasn't their job. "We're the authority figures on the street," Chris argued, "sometimes the only ones they can turn to. Why not make a phone call?" And they, in turn, were annoyed at him, for sometimes making them look lazy or indifferent.

He liked working the streets, getting to know the people, and he had become so experienced that he was once called to a meeting with the brass to discuss a bizarre problem. A street gang, a fraction of the Young Lords, had taken over a park at 145th Street—literally taken it over, erecting a sign that said PEOPLE'S PARK, then stationing two guards at the entrance so people couldn't come in, turning it into their private preserve for smoking pot, drinking wine and planning revolution. Storming the park was ruled out. "Heads would be broken," the chief of the Bronx, Tony Bouza, warned. "Go in and see what you can do about it, Chris."

At the stone steps leading up into the park, the guards looked at him with tight suspicion. "I don't have my weapon," he told them. "I want to talk to Frenchy." The guards huddled, then led him into the center of the park. Frenchy knew Chris from the street. Although Chris had locked up a few of the gang members, he'd gotten jobs for a couple of them, too, and had enticed one fellow into entering an addiction treatment center. Chris and Frenchy weren't friends, but there was a degree of trust. "I felt like John Wayne meeting with the Indians," Chris said, back at the station.

He and Frenchy negotiated a truce: The gang could use

the park, undisturbed, from six to ten A.M., then they were to clear out, leaving it to the neighborhood kids from eleven to four. All summer Chris visited the park twice a day, maintaining that fragile but workable peace. No heads were broken. He didn't delude himself about his relationship with the gang, at least not after his picture turned up in their newsletter captioned PIG OF THE WEEK. But he didn't take it personally. He felt they were just gloating in the knowledge that they could finger him as a cop, even when he felt so thoroughly disguised: in that photo, wearing a raincoat and a floppy hat, leaning against a lamppost, smoking a cigar.

In spite of such successes, and partly because of them, Chris was not the most popular cop at the 4-oh—although he was not deeply disliked, and he'd made some close friends, especially his first partner, Phil. But quite a few of the guys on the roster regarded him with puzzled skepticism as a loner, an oddball, hard to figure out. It didn't help that he was a Greek among Irish, he opposed capital punishment, he carried *Bulfinch's Mythology* in his car at all times, and his heroes were Thomas Jefferson and Alexander the Great.

Yet he wasn't a philosopher or a scholar; he'd scraped through high school—three schools in four years—mostly because of his splendid memory, paying attention only to the subjects that interested him: history, music, and art. He was sentimental—an operatic aria could bring tears to his eyes—and a romantic, though not in a conventional sense. When he got his first maternity call and had to deliver the baby, all went well—he wiped the baby when it emerged, hit it on the back until it began to cry, laid it on the mother's thigh until the ambulance arrived, and the mother vowed to name the baby after Chris—yet he never liked to talk about it. He'd felt dizzy and lightheaded, and he thought it had been an awful sight.

He had a reckless streak and, in the beginning, a capacity for serious drinking that enabled him to hold his own, and then some, with other cops at the end of a shift. He'd been a street kid in New York, and he was not naïve.

But the streets he'd grown up in, in the 1940s and 1950s,

were not the streets he patrolled in the late sixties and now, in the seventies. Street life for Chris had meant stickball, stoopball, peashooters, and skelsey, a game like shuffleboard: You drew boxes with chalk on the pavement, filled bottle caps with melted wax, then tried to knock other kids' bottle-caps out of the squares. He wasn't a sissy: He belonged to a tough-enough gang, the Dukes of Manhattan, for about a year, wearing a black-and-yellow sweater with his name stitched on the pocket. He'd pulled fire alarms and opened fire hydrants. He'd broken off car aerials to make weapons for use against a rival gang, The Sportsmen. On a dare, he'd sauntered into a Woolworth's, grabbed a red-and-yellow magnet from the toy counter and dashed out of the store. He hadn't been caught, but he hadn't ventured back into that Woolworth's for two months; he was sure the manager would recognize him from the guilty look on his face. One summer he and a pal, Carlos, had made regular trips to a leather factory, where they'd scaled the high fence, dropped down into the yard and snitched scraps of leather. But they'd used the scraps to make wallets and wristbands, cutting their own patterns and sewing them by hand, with a commitment that would have warmed the heart of a youth worker. He was an innocent in a thoroughly innocent time.

When he came to the 4-oh, a street kid was one who used dope or sold it or both; heroin was the choice, then. A street kid no longer stole dime store trinkets, but television sets, and the store manager had reason to be afraid of *him*. The carpet guns of Chris's boyhood, though not innocuous—a piece of wood whittled into a gun shape, and a heavy piece of linoleum latched into place with a rubber band—were no match for the pieces flaunted by teenagers in the South Bronx.

In the twenty years between Chris's boyhood and the time he was sworn in, the world had changed. He found it amazing that the change had come so swiftly—not gradually, so a person could see it coming and maybe have time to prepare, to come to terms with it, but drastically, overnight. Innocence was trampled on streets that had been playgrounds and were now battlegrounds, sometimes killing grounds. In one short period, four bombs were discovered, planted in police cars. So many police call boxes were booby-trapped that the order came down not to use them; patrolmen were to carry a dime pasted in their memo books at all times, so they could telephone the station. A New York City Councilman asked the Governor to send in the National Guard at least part-time to supplement the police who, just after the assassination of Martin Luther King, Jr., were put on emergency schedule; twelve hours a day, six days a week.

Although it seemed to be the worst of times to be a cop —a season of pervasive despair—it was, in a way, the best of times for Chris. A season of possibilities. The need for law and structure was so visible that it gave him the sense of purpose he'd never known in his first assignment, the Rockaway Beach precinct, where his main job was chasing unlicensed vendors off the beach. He didn't care that the young hustlers were selling beer from coolers, but the merchants along the boardwalk complained so vigorously to the precinct boss that Chris had been given a quota. "If you don't give out ten summonses a day, I'll know you're taking a payoff," the boss warned. So Chris had no choice but to stalk the guys on the beach, who would hastily close their coolers and sit on them, trying to act nonchalant, when they saw him coming. He hated seeing that guilty look on their faces. He hated the tediousness of writing out each two-dollar summons. He hated getting sand in his shoes.

Chris didn't feel like a cop, and he didn't even look like a cop, much of the time; with a shortage of lockers at the station, he had to carry his uniform back and forth from home. He was so aggravated at the whole setup that he didn't bother with a garment bag; he just folded the uniform and carried it in a brown paper grocery bag in the trunk of his car.

He got so fed up with answering endless questions— "Where's the Ferris wheel?" "Where's the subway?" "Where's the toilet, Officer?"—that he filled out a Form 57, Request for Transfer, specifically asking for assignment to either Harlem or the South Bronx. Hearing stories of the work other cops had done there, or the work that cops they knew had done, made him envious; by comparison, he felt he wasn't doing police work at all. "If I'd wanted to spend my days on the beach, I'd have gotten myself a wagon and sold ice cream," he grumbled to guys at the precinct, who usually told him to shut up and count his blessings, usually in more colorful terms.

When summer ended and the beach emptied, it was even worse: the seemingly aimless patrolling, standing on deserted street corners. Until he finally got the long-awaited call from the guy who monitored the teletype—"Hey, Chrissie, you're going to the 4-oh in the Bronx!"—he had plenty of time and energy, after work, to play. He and a bachelor buddy dropped in one night at a lively place, a cocktail lounge with a bowling alley attached. They were in partial uniform—raincoats over uniform pants and shirts—and after they'd been drinking and laughing a while, they became friendly with a woman at the bar, Josie. She had a girlfriend with her.

Pretty soon, the women invited Chris and his buddy to come home with them, to Josie's friend's apartment. The women said they lived right next door to one another, on the same floor in the same nearby building. Josie seemed especially gleeful that Chris was a cop, and assured him that her husband would be out all night, playing cards. "Hey, I don't get involved with married women," Chris protested. But by and by, after some more drinks and some more laughs, the four of them went over to the girlfriend's apartment. They were all drinking, laughing, fooling around, when Josie's husband began hammering at the door, cursing, yelling, looking for his wife. Chris and his friend made an immediate exit through the second-floor window. Chris felt daredevil and rakish, rather like Errol Flynn. He felt he hadn't been in any great danger—although he knew, even then, that the place was a mob hangout.

In his very first week at the 4-oh, he'd made an arrest. It wasn't a big arrest; in fact, it was a measly little arrest. But as his first arrest, it was the first proof that he was indeed a cop, protector of the right, avenger of the wrong. And, as measly little arrests go, it was rather colorful.

He was assigned to duty at an elementary school where there had been serious discipline problems. He was standing at the window of a classroom when he saw a man opening the hood of a car and removing the battery. Chris knew that the teachers parked their cars there, and he knew the guy wasn't a teacher.

He raced out to the street. The thief saw him, dropped the battery in the snow, slammed the hood of the car and took off. Chris caught up with him and tackled him from behind. They fell down together. Chris's hat fell off, and they both rolled over it. The hat was bent totally out of shape. Chris pulled out the handcuffs and put them on, just as he'd been taught, the lecture running through his head: When you put the handcuffs on, be careful, because that's their last moment of freedom. If they're going to try anything, they're going to try it then. Do it as quickly as possible. Try to get the cuffs on one hand, at least, very quickly. Always cuff them behind their back, which makes it much harder to run. Besides, if they're cuffed in front, they could raise their cuffed hands and swing at you, or smash you in the face with the hardware. Try to get them down on the floor, facedown, with your knee in their back.

Chris did all that. He was just pulling the guy back up to his feet when a man came running toward them. "That's my car, Officer, and he was stealing my battery!" the man cried. Whereupon he took a swing at the man in handcuffs. "Hey, hold it, hold it, take it easy!" Chris yelled. "But that's my car, and he was stealing my battery!" the man cried. He was trying to throw more punches, as the shriek of sirens pierced the street. Someone from inside the school had called the precinct, saying a policeman was in trouble. The call had gone out as a ten-thirteen—assist patrolman—which cops respond to without delay. And thus half a dozen radio cars, sirens screaming, lights flashing, were converging on the crime scene, bumping into one another, skidding in the snow, hurrying to help the cop in such danger from a guy trying to steal a car battery.

At the station, Chris stood with his prisoner at the big desk on the raised platform in the front hall. "What do you have there, son?" the lieutenant asked.

"I have an arrest for petty larceny," Chris said proudly.

"Oh, so it's just a petty larceny you have there," the boss repeated in his thick brogue. He sounded disappointed. "But did he try to assault you, Officer?"

Chris hesitated. "Well, I had to tackle him," he said. The boss beamed. "Oh, so he assaulted you, isn't that correct?"

"Well, I guess so," Chris said uncertainly. The boss stepped down from the platform and put his arm around him. "Nice work, son," he said. At the end of the shift, a bunch of the guys took Chris across the street to McSherry's, the cops' 19th hole, where he was initiated as a member of the tribe.

He got his first medal when he was working temporarily in a car with another rookie, Andy Glover, one of the few black guys at the precinct then. They were the same age, with the same amount of experience: none. Andy had married young; he had a nine-year-old son and an infant daughter. Chris enjoyed working with Andy, who always seemed to see the bright side of life. Andy had an ear-to-ear grin, a sensational grin that split his face in half.

They were cruising down Willis Avenue one afternoon when they spotted a guy running out of a clothing store, a knife in his hand. Right behind him, a woman appeared in the doorway of the little shop, waving her hands wildly and screaming, "Holdup! He gimme holdup!"

Andy jumped out of the car and gave chase. Chris drove the car around the corner, up over the curb, and boxed them in. Andy tackled the guy and was trying to wrest away his knife when Chris rushed over and fell on both of them. Between the two of them, Chris and Andy disarmed the guy.

Andy cuffed him while Chris dug into his pocket for a tattered scrap of paper and read him his rights.

Chris and Andy took their prisoner in, and that was about it. They hadn't been in grave danger; still, the guy was armed, so they wrote a suitably interesting account of the incident for the lieutenant, who okayed it, added his comments and sent it downtown. Months later, a set of orders came up from Headquarters: GLOVER AND ANASTOS AWARDED EPD. The EPD—the Excellent Police Duty medal—was the lowest a cop could get, and there was no ceremony involved; Chris just went down to the Equipment Bureau and filled out a form for the property clerk, who handed him a medal as though Chris had just requisitioned a box of paper clips. Still, a medal was a medal, the first for both Chris and Andy. It was a small bar, green and white, worn above the badge on the uniform jacket. As a cop gathered more medals, the number on the bar would change. Chris would eventually earn thirty-two medals of varying degrees, but that first medal, the EPD, was always special to him, and so was Andy Glover.

When Chris was assigned to regular car duty with Phil, others considered them an extremely odd couple. True, they were both Greek, but after that, whatever did they have in common? Chris was a playboy, a regular at McSherry's; Phil was so straight that Chris teased him he should have become a priest.

Phil had wanted to be a cop as long as he could remember, since he was a schoolboy passing the policeman who stood at the corner of 85th Street and Third Avenue in Manhattan. When Phil was ten, he'd gone with his mother to visit his godmother, who lived at 68th and Third. While the grownups were visiting, Phil walked around the corner to the 19th Precinct on 67th Street, where the sign on the door said VISITORS WELCOME. Phil went in. "I'm a visitor," he told the man behind the desk. "Please take me on a tour of this police station."

The cop stared at him. Looking back on it, Phil thought he must have looked like Opie from *The Andy Griffith Show*. "Well, sure," the cop said. He showed Phil all around the first floor, including the holding pens in the back. "This is where we put the bad people," he told the wide-eyed boy. At the door, they shook hands. "I'm glad you want to be a policeman when you grow up," the cop told Phil. "Don't let anybody change your mind."

Phil took the exam as soon as he could, when he turned twenty, though he wasn't eligible for the Academy till twenty-one. He was doing an army stint as a medical corpsman when he flew back to New York on a furlough to take the exam, and he enrolled at the Academy just after his next birthday. Phil was serious, kind of old-fashioned: Describing how careful he'd been not to make any mistakes at the Academy, he said, "I was determined to mind my Ps and Qs." He was amazed at the kidding around that went on, even about weighty matters, and at what he considered "childish horseplay." But he kept a wry perspective on himself. "You have to remember," he told Chris, "I was considered a serious person when I was four years old."

Chris didn't find it surprising that he and Phil got on so well. He thought they were alter egos. Chris envied Phil for his stability; he thought Phil envied him for being so carefree. They made more arrests their first year, in uniform, than were made by plainclothes teams at the precinct. Phil called Chris "Butch" or "Partner." He was going to college at night, determined to earn his degree and thus qualify for the FBI. "You'll never make it," Chris teased. He knew Phil would do just about anything he made up his mind to do, but he kept hoping Phil would change his mind.

One sweltering summer day, another radio car pulled alongside theirs. A cop in that car handed Chris two cans of soda. Chris took the icy cans gratefully and passed one to Phil, who was driving. Chris pulled the tab and was about to drink when Phil spoke sternly.

"Did anybody pay for these sodas?"

Chris looked at the cop in the other car. "Did anybody pay for these sodas?"

When that cop shrugged, Phil threw his unopened can

out the window. Chris pressed the cold can wistfully against his cheek, then threw his can out the window, too.

Phil drove around the corner and stopped.

"Those sodas weren't paid for, and we don't accept anything that isn't paid for," Phil said.

"Right," Chris said.

"I'm not saying it's corruption to take a soda," Phil went on, "but it's better to make it an absolute rule not to take anything that isn't paid for."

"Right," Chris said.

"If you never take anything—anything at all—that isn't paid for, the other person is going to have more respect for you."

"Right," Chris said.

"I'm not criticizing you, Partner," Phil went on. "I'm just telling you this for your own good."

"That's right," Chris said.

"Now, if we're in a diner or someplace," Phil continued earnestly, "and somebody wants to give us a cup of coffee, we don't want to hurt his feelings. But if we have enough scruples not to take anything free, then we also have enough manners and tact to be able to say, 'Thank you so much, but I know you'll understand why I can't accept.' "

"Oh, you are *so* right, Dad!" Chris said to Phil, who was four years younger. "Can we please go home now?" And they both broke down laughing.

Chris wasn't such a stickler as Phil; he'd have drunk that soda without a qualm. But on his own, he'd confronted the issue already. On his first post in Rockaway, he'd walked the boardwalk one late shift, then had gone to the only place still open in the predawn hours, a tiny deli. "How are you, Officer?" the deli man said in a friendly way. "Fine," Chris said. "Give me a roast beef on rye with mustard and lettuce."

The man looked embarrassed. "Well, how about a cheese sandwich?" he said.

Chris stared at him. "I said a roast beef sandwich."

The man wiped his hands up and down on his apron,

nervously. "Well, Officer, roast beef—I mean, it's—it's very expensive."

Chris felt a little sick with humiliation, as he understood. "Look, I'm going to *pay* for this sandwich!" he said loudly. "And I want roast beef!"

After that, he was careful always to have his money in plain view, when he ordered something, though that didn't always work. At a coffee shop, a cashier told him, "We charge policemen half price." To make it worse, she said it very loudly, so that everybody in the line behind him heard her.

"You charge me the price you charge everybody else!" Chris said, just as loudly. "How much do I owe you? Five dollars? Here's the five dollars!" He threw the bill on the counter and stalked out, not waiting for change.

Although Phil was always willing to lecture Chris, and Chris was almost always willing to listen, neither lectured other cops. They went their own way together. Chris tried to get Phil to laugh a little more, with considerable success. Phil tried to get Chris to clean up his act, with somewhat less success. When Chris would open a pack of cigarettes in the car, Phil would reach over, grab the pack and crumple it, saying, "That's bad for you, Partner," and throw it out the window. Later, Chris would have to buy a new pack. Phil was constantly dieting, while Chris, slim and wiry, never had a weight problem. Sometimes they'd stop at a diner, where Chris would buy a burger and fries, take-out. He'd eat in the car, and when the bag was empty, Phil would stick his face in the bag, taking deep breaths.

Together they knew the satisfactions of police work, the unexpected adventures. One morning they stopped their car, seeing a crowd gathered in the middle of a block. A boy about ten years old was kneeling in the street, cradling a dog in his arms, crying. "My dog got hit," he told them. "Please help me and my dog." "Are you okay?" Phil asked. "Yeah, I'm okay, but something's the matter with my dog," the child said.

They put the boy and the dog in the backseat of the car

and drove to an animal hospital in the Bronx. "We don't take injuries," the receptionist told them. "We only take sick animals. We don't take accidents." Phil and Chris looked at one another; without speaking, they knew they were thinking the same thing. They all piled back in the car. With lights flashing and siren wailing, they hit the FDR Drive down to the Animal Medical Center in Manhattan, doing about a hundred miles per hour, Chris figured. They had the leeway to do whatever they thought necessary in an emergency; he radioed that they had an emergency. The Center took the dog and three days later, Chris drove back down, without sirens, to pick him up.

And together they knew the sorrow. Following an anonymous phone tip, they drove to an address just a few blocks from the station. It was an abandoned tenement building. There was no front door; the hallway was piled with rotting garbage and had been used as a toilet.

The upper floors were burned out; those stairs led nowhere. But there was a flight of steps leading down. Chris went first, picking his way carefully down the sagging steps to the basement. There was another long, narrow hallway, stretching toward the back. In the blackness, Chris shone his flashlight ahead as they walked cautiously along. Its beam picked out what seemed to be a large doll hanging from an overhead pipe. They got closer. A little girl in a white dress, barefoot, was dangling from the pipe, strangled with a coathanger.

Chris's second partner, Mac, was very different from Phil, more like Chris in his rambunctious nature. Working together in the anticrime unit, Chris and Mac were so effective, sometimes so colorful, that they'd caught the attention of the press. After they'd thwarted an ambush of a police car by members of The Bachelors gang—firebombs from a rooftop—and after they'd broken up a confrontation between The Bachelors and The Black Spades, one newspaper story labeled them "The Mod Squad." If they weren't quite the supermen one piece suggested—"After a few quick punches by Chris, the gunman was subdued and disarmed"—they were undeniably successful. They made a hundred arrests, from disorderly conduct to homicide, their first year.

Mac agreed with Chris that cops sometimes should go beyond the drawn lines of duty. One arrest they made—a fourteen-year-old boy who'd confessed to setting a schoolmate on fire—began to bother them. Although the boy insisted he'd done it, and even his parents said so—"Take him, he is bad!" the boy's father cried—Chris and Mac began to have doubts. They'd heard bits and pieces of information on the street, so they kept on the case for five months, mostly on their own time since, officially, the case was closed. Finally they were able to prove the boy innocent. He'd been too terrified and inarticulate to explain what had really happened: Both boys had been playing with matches, but the boy who was burned had started the fire, and an old feud between the families had led the injured boy's parents to accuse the other child. The Legal Aid attorney praised the cops in court, and a long newspaper story carried the banner headline: HERO COPS TIP SCALES OF JUSTICE FOR SLUM CHILD.

"I got lucky," Chris would mumble, embarrassed, when people congratulated him. Although he knew it was more than luck, and so did they, and he knew they knew, he did really believe that luck had been a factor in his life. He'd been lucky with Phil, who'd helped him get off to a good start in the department, which Chris felt had enabled him to take advantage, then, of his lucky break in being teamed with Mac. He was lucky to have met and married Liz. Before that, he was lucky to have had a father who, though Chris hadn't realized it at the time, had turned him in the right direction.

On the subway, heading down to the meeting, he hoped his luck wasn't running out.

He knew he wasn't in trouble, so he wasn't worried about a reprimand. He was clean as a whistle. What could they get him for? Coming back late from lunch? Not having his shoes shined? He'd been warned that, as an active cop, he could expect to be called down often to appear before the Civilian Complaint Review Board. But in seven years—nearly four hundred arrests—Chris had never been called down.

He was worried that this meeting might have something to do with the department's problems. The NYPD was still recovering from the revelations of widespread corruption that had led to the Knapp Commission hearings, which still cast a long shadow. Chris was angry that, in the public mind, all cops had been smeared. He'd heard one cop testify, on TV, that all cops commonly took money at Christmastime.

Chris was not deaf and dumb; he knew many cops who did. He knew payments on the side were often considered routine; under city law, a police officer was required to stand by when a marshal was carrying out an eviction order. Because the marshal needed that uniformed presence in order to do his job, the marshal customarily handed the cop a five-dollar bill. That sort of payoff was considered "clean money," as opposed to a payment, say, for letting someone continue to deal drugs. Chris wanted no part of any payoff, clean or otherwise, but when it came to corruption, he felt politicians were guiltier than cops, especially in the Bronx, where he felt they were bleeding the place dry. And you didn't see those politicians laying their lives on the line every day. You didn't see them chasing a guy down the street, knowing that, any minute, that guy might turn and blast them in the face.

When it came to police corruption, Chris didn't want to get involved. He just wanted to be left alone, to go his own honest way. But it was that attitude that Frank Serpico, the cop who'd gotten the investigation rolling, had considered a big part of the problem: squeaky-clean guys who looked the other way, out of a misguided sense of loyalty, when comrades messed around with shakedowns. Who didn't want to get involved. Chris had met Frank; the 4-oh was part of the 7th Division in the Bronx, where Serpico was mostly based. Because Chris had spent nearly all his time there, in both pre– and post–Knapp Commission days, he was afraid he was going to be assigned now to the Internal Affairs Division, whose job it was to sniff out corruption, to dig out the bad apples from the big blue barrel. He dreaded the idea of being asked to spy on other cops. He hoped desperately that nothing was going to happen at this meeting that would alter his life as a cop, the life he'd come to like so much.

Sometimes he was surprised he liked it so much, considering he'd never wanted to be a cop and, in fact, had never liked cops. He'd seen them come into his father's coffee shops, always looking for a free meal or a sandwich, a cup of coffee, just hanging around, and he'd complained to his father that he shouldn't let the cops take so much from him. George shook his head in rebuke. "The policemen are our friends," he told his son. "They protect us."

Chris just shrugged and said no more. He and his father seemed to have little to say to one another, as Chris was growing up. For long stretches, they didn't even see much of one another. George worked from before dawn until late at night, six and sometimes seven days a week. He never stopped working. He'd washed dishes in restaurant kitchens, scrubbed the floors of restaurant toilets, determined to buy a place of his own someday.

The family was living on East 117th Street, in the Italian section of Harlem, when Chris was born in 1941. But George was planning to move from the neighborhood as soon as he could manage it. He thought the area was not respectable enough. Men said to be gangsters strolled the streets, hanging out at the restaurants, conducting their shameful businesses, playing cards and drinking, even during the day, at their social clubs. Chris was only nine when George moved the family to a better neighborhood on the west side of Manhattan, a block from Central Park, but he'd already heard a name he thought was funny: Three-Finger Brown. All he knew then was that it was a silly name, and that his father had great contempt for this man and all of his kind. "I spit on them!" Chris heard his father say, one day, and although Chris never knew if any specific thing had provoked his father's unusual outburst, the depth of George's scorn for men who dishonored their family name was abundantly clear.

Family was not just an important thing to George and to Chris's mother, Katrina; it was everything. George never sat down and talked to Chris about it, but from conversations Chris overheard, through the years, scraps of information he picked up, he was able to piece the story together.

George was born in Cyprus, though he didn't know the exact date, and he had several brothers, though he didn't know exactly how many. Their mother died when George was young, and his stepmother whipped him. He never went to school. He spent his days tending sheep, until he ran away when he was about fourteen, working as a deckhand on a freighter that just happened to be going to Argentina. He spent about ten years there before coming to America. Chris was always impressed that his father spoke Spanish so fluently.

At home, everyone spoke Greek, although as Chris and his two sisters got older, they spoke English to one another. When Chris went to kindergarten, he didn't know a word of English. When his teacher said something to him, and he didn't respond, she gave him a little push, and he began to cry. His mother just stood there, looking frightened. The teacher pointed Katrina toward the door, indicating that she should leave. When Katrina didn't move, the teacher gave her a little push, too. By then, Chris was crying hysterically.

He settled down when Mrs. Fletcher handed him a box of crayons and a sheet of drawing paper. Crayons and paper were the only art supplies available in public school kindergartens in the forties, but that was all Chris needed. He had a natural ability in art: When the other children were drawing stick figures, Chris was drawing faces, with eyes and ears, noses and mouths and hair, everything in proportion. When the class picture was taken at the end of the school year, Chris was standing right next to Mrs. Fletcher, who had her arm around him.

Chris's liking for school continued through the early years, thanks to his talent for drawing and music. By third grade, he was designing the sets for class plays. The teacher would lay out large pieces of posterboard and tell Chris what to draw—for a Western setting, some trees, mountains, a campfire—then the other children would color in the drawings. In fifth grade, he joined the drum-and-bugle corps. He'd had a set of drumsticks since he was three years old—no drums, just the sticks—and he'd gone around the house banging enthusiastically on pots and pans, tables, chests of drawers, any available surface. His first public performance with the drum was disastrous: At a school parade, he banged his drum so fiercely that he put a hole in it, and marched with his arms at his side, crying. It didn't occur to him until it was too late that he could have turned the drum around, as it hung around his neck, and beat it on the other side.

Except for music and art, he was uninterested in school, restless and fidgety. He was always embarrassed, at the beginning of each school year, when the teacher would ask each child, "And what does your father do?" As it got close to his turn, Chris would begin to squirm. George was cook and counterman and part-owner of three coffee shops, and Chris would mumble, "My father works in a restaurant." He thought that sounded dumb, and he envied a kid who could say, proudly, "My father drives a truck!" Chris knew that his father spoke several languages—Turkish and Armenian, as well as Greek and Spanish—but he also knew that his father didn't understand how baseball was played. One Sunday, though, when his father walked over to Central Park with him, they ran a race, and George won. Chris was so delighted to see how fast his father could run that he didn't even mind losing. He talked about it so much at school that the other kids finally told him to shut up about it, they were tired of hearing him say that his father was the fastest runner in the whole world.

Katrina never learned English, but she spoke Italian as fluently as Greek. When she was orphaned in Greece, as a young child, she'd gone to live with relatives in Italy, before coming to this country. She lived with her Uncle Gus, who had a barbershop at 106th Street and Broadway. In tribute to the family roots, the shop was named The Riviera. George was living in a rooming house on the Upper West Side, getting haircuts at The Riviera. Katrina was earning money as a seamstress. Their marriage was arranged when she was eighteen and George was thirty-two.

As the only son, Chris felt a special responsibility to succeed, and he hated the feeling. His carefree, happy-go-lucky personality contrasted sharply with his father's sense of duty and discipline. Chris loved his father, and he didn't doubt that George loved him, but it was a remote, silent love. His mother told Chris that when he was an infant, George would pick him up from the cradle and hold him close. But the only time Chris remembered being in his father's arms was one Sunday morning when he was nine or ten. He had a terrible stomachache when he woke up. Katrina thought he was just trying to get out of going to church, so she told him to get up and get dressed, the pain would go away.

When Chris tried to get out of bed, his legs felt numb, and he vomited. His father picked him up and carried him down the stairs to the street, where he got a taxicab to take them to St. Luke's. Chris was operated on that afternoon for appendicitis. Except for that one time, Chris could not remember ever being physically close to his father. He could not remember hugging his father, or embracing him as men in the family embraced one another in greeting. Chris and George never seemed to be able to exchange any comfort with one another. They had never kissed.

When Chris was fourteen, George paid sixteen thousand dollars cash for a house in Queens. After that, Chris saw his father even less. George worked mostly at the coffee shop on West 45th Street in Manhattan, that he'd bought in partnership with Katrina's sister's husband. Chris barely tolerated junior high school, living for his music. He took drum lessons at a music studio in Astoria, and practiced for hours at home on a rubber pad glued to a piece of wood set at a slight angle, to strengthen his wrists and fingers and to perfect his timing. By sixteen he'd outgrown the Astoria teacher and was seeking out Gene Krupa clinics all over the city. He had acquired his first set of good drums—the bass, the snare, the floor tom, another pair of tom-toms, and the high-hats.

He passed the test for The High School of Music and Art, but a couple of his friends were going to Stuyvesant, where Chris had been accepted, too. So he went to Stuyvesant, and flunked out at the end of his first year because he didn't bother to keep up with the work. He went to a technical high school for a year, and found it tedious; since he didn't intend to be a greasemonkey all his life, he said, he transferred again, to William Cullen Bryant, where he graduated with a 2.8 average of a possible 4.0. He felt that was okay; George felt it could have been better. Chris didn't care, because his ambition was to play drums in a big band.

Two months before graduation, when he turned eighteen, Chris got a call from his father, telling him to come into the city. Chris tried to get out of it, but George insisted, so Chris took the subway in from Astoria and met George at his coffee shop near the Times Square stop. George was watching for him, and when Chris arrived, George told one of his helpers that he was going to take the rest of the day off. Chris was astonished, and a little aggravated; whatever George had called him in for was going to take the rest of the day. "What's going on, Pop?" he asked grumpily. "Why did you make me come in?" George said nothing, but led him outside, over to Broadway, then up Broadway to the Don Allen Chevrolet showroom at 58th Street. "Pick out a car," George said.

Chris was stunned. He knew his father was serious, because his father was always serious. Still, he felt dazed as he looked around the showroom. He couldn't keep his eyes off the red convertible, and he was just wondering if he dared mention it when his father, who had been watching him, spoke quietly. "You know something?" George said. "I like that red car, don't you?"

Chris watched his father pay cash for the car, $3100.

George sat in the front seat as Chris drove home. They didn't talk much; Chris was only thinking of showing off his car to all the girls. His father didn't lecture him about his driving; even going over the Queensboro Bridge, George didn't say, "Be careful."

With not the slightest desire to go to college, Chris floundered around. Using a forged cabaret license, he played drums at a strip joint on West 52nd Street, earning five dollars a night, telling his father he was playing at school dances. At home he practiced till his hands blistered and bled; he taped them and kept practicing. He had his union card—Local 802—but work as a freelance musician was so sporadic that when somebody suggested, "Why don't you get a hack license?" Chris thought, why not?

He drove a cab from three o'clock in the afternoon until three o'clock the next morning. He hated the way passengers treated him as a subordinate, the way they ordered him around. "Don't drive so fast! Don't drive so slow! Make a right! Make a left! Hey, what are you *doing?*" Sometimes people would peer at him and say, "You don't look like a cab driver." Usually he didn't respond, though he wanted to yell, "You're right, I'm not really a cab driver, I'm a musician!" He didn't, because he thought it was none of their business. If somebody pressed, he said he was married, with a wife and five kids, and was working to put himself through law school. He enjoyed making up bizarre stories, but he hated the job so much that at the end of two weeks he turned in his hack license.

When George put him to work in one of his restaurants, it was a disaster. As a cashier, Chris couldn't keep the tapes straight. As a waiter, he was so careless that customers complained. As a potato peeler, he was so bored that he paid some bums on the street a few dollars to come around to the back entrance and peel the potatoes for him.

When a guy he knew said he needed a drummer for a jazz combo, Chris thought it was the start of a solid musical career. They were booked at the Copa Lounge two nights a week—only big names played on weekends—and Chris loved it, though he didn't think much of Julie Podell, the owner. Podell wore a big ruby ring that he would bang down hard on the table when he wanted service. Chris thought Podell was a mean SOB, so he made it a point never to have a drink at the Copa. Instead, he'd go down the block to Chez Joey to have a drink and listen to the waiters sing opera. But the Copa was an interesting, lively place. Lots of off-duty cops came around, and so did flashy guys who wore diamond pinky rings and spent money so lavishly that Chris couldn't help but be impressed.

But that job ended, and he couldn't get another date. Jazz drummers, in those days of Elvis Presley and early rock, were not in demand. He enrolled in a course on how to sell life insurance and learned a remarkable pitch in which he never uttered the word "death." At the point in the pitch where the subject inevitably came up, he was to say, "And then, if anything should happen, God forbid . . ." He watched sales films and listened to a lecture by a super-salesman who flew in from California to display his style. Among other tactics, Chris learned always to have a crisp new ten-dollar bill sticking out of his jacket pocket, and when the potential customer mentioned it, Chris was to whip it out and declare, "Yes! and this money can be *yours*!" When he went out to sell, he liked the freedom of motion in the job, which gave him time for practicing drums and hanging out at the beach. "You have a marvelous tan," the office manager said to him suspiciously. "Well, I have a convertible, and I drive with the top down," Chris said. But he knew his days were numbered. He knew his father felt he was going nowhere; though they rarely saw one another, Chris could feel the weight of George's disappointment all around him, like a sad, heavy presence in the house. When he ran out of friends to sell insurance to, he joined the army.

When he came home on furlough, he spent his days playing drums, his nights drinking and hanging around clubs, sleeping late. He was sound asleep one morning when George came into his room and shook him awake. "Get up," George said brusquely. Chris followed him out to the kitchen, where George poured coffee for him, cooked eggs and made him eat, then showed him the notice in the morning paper about a walk-in test for the New York Police Department being given that day. "I want you to go down and take this test," George said.

Chris didn't care, one way or the other, and he was in no condition to argue. It was easier just to go down and take the test. He didn't take it seriously. He had no intention of becoming a cop. He'd never understood his father's fondness for cops, anyway.

Two mounted policemen had just tethered their horses on West 45th Street when a man in a stocking mask, with his gun still in his hand, ran out of the coffee shop. When he fired at them, they shot him down on the sidewalk. Inside, the masked man had fired just one shot from his .22-caliber Beretta, hitting George in the chest.

Chris immersed himself in police work with the fervor of a man who wanted no context for remorse, no time to ponder ironies.

2

When he daydreamed of becoming a gold-shield detective, Chris always saw it very clearly. He was wearing a trenchcoat. He was knocking firmly on a door. When the door opened, he was saying, also firmly, "Good morning. I'm Detective Anastos. I'm here to solve the homicide for you."

That spiffy image didn't survive the grittiness of the 4-oh, where he went from uniform into torn blue jeans and none-too-clean T-shirts, the better to make drug buys. So Chris always enjoyed going down to one of the police buildings in lower Manhattan, where the air of crisp efficiency and polish revived that old image. When he was recovering from hepatitis, he'd spent a few weeks on desk duty at headquarters, and although he hated the tedium of paperwork, he'd liked the feeling of the drafty old place. One day he'd run into a chief he'd known uptown, who was then a deputy to the police commissioner. They talked, then Chief Devine said, "Come with me." He led Chris through an outer office, past a couple of secretaries, into a huge room that reminded Chris of a magazine picture he'd seen of the Oval Office in the White House.

"See that desk?" Chief Devine said. "Know whose that is?"

"Yes, I know that desk," Chris said. "That's Teddy Roosevelt's desk."

"Oh, so you know about it," the chief said. "Good. This is the desk every police commissioner has used since before the turn of the century. Now you sit there."

A little hesitantly, Chris walked around the big desk and sat in the leather swivel chair.

"Put your feet up," the chief said. Chris wondered briefly if he should take off his shoes. "Put your feet up," Devine repeated.

Chris pushed back the chair a little and stretched his feet up on the desk. He leaned back in the chair. He grinned.

"Okay, that's enough," the chief said. On the way out, he put his arm around Chris. "You'll never be police commissioner," he informed him. "But now, when you're talking to somebody, you can truthfully say, 'Well, when I was sitting at the commissioner's desk . . .' "

At the Operations counter, separated from the foyer by a glass partition, Chris showed his ID and was given a visitor's pass. Not even seasoned veterans were allowed to roam freely at the Intelligence Divison, with its sensitive offices and sometimes explosive files. He was directed upstairs, to a conference room where the inspector and three other men were sitting at a long, rectangular table.

"Sit down, Chris," the inspector said casually, waving him to the chair opposite him, at the other end of the table. Chris gave a kind of semisalute, to take in all the men, and sat.

"I hear you speak Greek," the inspector said.

Chris was startled. "Uh, yeah. Yes, sir. I speak Greek. I mean, I'm Greek."

The inspector smiled. He folded his hands in front of him on the table. "Tell us about yourself, Chris," he said.

Chris was so taken aback he didn't know where to begin. You already know all about me, he felt like saying. He was sure the file folders on the table, in front of each man, were his reports, his entire dossier. One man, in fact, was reading something from the file, not even looking at Chris.

"Well, I started in Rockaway," Chris began. He sketched over his time there, and was talking in a rambling way about cases at the 4-oh when the man who was reading from the folder looked up.

"Do you consider yourself a hero?" he asked, not smiling.

Oh Jesus, Chris thought; he's seen that clip. He was stammering for a reply when the chief—Chris knew he was a chief from the stars on his jacket—spoke again. "We don't want a hero," he said sternly. "We don't need a superstar. We just need a good man."

"We need *you,* Chris," the inspector said. "And here's why." He listened intently, with growing amazement, as the inspector explained. They had reason to believe that crime within the Greek community, centered in Queens, was linked with the traditionally Italian-dominated crime network. The mob. The Mafia.

"We want you to go undercover and find out how the Greek network is structured and what they're doing with the Italians," the inspector said. "If anything."

"What would I be doing?" Chris asked.

"Your job would be to gather intelligence," the inspector said. "The DA wants to know all there is to know about what's going on among the Greeks, how they're organizing, what they're up to. You would go in and find out."

"Well, but—I'm really happy where I am," Chris said. "I have a good partner and, well, I just think I'd rather stay put."

The inspector smiled. He was a marine captain in the reserves, Chris knew, but he didn't look tough. He had a round chubby face and a friendly smile.

"You'll have carte blanche," the inspector continued, as though he hadn't even heard what Chris had said. "You'll have money to finance the operation, as much as you need. We'll leave that up to you, because you'll be working alone."

"It's not that," Chris said. "I wouldn't mind working alone. But I'm really happy where I am. I'm a street cop, and I really don't want to do something else. But thank you, sir. Thanks anyway." Nobody spoke. "Thank you," Chris said again.

"Chris, we have interviewed twenty men for this job," the inspector said. His voice was quiet. "And we don't want any of those men. We want you."

"I'd really rather stay in the Bronx, Inspector," Chris said, a bit desperately. "I like what I'm doing there, and I think I'm doing a good job. But thank you, anyway." For God's sake, stop saying thanks, he told himself.

Nobody spoke. One man drummed his fingers on the table, frowning. Chris felt he had to say something more. "I do undercover narcotics and street crimes," he said, feeling idiotic for telling them what he knew they already knew. "I like my work, and I like my partner, and I think we're doing good work, I really do." He stopped talking, not knowing what else in the world he could possibly say.

"Chris, we don't just *want* you for this job," the inspector said. "I'm saying we *need* you."

Chris took a long, deep breath. "I just don't think I want to do it, sir," he said. "I mean, I really don't. I—I'd have to think about it."

The inspector stopped smiling. "All right then, Chris," he said abruptly, in an irritated voice. "You think about it, and get back to me."

"Yes sir, thank you, Inspector," Chris said, getting up quickly. He nodded at the stern-faced men around the table, who just looked at him. He left the room as hastily as he could. He hurried out the front door, not speaking to anyone, and up the block to the subway. He was halfway back to Forest Hills when he realized they hadn't offered him coffee.

Back home, he called the station to say he was taking some lost time—time that was coming to him—and he'd be in on Monday. He changed into jeans and a sweatshirt and made a pot of coffee. His mind was made up. He knew he didn't want the job. But he thought he ought to wait a couple of hours before he called the inspector.

No *way* did he want the job. He'd told the truth when he said he was happy where he was, and he didn't want to rock that boat. He liked his work, and he liked the camaraderie of the 4-oh. He wasn't thinking now of the times he'd felt like an outcast; all he could think of now were the good times there. When a cop who had worked there, then had been transferred, had a family tragedy, the guys at the 4-oh had still cared. Jeff's house had caught fire one night, when he was at work. His ten-year-old son had died in the blaze, and his wife and two other children were badly burned. Chris and some guys had been sitting around, talking about what they could do to help, when somebody thought of a benefit. Several cops at the 4-oh had boxing experience, some with Golden Gloves. Chris had boxed with the Police Athletic League, as a kid.

They set up a gym in the 4-oh basement and half a dozen guys, including Chris, went in for some serious training. He sparred two, three hours a day for six weeks and got himself in top shape. At 160 pounds, he was matched with a cop named Ralph, same weight. Flyers went out to other precincts; as the word spread, tickets were snapped up, and the match had to be relocated from the 4-oh basement to the auditorium of the Methodist Church at 141st Street and Willis Avenue.

Four days before the event, Ralph broke his wrist. Nobody seemed available to take his place. Then a guy named Nolan said, "I'll box you, Chris."

Chris stared at him. Nolan was a very big person. He had a farm upstate where he spent his days off, pitching hay.

"Nolan, you've got to be kidding," Chris said mildly. "You outweigh me by fifty pounds."

"What's the matter?" Nolan demanded. "You afraid to fight me?"

"Nolan, you're fifty pounds heavier," Chris repeated.

Then the other guys chimed in. "C'mon, Chris, it's for Jeff's kids."

Even though the auditorium held six hundred people, the crowd was SRO. The commissioner came, the mayor, newspaper reporters, TV crews, the works. A regulation ring was set up, all very professional. Emergency Service stood by with oxygen. Cops sold beer and peanuts among the noisy throng as a doctor checked out the boxers.

Chris and Nolan had the first bout, three two-minute rounds. Each fighter was introduced, to deafening cheers. Chris clenched his hands above his head, in the big, black gloves, and tried to wave. Mac was the timekeeper. He banged the bell. Chris and Nolan came out swinging.

Hey, I'm a boxer! Chris thought with delight. He threw a quick jab, another quick jab. Nolan was swinging wide. Chris was right-handed, but he could box southpaw, and he hit Nolan with such a counterpunch that the crowd went wild. The bell rang. "You boxed his ears off!" Mac hissed to Chris.

But as he sat sweating in his corner, a towel draped around his shoulders, Chris felt he was in trouble. When he and Nolan faced off for the second round, he knew he was. "It was like I'd waved a red flag in front of a bull," Chris remembered. "I'd embarrassed him, and he was going to get even. We were both cops, but that night we were just two boxers. He came at me like a tank—charging, charging."

The third round was even worse. Nolan hit Chris so hard that he dislocated his shoulder. "Mac, Mac, hit the bell, hit the damn bell!" Chris yelled. "It's not two minutes yet!" Mac yelled back. So Chris spent the rest of the round just trying, basically, to keep out of Nolan's way.

Melba Tolliver, a television reporter, approached Chris afterward. "What makes a man like you get in that ring and take such punishment?" she asked. Chris clutched his right shoulder with his left hand and tried to smile for the camera. "The police department takes care of its own," he said stoutly, as a guy waved a can of beer back and forth in front of the camera. "Hey, what are you interviewing *him* for? He lost!" The following Sunday, the photograph in *The News* showed Chris bent over, grimacing in pain, obviously trying to dodge Nolan, who was just as obviously beating the hell out of him.

Still, it was a wonderful night, Chris always said—mentally, spiritually and morale-wise. A night that had made him glad to belong to the 4-oh. A night that, as he remembered it, made him absolutely sure he didn't want to leave.

The inspector's secretary said he wasn't available at the moment. Was there a message? Feeling relieved that he didn't have to speak to the inspector, and a bit ashamed at feeling so relieved, Chris said yes, there was a message. "Please tell him thanks, I really appreciate it, but I have to say no."

He was glad when that was over. Still, he felt restless as he roamed around the apartment, not knowing quite what to do with the rest of the day. He put an opera record on the stereo—Maria Callas, one of his favorites.

He wished he had his drums, which were packed away in a closet at his mother's house, because you couldn't play drums in an apartment building. When he was still in uniform, his drums had been a good backup. When he'd waded into a crowd on a street corner at the 4-oh, suspecting trouble, he found a bunch of young guys setting up a combo, with conga drums, bass, and guitar. "Hey, man, you're not going to break this up, are you?" one of them asked.

Chris looked around at the faces surrounding him, in the sudden silence. "Hey, no, I like music," he said cheerfully. "Let me sit in." He didn't know the conga, but what the heck, percussion is percussion, he thought. He took off his hat, sat on a garbage can lid and hit the drums. The crowd was clapping and stomping, making such a racket that Chris didn't notice the radio car pulling up. By the time he saw the gleam of gold on the cap of the cop headed his way, there was nothing he could do but sit there.

"What's going on here?" the sergeant demanded.

Chris thought fast. "Well, this is good public relations," he answered. "Kind of like—like community work with the people, you know?"

The sergeant snorted. "What an answer," he said. "How could I write you up? But don't let it happen again!"

Chris felt relieved that he'd escaped a reprimand, and he felt even better when, as he walked away, he heard someone say to the drummer, "Hey, man, you better burn your hands—the cop is better than you are!"

He wished he could talk to Phil. They talked on the phone at least once a week. But with the hour time difference, Phil would still be at his desk in St. Louis, and Chris didn't want to interrupt him there. He felt he could tell Phil anything, even something he wasn't supposed to talk about, but if there were people around, Phil wouldn't be able to talk freely.

Phil had made the FBI, as Chris had known he would. Early one Sunday morning, Chris had driven him to Penn Station, where Phil was catching a train to Quantico for training. They laughed and talked and reminisced over coffee at the station restaurant, then had walked to Track 25. At the very last minute, Phil threw his arms around Chris and said, "So long, Partner." Chris thought it must have looked like a scene from some B movie: two macho cops standing there, trying to look tough, tears running down their cheeks. After training, Phil was assigned to St. Louis. He and his wife, Judy, had adopted a baby boy and named him after Chris.

He wished Liz would call, but he was pretty sure she wouldn't. She got as wrapped up in her work as he did in his. It probably wouldn't even occur to her to call. Although their second anniversary was coming soon, Chris still felt a little like a newlywed, partly because he had waited so long to marry, partly because even after they were married, their careers often separated them, and whenever they got together, it seemed new.

Chris had always liked women and felt comfortable around them. He thought that, in general, women were smarter than men. But somehow the notion of marriage had eluded him all through his twenties; he'd been a late bloomer. He had his first date when he was seventeen, with a nice girl, Beth, who was in his civics class. Chris remembered those days, the late 1950s, as "Archie and Veronica time," sweet, nostalgic days when boys wore chinos, girls wore angora sweaters and pleated skirts, and everybody wore saddle shoes.

In those fond days, "going steady" meant hand-holding at the movies, the privilege of planting a chaste goodnight kiss on the cheek. Chris went steady with Beth for nearly two years, partly because it was much easier to have a steady girl than to keep gathering up his nerve to ask girls for dates. As unlikely as it seemed, for such an apparently confident guy, Chris was shy. In his whole life he'd never approached a girl to say hello or to ask her to dance. He could never bring himself to say, "Hi, my name's Chris, what's yours? and what are you doing tomorrow night?" He knew other guys did that, and he wished he could too, but for some reason, he absolutely couldn't.

When his family moved to Queens, Chris was considered a smart, streetwise guy from Manhattan by the boys who had grown up in an area that Chris considered "East Cupcake, USA." Wearing the Dukes of Manhattan black-and-yellow sweater helped his image along. But he was never as experienced or daring as he was thought to be. He'd grown up without any serious romance, and only one close call.

The year he graduated from high school, he was at a party at somebody's house, in the basement rec room. The lights were low; in the darkness, Chris and Beth were dancing to a record by The Platters. Chris had had several beers, then some jug wine, and as he and Beth danced "The Fish"—a close, inside kind of dance—it suddenly seemed to both of them that it was a swell idea to drive down to Delaware or Maryland, where they could be married right away, without a waiting period. They were heading south in his red car, Beth snuggled up against him, when whoosh! his head suddenly cleared. What the heck am I doing? he asked himself, and he made a sharp U-turn at the next break in the divided highway.

Once he began playing in nightclubs, approaching women was no longer a problem. Women approached him. For some reason, women seemed drawn to drummers. He found it astonishing that they would just walk up to him and stand there, openly flirting, sometimes when they had a guy waiting back at their table. He remembered one lady who had kept reaching out to try to touch his hair, telling him over and over that his curls were very sexy.

That surprised him, too, because he'd always hated his curly hair. Once, when he was scuffling with another boy on the street, a neighbor had leaned out her window and, seeing Chris only from the back, with his black curls tumbling to the collar of the pink shirt Katrina had made for him, she had screamed at the other boy, whom she knew: "Jimmy! You, Jimmy! You stop hitting that girl!" Chris was so mortified that he'd gone to a barbershop to have his hair straightened. Afterward, though his hair wasn't really curly anymore, it wasn't what you would call straight, either; it sort of stuck out stiffly around his head, like jangled wires, and it stunk to high heaven. So he had let his hair return to its natural curly mass which, he came to realize, was a romantic asset, encouraging women to want to mother him or go to bed with him, or both.

Beyond the lure of the curls and the dark eyes, Chris was attractive to women because of his genuine empathy. In the late sixties and early seventies, with the women's movement just dawning, and particularly in the macho milieu of the 4-oh, Chris was a standout feminist, though he never would have used that term. He was especially sympathetic to women who had been raped. He thought it ridiculous and wrong that in order to get a conviction, eyewitness corroboration of a woman's story was needed. As cops put it bluntly, the guy needed a glass ass. Because rape victims tended not to have witnesses handy, and because so many suspects therefore went free, Chris was especially pleased when one didn't. After a series of rapes in the 4-oh neighborhood, with a blind woman and a fifteen-year-old girl among the victims, Chris and his partner at the time, Mac, had identified the rapist. When they heard on the street that the man had fled to Puerto Rico, their quest seemed futile. Still, they staked out his apartment, because they'd also heard his wife was pregnant. They had a hunch he'd want to be back for the birth.

Week after week, on their own time, they sat in their unmarked car, smoking cigarettes, drinking endless cups of coffee. When they saw a man appear in the lighted fourth-floor window one night, they almost didn't believe what they saw.

"What do you think?" Chris asked.

"Let's go up," Mac said.

They radioed the station, then Chris took the front door, while Mac went up to the roof. When the woman opened the front door, and the man saw Chris, he headed out the window. Chris dove out after him, and they grappled on the fire escape. Meantime, up on the roof, Mac was using his flashlight to fight off a guard dog. Chris was being pushed backward over the railing when Mac came bounding down the steps and pounced. Chris told a newspaper reporter that the man had been "as strong as a bull," so the story labeled him "The Bronx Bull Rapist."

Two women had made positive IDs, and one woman's husband had been able to finger the guy. That woman had been followed home from the subway and forced at knifepoint to the top-floor landing, where she was sodomized. When her assailant was running down the stairs, he passed a man coming up—the woman's husband, on his way home from work. Amazingly, the suspect had even boasted of his crimes. "If you put my picture in the paper, you'll hear from forty women I raped," he told Chris.

With the IDs and the admission, Chris felt they had a rock-solid case. But at the arraignment, the judge remanded the guy on only five hundred dollars bail. Chris was so enraged that as the judge stepped down, Chris hurled his briefcase at the bench, using both hands, and was nearly cited for contempt.

When the trial got underway, Chris thought the judge was more concerned with the well-being of the defendant than of the women. "Did you have anything to eat, Mr. Rodriguez?" Chris parroted him later. "Did the police officer read you your rights, Mr. Rodriguez? Did you understand the police officer when he read you your rights? Are you very sure you understood, Mr. Rodriguez?"

Chris had decided, early in his career, that a detached cynicism was his most viable response in a courtroom. It was theater of the absurd, he felt, with stock players saying the same lines over and over; an unbalanced chess game with too many pawns. So he'd trained himself not to get upset when somebody he'd nailed was turned loose, for one reason or another. Thieves, muggers, pushers were going to be back on the street sooner or later, probably sooner, so Chris had developed his own simple philosophy. "My job is to take the man off the street and see that he's locked up. Then I have to do the paperwork, get to court on the right day, be there on time, bring in the evidence, and make sure my testimony is correct. After that, what happens, happens. My act is over."

Only once had he screwed up his act. "Did you advise my client of his rights?" a defendant's lawyer asked.

"Yes, I did," Chris said.

"And how did you advise my client of his rights?"

"Well, I just advised him of his rights."

"You just *told* him?" the lawyer pressed.

"Yes, I did."

"You didn't *read* them?"

"No, I didn't."

"Do you know them that well, Officer?"

"Yes, I do."

"Then please recite the rights for this court now," the lawyer said, as Chris went blank. Totally blank. He knew the rights upside down and backward, and he also knew that he could sit on that witness stand forever and a day without being able to recite them. He felt like a total jerk, especially when the lawyer then made a motion to suppress.

From then on, he carried the scrap of paper with the rights written out everywhere he went. When a lawyer asked, "How did you advise my client of his rights?" Chris would say, "I read them from this piece of paper," and he would whip out the scrap. If a lawyer then tried to trip him up by sneering, "You mean you don't even know the rights without reading them?" Chris would smile and say, "Yes, I know them, but I wanted your client to have the best possible presentation."

Chris had absolutely no use for lawyers. "Even Shakespeare said, 'Get rid of all the lawyers and we'll have a better society,' or something like that," Chris pointed out. "I think maybe Christ said something like that, too." He felt cops were often trapped in a tough, even an impossible situation. "Legislatures take months to put something into law, then they expect a cop to make a split-second decision, with no time for a committee meeting or a conference or any kind of huddle, and then enforce the law instantaneously and exactly right. And they say to a cop, 'If you make a mistake, we'll prosecute *you*.' " One way or another, Chris felt, a suspect was likely to slip through—by copping a plea, or claiming mitigating circumstances, or by having some sharp Legal Aid guy confuse the issue enough so that the case got thrown out. And Chris had learned not to take it personally.

Except in the case of "The Bronx Bull Rapist." Chris remembered how terrified the fifteen-year-old girl had been, how she'd backed away from him, whimpering, her face quivering, when he tried to talk to her. "Once a woman is raped, she's never the same again," Chris said moodily. "A part of her is stolen and she will never get it back." He'd handled a rape case in which the woman had just sat there as he tried to get her to speak, with her jaw so tightly locked, the doctor found, that she physically couldn't open her mouth to get the words out.

Chris was determined that the Bronx Bull not get away. He called up some women he didn't know but knew something about, whose bylines he'd seen, including "the one with the glasses," Gloria Steinem. "I think the judge is coddling this guy," Chris told them. "I think he's completely insensitive to the women who were raped, and I'm afraid he's going to sabotage this case and let the guy go." On the next trial day, Chris's team was lined up in the front rows. Each woman had a notebook and pen in hand, and kept her eyes riveted on the judge. Chris watched happily as the judge's attitude changed, "from night to day. He got sixty-five years, baby!" Chris told Liz.

Liz had been singing at a nightclub in Manhattan, when

Chris dropped in one night to hear the flute player in the combo. He'd always liked the flute. The owner of the place knew Chris and, between sets, brought Liz over to say hello.

"I hear you're a policeman," Liz said lightly.

"Well, yeah, I am," Chris mumbled awkwardly.

"Well, I feel real safe now," Liz said, and everybody laughed. Chris stayed until she was finished, then drove her home to her apartment on the upper east side. When he dropped her off, he didn't ask for her phone number.

When he went back to the club a few nights later, she asked why not. Chris mumbled something vague, because he didn't have an answer. Liz was lovely, with blond hair in a classic pageboy cut, wide blue eyes and, in her black dress with a ruffled skirt and a string of pearls, she was sexy in a cool, sophisticated way.

"Well, here it is," she said, handing him a slip of paper. "Call me up sometime." So he called, and they went to dinner. When she got a part in an off-Broadway revue, he went to see it twice. When the show closed, she invited him to Massachusetts for the weekend, to the small town where she'd grown up and where her parents still lived. Chris enjoyed the trip and he liked her parents, who seemed to like him, too, even though Liz's dad was an avid golfer and Chris had always hated golf, along with most sports. As a kid, he'd always been the last to be picked for a team, any team, in any game. When he was the only kid left, just standing there, one team captain or the other would shrug and say, okay Chris, you're with us. On Saturdays and Sundays, when other kids were playing ball, Chris was at home, practicing drums.

Chris had never said "I love you" to anyone. Even when he felt that he loved someone, he didn't say it in those words, not even within the family. He'd never told his mother he loved her, and certainly he'd never told his father. In a romantic relationship, he just couldn't seem to get the words out. He hated the way people said "I love you," so loosely, sometimes so falsely: At the station he heard guys on the phone, talking to their wives, saying they were working late, don't wait supper, just go on to bed, see you tomorrow, I love you, then hanging up and heading out to meet their girlfriends.

So Chris went to the other extreme and never said it. He assumed that people who knew him would know how he felt and, if he loved them, they would know it without him saying so. When Liz asked him, "Do you love me?" he was embarrassed and mumbled, "Well, yeah." He knew certainly that he'd never met anyone so talented and glamorous, while still being so nice and so easy to talk to. He'd never known anyone like her. "Why are you interested in me?" he asked her. "I'm just a cop." While the question was a trifle disingenuous—by now he was no longer oblivious to his masculine charm—he really did want to know. "I don't meet many straight, normal people in my line of work," Liz told him. So maybe she hadn't known anyone like him, either.

Chris liked being married. He no longer needed to spend so much time after hours at McSherry's, now that he had a wife to come home to, share his day with. Shortly before he met Liz, he'd had the bout of hepatitis that the doctor blamed on alcohol. Getting married and settling down was a good way to straighten out, Chris thought. And as long as he'd stopped drinking, he thought he might as well go one step further, and he'd stopped smoking.

Liz seemed content, too. She'd had a couple of roommates, each of whom had married and moved away. With the instability built into her profession, she welcomed some emotional and social security, too. She was understanding of Chris's irregular schedule, because hers was. When she got a part in the road company of a Broadway musical, Chris flew out to Cleveland to see her.

At home in Forest Hills, Chris discovered a domestic streak in himself that surprised him. When he was living with his mother, he'd been accustomed to not lifting a finger. Now, when he had a day off, he enjoyed doing the laundry. Liz liked to sleep late; he liked to bring her breakfast in bed. He could whip up a fine Greek salad. He especially enjoyed their trips to Massachusetts. Every year since they'd met, they'd gone there at Christmastime. Chris would spend Christmas Eve with his mother, then, very early on Christmas morning, he and Liz would pile into his car, loaded with gifts, and set off for the country, lighthearted as children, singing. Chris couldn't match his wife's trained voice, but he managed to hold his own. He thought that the more he sang, the better he sounded.

There was always snow in the country. Liz's parents didn't have a farm, but they had a lot of ground, with birch woods stretching behind the house. Sometimes Chris got up very early, the morning after Christmas, and walked in the woods alone. He never chopped wood—as a city kid, he was sure he'd cut off a foot had he tried to wield an ax—but he learned to make a good long-lasting fire, poking and stoking it late into the night. The rambling old Victorian house smelled gloriously of pine, of roasting turkey, and pies in the oven. He liked to lie on the floor in front of the fire, listening to the murmur of voices all around him, sometimes dozing, sometimes just dreaming. He liked the way he and Liz seemed to laugh a lot, in the country. At home, in the city, there didn't seem to be as much time to laugh. They had busy schedules. Sometimes they met in the city for dinner, then went to a club to hear jazz. Chris could never persuade Liz to go to the opera, though. As much as she loved music, Liz didn't like opera, so he went only once in a while, while she was out of town, and he played his opera records at home only when he was there alone.

The Maria Callas was so loud that he almost didn't hear the shrill ring of the phone.

"Chris, don't be stupid," the man on the phone said bluntly. "Do you realize what you're doing, if you turn this down?"

It was Captain Selzer, whom Chris had known in the Bronx, who now worked downtown. He hadn't been at the morning meeting, but obviously knew all about it.

"Hey, Cap," Chris said. "I've already turned it down. I just don't want it, you know? I'm really happy where I am."

"Chris, listen to me," Selzer said. "Just listen to me for a minute. I'm telling you, don't say no to this. You know Intel is the elite unit. I don't have to tell you that, and if you do a good job, Chris, you can make the gold."

"And what if I don't?" Chris countered. "What if I screw up? Would I get busted back to the bag?"

"No, no you wouldn't," Selzer said. "I give you my word, you wouldn't go back into uniform. You could just go back to what you're doing now."

"Hey boss, you know I want the gold," Chris said. "But I think I can get it anyway, with what I'm doing, sooner or later. And I really don't want this job."

"I'm telling you again," Selzer persisted, "don't turn this down. You'd be making a big mistake."

"Hey, I don't even know what they want me to do, exactly," Chris said. "Gather intelligence, they said. But that sounds real vague, and I don't really know what they want me to do. I'm not sure *they* know what they want me to do."

"Here's what I want you to do, Chris," the captain said. "Take the job for a little while. Ninety days. How does ninety days sound? Then, if you want to drop it, you drop it, no questions asked."

"I still don't think . . ." Chris began, when the captain cut in. "Think about it some more," he said briskly. "The inspector wants you to think about it some more. He thinks you haven't thought about this sufficiently, Chris, and he wants you to take the weekend to think about it. So you do that." He hung up before Chris could say anything more.

Chris turned the record over and walked out to the kitchen. He got another cup of coffee, took a sip, then poured it down the sink and opened a diet cola. He went back into the living room and sat at the end of the sofa.

He'd started out as a mediocre cop, then he became a good cop. Not a superstar, just a very good cop. He was satisfied with what he was doing at the 4-oh. After coming close to messing up his life, all the drinking and the drifting, he was straightened out. As a good cop, he was making something of himself. Redeeming himself.

Early in his career, he'd been lazy. Once, Chief Bouza in the Bronx had called him up to his office. Bouza was an impressive-looking guy, very tall and lanky, six five, with a wonderful way of speaking. Some people thought he was arrogant, but Chris liked him a lot. The chief had a fabulous vocabulary; talking with him, Chris thought, was like talking to a professor.

The chief pointed a finger at him. "What are you doing in terms of education?" he demanded.

"Well, I take some classes at John Jay," Chris began. Then he stopped. He didn't want to bullshit the chief. It was true that he'd signed up for classes given at the precinct through the John Jay College of Criminal Justice. But it was also true that he didn't pay attention, didn't do the assigned reading, and often dozed in class. "Well, nothing," Chris admitted.

"You know, Chris," the chief said, "I'm a dropout from Manual Trades High School. And now I have my Ph.D. in Police Management." Chris was wondering how to respond —should he congratulate the boss?—when Bouza pointed dramatically to the bookshelf behind his desk. "See those books? Those are *my* books, Chris. I wrote them! And yet I was a dropout from Manual Trades!"

Chris could see what the chief was driving at, then, and for a while he tried to pay more attention to the classes. But his heart wasn't in it. He didn't need a college degree to get the gold shield of a detective. For that he needed a hook or a "rabbi"—either a high-ranking cop who could give him a strong reference and hook Chris up the ladder with him, or someone who would press his cause, perhaps using political connections. Chris had neither, so he needed lots of arrests, lots of medals. He was working on it.

He went back into the kitchen for the rest of the soda. He stood again at the kitchen window, looking down at the courtyard. The overhead lights had just gone on; in the early dusk, a man was walking along the path, swinging a briefcase, probably on his way home from work. Heading home to his wife and children.

Chris and Liz had talked about having children, then had put it on the back burner. For one thing, Liz had worked hard to get where she was in her profession; she'd taken lessons for years—dancing, singing, acting; she'd gone to auditions constantly, answered "cattle calls," and she seemed to be just on the verge of getting some big breaks. She had time—she'd be just twenty-eight on her next birthday, around Christmastime. Chris was a great believer in letting people do what they had to do, so that years later, one of them couldn't say to the other, "If it hadn't been for you . . ." If Liz didn't want to interrupt her career now by having babies, it would have been selfish and wrong of him to hassle her about it.

He thought of calling his mother. Katrina still lived in the house in Queens, where Chris had lived until he was married. He'd never thought it strange that a bachelor over thirty still lived at home; his father had always stressed that family was the most important thing in life. When George became a successful businessman, people had come to see him, to ask him to sponsor a family member in the old country who wished to come to America. Because George had an established business, his vouching that the immigrants would work in one of his restaurants, or in some other job that he would arrange for them, and not have to go on relief, was often their key to entry.

George never refused such a request, even though so many people came to see him, some Sunday afternoons, that they had to form a line. Sometimes people were so grateful that they would kiss George's hand, which Chris thought was weird. Chris had never taken part in those Sunday rituals, but he remembered the people coming, paying their respects to George, asking a favor. He remembered Katrina bringing out the homemade cookies, with small servings of wine in her precious cordial glasses, dark red with silver rims.

Sunday was always family day. When it got to the point

where George didn't work on Sundays most of the time, they all went to church for the long Greek liturgy, then came home for dinner. Katrina always cooked lamb. Often, relatives came by for a visit. George had brought Katrina's brother Michael and her sister Rosa to this country; Rosa had married a friend of George's, from his old rooming house on upper Broadway, near the Riviera barbershop, so there was a collection of aunts and uncles and cousins. Those Sundays were the only days Chris remembered seeing much of his father, those Sunday dinners the only meals he remembered sharing with him. During the week, Chris and his sisters would have eaten and were usually in bed by the time George got home. Katrina always had George's meal ready, no matter what the hour, and after he'd eaten, George would go straight to bed. He never went to a restaurant except his own, except to work.

Chris still visited his mother almost every Sunday. Even when Liz was home and wanted Chris to do something else on Sunday, Chris tried never to let his mother down. Katrina never would have complained if he hadn't come, which is why he tried hard to make it.

Katrina was only fifty-one when George died, but she'd worn black from that day on, and would wear it, Chris knew, to her grave. Chris had spent the three days of his father's wake at a bar down the block from the funeral home. He'd walked up to the open casket, one time, to look at his father, and that was it. He knew his sisters were taking care of Katrina, and he knew somebody was making the arrangements—probably Uncle Mike—so Chris had just kind of drifted through those three days. He could remember people seeking him out at the bar, from time to time, coming up to him, putting a hand on his shoulder and saying, "How are you doing?"

On the day of the funeral, Chris stood on one side of his mother, Uncle Mike on the other side, as the pallbearers carried the coffin out of church. Chris didn't know those men; he guessed they were from the funeral home. Suddenly Uncle Mike stepped over to one of them, tapped him on the shoulder, and took his place. Chris wished he had done that, too.

Nobody had asked him, but then, nobody had asked Uncle Mike, either.

At the time, Chris hadn't thought much about it, but later it bothered him. He thought George would have been pleased if Chris had done that, as a sign of respect.

George would have been pleased, too, that Chris was respected as a very good cop, that he was redeeming himself. And if he knew that Chris had been singled out, asked to join Intelligence, where they took only the best men, he could even have been proud.

3

His code name was Jason.

Only one man at the Intelligence Division would know him. "This is Jason," Chris would say when he telephoned Harry, his control officer, his only link with the department. The inspector and a few other men would know about the assignment, of course, but only Harry would know on a regular basis where Jason was and what he was doing. Chris would send his reports to Harry, signed only with the code name. In his new life as a jazz drummer, just back from Vegas, looking for some action, he would keep his first name, so he would respond naturally, but he had a new last name. In his real life at home with Liz, with his mother and his sisters and friends, who knew nothing about the other names, he would still be Chris Anastos.

Already he was three different people, and he hadn't even started the job.

Before going under, he spent one more week at the 4-oh, to make his leaving there seem reasonably normal, not particularly irregular or dramatic. It was a strange week. He didn't want to make arrests, which would have tied him up in court, but it was difficult for him to walk around the neighborhood without sniffing trouble. Were those guys huddled around a table in the pizza parlor planning something more complex than whether to get mushroom or pepperoni? One of them had a long record of stickups. Maybe that young woman pushing a baby carriage very slowly, up and down the block, not seeming to be going anywhere, was pushing something else, something slipped into the pillowcase, or inside the baby's bonnet. It had happened.

And it would happen again, Chris knew, when he spotted the man he'd nicknamed Pumpkin. He was wearing an orange jacket, a bright-green cap with a black visor, and a swaggering smile that said he owned the block—which, in a very practical sense, he did.

Chris swore angrily. He'd caught up with Pumpkin, less than two months earlier, after stalking him for weeks, trying to figure out where the guy stashed his junk. He'd approached the pusher a few times, in various disguises—once, even sporting a chestnut-colored wig—but Pumpkin was tuned in to trouble and had never been willing to deal. Then Chris had put on a master act. Wearing a red bandanna tied around his head gypsy-style, a stained fatigue jacket, with a canvas pouch dangling from his shoulder, he'd stumbled down the block, appearing to be drunk, sick, stoned.

Past the liquor store, where sales were made from behind a thick Plexiglas shield, past the vacant lot piled with rubbish, he had stopped in the middle of the block, where Pumpkin was leaning against the brick wall of an abandoned tenement.

Chris lurched toward the curb, reaching out to grab on to a parking meter for support. When he seemed to regain his balance, he turned and shuffled across the sidewalk.

"Hey man," he mumbled, "you got something for me today?"

Pumpkin said nothing. His eyes were hidden behind mirrored dark glasses.

"I'm sick, brother," Chris pleaded in a rasping voice. "I gotta get high."

"I don't know you," Pumpkin said shortly.

"Hey, I just want to cop some junk, you know?" Chris moaned.

"Who sent you down?"

"Oh, some brother—hey man, what difference?" Chris turned, as though to move away. "Okay, okay, I don't need to buy from you, man."

Pumpkin called him back. "How much you want?"

"Gimme a dime bag." Chris groped in his jeans pocket and brought out a folded ten-dollar bill.

Pumpkin eased down the side of the building, very slowly, his long legs bending as gracefully as a dancer's. Near the bottom of the wall he turned slightly, sliding his hand along the wall. He removed a loose brick, took a glassine envelope from the hole, and deftly pushed the brick back into place. In a swift handshake, the envelope and the money were exchanged. "Move," Pumpkin hissed.

Chris moved, bobbing his head as he turned away. At the curb, he stopped. He stood up straight. The handcuffs in his pouch made a satisfying clank as he walked briskly back to Pumpkin to deliver the curtain line. "I forgot to tell you: You're under arrest."

It was a very good line, but clearly it had merely been the end of the first act, in what looked to be a long-running show. Here was Pumpkin, back on the street, having breezed through the judicial revolving door. Frustrated and depressed, Chris decided to stay off the streets until it was time to go downtown.

Yet he didn't like hanging around the precinct, either, in the midst of the everyday activity, the hustle and bustle that had nothing to do with him. It was disappointing to be leaving without a transfer party, the traditional sendoff that reminded cops of their indissoluble fellowship, that reinforced the feeling that even when they left, they belonged. When Chris left, he didn't know where he would belong.

It was tough not to talk about his assignment, not even about the meeting, among guys who talked incessantly about what they were doing, the collars they'd made, and the ones they intended to make. "What should I tell people?" Chris had asked Harry. "Tell them you can't tell them," Harry said shortly. When the message came over the 4-oh wire: P O ANASTOS TEMP REASSIGN—everybody knew the terseness meant they shouldn't ask questions, but not everybody could resist. Chris had never been much of a liar, probably because his father had always made lying sound like the deadliest of all deadly sins. "If you do a wrong thing you must say so," George had lectured his children. "No matter how bad, it is not so bad as a lie. My daughters do not lie. My son does not lie." For all the faults and character flaws he'd accumulated over the years, Chris thought wryly, he found it hard to manage a straight-out lie, though surely it could be justified now. So he just evaded the questions with a shrug of the shoulders, a shake of the head. "Okay, then," some of the guys said. "Good luck." Only Mac pressed a little more. "Hey, what's going on? Is the Mod Squad breaking up for good?"

"They just want me to do some special job for a while," Chris said. "I really don't know much about it."

He really didn't. "You'll be our eyes and ears," Harry told him, leading him into a small room at the Intelligence Division. The room had a rectangular table, with a chair on either side of it. Nothing else. There was no window. The door could be locked from both the inside and the outside.

The inspector greeted him on the first day with a warm handshake. "Welcome aboard," the inspector said. "If you have any problems, let me know." Chris didn't see him anymore after that, and didn't talk to anyone but Harry.

The hall was lined with rooms like the room Chris was using, some of them empty, with the door open, some with the doors closed. Other men, other jobs, probably. But that was only a guess, based on seeing guys either coming or going from a room, often wearing dark glasses. Undercover work had not even been mentioned at the Academy, let alone taught. Maybe it couldn't be taught, as the Internal Revenue

Service had learned, to its great embarrassment. In the early 1960s, when the IRS had tried to teach agents how to act like criminals in order to run down tax evaders in the world of organized crime, they'd ended up a laughing stock. They'd set up "stress seminars" at various motels around Washington, testing guys with liquor and women to see if they'd keep their mouths shut. The operation came to light when one totally drunk agent was picked up by the Maryland State Police on a highway near a motel. At first he was so drunk he couldn't answer their questions. When he sobered up enough to speak, he still wouldn't answer their questions because he thought it was part of the test.

Obviously, undercover work was going to be OJT—on-the-job training. Chris hadn't even taken the month-long Criminal Investigation Course that was routinely prescribed for cops who went into plainclothes. The CIC was designed for the morals squad, mostly; Chris's plain clothes unit had not been an investigatory body. For the stuff he dealt with, categorized loosely as "violent street crimes," he didn't need a special course. He just needed to be in the right place at the right time.

Harry brought in stacks of folders, so many he had to make more than one trip from wherever he got them, to Chris's room. The folders bulged with reports, photographs, clippings—an array of information on men who came under the general heading OC: Organized Crime. Gathering information on their comings and goings wasn't difficult, Harry said, especially since the Organized Crime Control Bureau had been set up by Commissioner Murphy in the reform, post-Knapp days. And Intelligence had its own squad, the Organized Crime Monitoring Unit. Some OCMU guys did nothing all day, every day, but keep a target in view. Where does he go? Who does he see? What are his habits? The feds did the same thing, but all this tailing and monitoring didn't amount to much unless they had evidence. The guys in the folders knew that, just as they knew, more often than not, when they were being tailed. Sometimes they would taunt the guys tailing them, strolling over to the car, knocking on the window. "I'm going to be inside this place for a couple of hours, you can relax, go get yourself some coffee and a doughnut."

Five years earlier, the Racketeer Influenced and Corrupt Organization act—RICO—had been adopted by Congress, and law enforcement people were just beginning to learn to use what they hoped would become an enormously important tool. RICO had created a crime category, "racketeering," based on two or more crimes being committed within a ten-year period as part of a "criminal enterprise." Lawmen and lawwomen were trying to gather evidence of these enterprises, trying to show that crimes were joined in by members of various crime families. Specifically, Harry said, the NYPD was looking for evidence that would justify a wiretap, or the planting of a bug. For that they needed "probable cause," and for that, they needed to wire Chris. He was outfitted with a Nagra, which he hated.

He was given a small, flat box about four inches square and shown how to tape it to his body—under his arm, or in the small of his back. A thin wire about three feet long was laced over his shoulder. One end of the wire connected to the box, the other end to a tiny microphone that was no bigger than the eraser at the end of a pencil. The mike was taped to his chest, just above the muscle. The reels of recording tape ran for three hours; when Chris was alone, he could switch off the recorder with a remote control button in his pocket.

Every week or so, he was to send the reels to Harry, who would vouch for them and put them in a vault at the NYPD, for future use, unless the information couldn't wait. If a hijacking seemed imminent, or if guns were moving in preparation for an immediate job, perhaps even a killing, Chris was to get in touch with Harry at once. When it was necessary for them to meet, they'd pick the lobby of a bank, or a post office, sometimes a hotel room; the locations would change.

Chris was to use his own judgment on when and where to be wired. When he wasn't wired, he was to make notes in any way possible and send those to Harry, too. "You won't make arrests," Harry emphasized. "Your job is to gather intelligence and send it in. We'll take it from there. Even it it doesn't mean anything to you, send it in. It may mean something to us."

But Chris was not being sent in as a cleanup hitter against the Mafia, Harry stressed. His job was simply to infiltrate the Greek community and figure out the organization and structure of its criminal element. Harry said that arrests had been made among the Greeks in Queens, but they seemed disconnected. A cop at the 114th Precinct in Astoria had tried to do some digging, but his name was Sean, with a face to match, so he'd made no headway among the clannish Greeks. There was a man at the top, Harry told Chris, a kind of Greek godfather, Kostos. Harry called him "The Big G," pronouncing it with a hard G, as in Greek. Chris was to get close to Kostos, find out whether he headed an organized crime family, and whether that family was linked with organized crime among the Italians.

A handful of names and faces in the folders were familiar to Chris. When he'd worked as a musician, sometimes playing at a club, sometimes just bouncing around, he'd met people who were on the fringes of organized crime, sometimes well beyond the fringe, which is why his father had objected so strenuously to that career. Now, in a folder, Chris recognized Tony. When Tony had opened a bar in Queens, Chris had brought his combo to play on opening night, and he'd done that again at the christening party for Tony's baby daughter, Amanda. When Chris wouldn't accept any payment, Tony had given Chris an unusual gift, a huge soap sculpture in the shape of Buddha. Over the years the soap had fallen on the floor several times, with pieces chipping off, but Chris had always managed to glue the pieces back together, so that the Buddha shape was still clear. When Tony's brother was gunned down, Chris had hurried over to Tony's club. Tony was secluded inside, refusing to see anyone. But when he was told that Chris had come, he told the man at the door to let Chris in. Chris was the only person Tony wanted to talk to at that time.

He knew Dino, Les, Arnie, and that crew. He'd played at Dino's place, the Starglow Lounge, and had enjoyed it. Chris thought that Dino and his pals had been involved in the "French Connection" job—not the original operation, but afterward, when drugs that had been recovered and vouchered at the NYPD just disappeared.

He knew Bing and his father, Sal. One night Chris and Bing were at a bar, drinking, when Sal came by. Sal was a tough old bird, in some kind of racket, though Chris wasn't sure exactly what it was, then.

"I hear you're going into the police department," Sal had said.

"That's right, I am," Chris replied.

"Good," Sal said firmly. "You'll either be a first-grade detective, or you'll be thrown off the force. One or the other." Bing laughed, but Chris could see that both father and son were pleased for him. "Good luck to you," Sal said, gripping Chris's hand. Chris never saw Sal, after that. The old guy died about a year later, and Chris hadn't seen Bing since then, though he'd heard from him once. When Chris's picture appeared in the paper, in the "Hero Cops" story, Bing had telephoned him. "Chris, babe, I'm so proud of you! My Pop would have been proud of you, too. That's great! That's just great!"

When he became a cop, Chris had to cut off those old acquaintances. "Consorting with Known Criminals" could get a guy thrown off the job. So he didn't know what had become of most of them. "What happens if I run into somebody?" he asked Harry. "Some of these guys might know me, and they'll know I didn't just come out of an Easter egg."

Harry explained that Chris's file would be pulled, sealed, and locked in a safe at the DA's office. A red flag would be posted on the police roster, the wheel. If someone called asking for Chris, or asking about him, the switchboard would note the warning and refer the caller to an extension, where the caller would be told that Officer Anastos had been terminated. Thrown off the force for extortion and bribery. A bad cop. Chris needed this protection, not only from the mob guys who might be checking him out—theirs was a world of paranoia and suspicion, not without reason—but from people who should have been trustworthy, throughout the NYPD, both cops and civilians. "We do have people who sell information," Harry told Chris, simply.

Most people in the department would have no reason to think that the story was fake. In fact, Chris reflected ruefully, some guys might find it very easy to accept. We could see it coming, some guys at the 4-oh might say. Anastos always seemed a little reckless, a little weird, something funny about the guy. Just as the brightest leaves on an autumn tree were the most rotten, guys like Anastos were the first to fall.

Chris asked only that his mother not be told he'd been expelled from the force. Katrina was not an old woman, but she'd grown somber and frail since George's death. Chris thought it might actually kill her if she thought he had dishonored himself and his family, and the memory of his father. He persuaded Harry to allow him to tell Katrina that he'd been transferred someplace where he could not be reached, that she was never to try to reach him, that he'd call her often and would see her as often as he could. Katrina would ask no questions, Chris assured Harry, and she would follow his instructions perfectly. A Greek-Italian woman took a man's word without protest.

Liz was a different woman. "I got a new assignment," he told her simply. "It's with the Intelligence Division, but I can't tell you anything about it." Liz was about to speak, so Chris continued quickly. "Intelligence is the elite unit in our department, and this will be very good for my career. But I can't tell you where I'll be or what I'll be doing, so please, just don't ask me any questions." So Liz didn't, though her expression reflected a clear question: Don't you trust me?

The harsh truth was that he didn't. He couldn't. Not even a wife was welcome in the secluded world of the undercover cop, in which even a casual comment, unexceptional in itself, could be literally a matter of life and death. If Liz knew anything at all about his work, she might know too much.

Chris himself didn't want to know too much. As he studied

the material Harry gave him, he realized he might be learning something that nobody else knew. In a conversation, he might let something slip. Then the guy would wonder, how does he know that? Chris didn't want anybody to wonder about him, at least not to the extent that questions would be asked to which there were only impossible answers.

Near the end of his second week in the closed room at Intel, Chris and Harry agreed that he knew as much as he could, or should, know. In fact, Harry pointed out that some of the men the department most yearned to nail were hidden behind a curtain of legitimacy that seemed impassable. Their names might be known, their games suspected, but in police language, it had never been possible to "get them good." They kept a low profile. As high-level managers of their shadowy world—arranging things, settling problems—they were, in a way, more of a menace than the hoods on the street, because of the depth of their knowledge and experience, their executive expertise. Such a man, Harry said, would typically be in his late fifties, early sixties, probably having moved up from the violence of Prohibition days to a position of relative respectability. He likely would have moved from one of the city's notorious neighborhoods to the suburbs, where he would be, not exactly a pillar of the community, not a polished Wall Street type, but not a crude, cigar-chomping figure, either. He was as desirable a target as he was difficult to describe. "You'll know him when you see him," Harry said.

When Chris arrived for his last day of briefing, Harry had no new material for him to sift through. Instead, he locked the door from the inside and sat down at the table, across from Chris. From his briefcase, Harry brought out a large manila envelope and spread its contents on the table.

There was a new social security card and a checkbook in his new name for an account at a bank where Chris's paychecks would be deposited for him. Those paychecks would not come through the city comptroller's office, but from some corporation Chris had never heard of; his salary would be laundered, in classic style. There was not just one fake ID, but a handful, with various addresses. One address was a safe house outside New York, but the address in Valley Stream was an abandoned warehouse.

Inside the big manila envelope was a smaller envelope stuffed with cash: two thousand dollars in tens and twenties, mostly, with some fifties and a couple of hundred-dollar bills. Harry insisted that Chris count it and give him a receipt, which Chris did, feeling a bit ridiculous. There was a car registration in a corporate name, so that if anyone took down the plate number, it would either come up as a "no-hit"—too new to be filed—or, if someone really persisted, it would lead to some business in Brooklyn. And there were the car keys.

"I already have a car," Chris pointed out. "Why don't we just change the plates on my vehicle? I don't need another car."

Harry laughed. "You need this car," he said. "C'mon."

He led Chris out of the room, down the stairs and out of the building, around the corner and down to a parking garage near the Hudson River. Harry spoke to a man at the garage and handed him the keys. A few minutes later, that man drove up the ramp in a gleaming new Buick, dark brown with a light-tan roof.

Harry shook Chris's hand. "Good luck, Jason," he said. "Keep in touch."

As he drove east across Manhattan, Chris couldn't help grinning. The flashy car smelled new and leathery and expensive. He had two grand in his pocket. He felt excited and sort of thrilled, very much as he'd felt when he was driving the red convertible across Manhattan, heading into Queens. And just as George hadn't lectured him that day, as he drove across the Queensboro Bridge, neither was there anyone now to warn him, to say "Be careful."

More Greeks live in the Astoria section of Queens than anywhere else in the world, outside Athens. Only a twenty-minute subway ride from Bloomingdale's, in mid-Manhattan, it's also so far, in a sense, that someone who isn't Greek can never complete the distance.

Chris stopped at the newsstand, in the shadow of the

elevated train, with racks of both Greek and English newspapers and magazines—*Ethnikos Kirix, Proïni, The Greek National Herald*. He bought a racing form; knowing that Greeks liked to gamble, it seemed a likely approach. He'd never been to the track, though, and as he settled at a table in a coffeehouse, struggling to decipher the language of the racing sheet, the wry catch-phrase came to him: It's all Greek to me.

He hadn't spent time at the *kafeneia*—the coffeehouses—when he lived in Queens; as a teenager then, he'd had other things to do. His father had never had time to spend in coffeehouses; the only time George went to a bar was when he closed on a restaurant. Once he had taken Chris with him, set him on a stool near a dish of hardboiled eggs, and let Chris take a sip of his beer. Katrina had come to the commercial center of Astoria occasionally to buy groceries; Chris remembered the butcher shop with a full-size goat hanging head down in the window, and a hand-lettered sign: ALL YEAR ROUND, BABY LAMB PIG GOAT. Katrina had sent Chris a few times to the grocery story with gleaming green-and-gold cans of olive oil stacked in pyramids in the window, pungent with spices, dried apricots, and figs. Chris had dropped in at the Steinway branch of the public library a couple of times, but he never could remember when the books were due; he'd get a postcard from the library saying he owed them money, so finally he'd said the heck with it, and just stopped going.

He'd gone to movies in the neighborhood as often as he could. Chris had always loved movies. When they still lived in Manhattan, when he was too young to go by himself, he used to go with his uncle Byron, who invariably fell asleep within the first twenty minutes. Chris would stand on the seat and watch the movie a couple of times over, or as long as Uncle Byron slept. When he was in the fifth or sixth grade, his teacher, Mr. Zuckerman, had worked as weekend cashier at a theater on upper Broadway, and let kids who behaved themselves in school all week get in free. Sometimes his mother even went to the movies with him. Katrina didn't understand much English, but she loved westerns, and was especially fond of Gene Autry, who had such a lovely singing voice.

Chris liked gangster movies and detective movies, though he suspected, even then, that they didn't really go around snarling things like "You dirty rat!" Two detectives had come to the house once, at George's request, to observe a man in the apartment across the street. The man had a habit of coming to the window, taking off his trousers and just standing there. Katrina and the girls were banished from the front room, but Chris was allowed to stay. He was very impressed by the detectives in their dark suits and soft hats, who talked in deep, smooth voices.

With its tidy rows of tidy houses on clean streets, Astoria was a family community, not a high-crime precinct; the 114th was known as a "good house" to work in. During the day, its streets were filled with old women picking out fruit, piece by piece, at the produce stands, young women with toddlers in tow. At night the climate changed, but even in the daytime, Chris knew he had to stay alert, on the lookout for someone he knew. His mother lived just ten blocks away. He and Liz had been married at the Byzantine church, St. Demetrios, within walking distance of the coffeehouses where he was now hanging out.

Liz wasn't Greek—her ancestors were mostly German—but Chris knew his mother would be deeply distressed if they didn't have a church wedding, and Liz had said it didn't make any difference to her, Greek was fine. Katrina had seemed pleased that her thirty-two-year-old son was finally settling down, though Chris suspected she was less than thrilled with his choice of a bride. She never said so; she was so accustomed to the old-world tradition of not questioning the men of the family that she never discussed such things with him, and Chris was so used to not having to explain his feelings or his actions that he'd never brought it up with her.

He didn't think Katrina minded so much that he wasn't marrying a Greek girl. Any bias she may have felt was more likely based on Liz's career. Even Chris's sisters had had their marriages arranged for them, in the old-world way. Katrina's two-family house had been converted to three-family to accommodate his sisters, who lived the sort of traditional, housewifely lives that Liz clearly would not.

In any case, it had been a festive wedding, an elaborate Greek service with a lot of music and chanting. The priest had spoken in English as well as in Greek, probably out of consideration for Liz and her relatives, who had come down from Massachusetts in such droves that they'd chartered a bus, making it unnecessary for anyone to drive back after a long day of partying. Chris's cousin was his best man, because Phil was in St. Louis.

Heads turned when Chris came into the coffeehouse, a stranger among the regulars. Late in the morning on a weekday, the place was filled with customers, mostly male, from young men in their twenties on up to elders in ther sixties and seventies. Some of them sat at tables for two, others were grouped at tables seating four, with sometimes a fifth chair drawn up behind one of the chairs, in the consulting position.

For the first few days, Chris didn't stay long—an hour, maybe an hour and a half. Sometimes he came back in midafternoon, and sometimes he didn't reappear until the next day. He didn't want to appear to be in a hurry; he wanted to arouse interest, not suspicion. When he ordered coffee, or a rectangle of silky baklava, he always spoke in Greek. Since Greek men smoked a lot, he bought cigarettes, and soon was back to a pack a day. He wore dark glasses, a crisp sports jacket and slacks, no tie, a few gold chains around his neck, but no diamond ring on his little finger. He wanted to look flashy but in a restrained way. He didn't wave money around flamboyantly, but he paid for a magazine at the newsstand with a twenty, a coffeehouse check for nine dollars with a fifty, and when he ate lunch at Stani Sistaria, the neighborhood restaurant with plaintive Greek music in the background and sentimental oil paintings of Mediterranean scenes on the stucco walls, he gave the cashier a hundred-dollar bill.

Then he stayed away for three consecutive days, hoping that his reappearance would spark something. Sure enough:

When he turned up at the place, a man speaking with a thick accent approached and sat down at his table. His name was Bennie—no last names exchanged. They talked about the day's races, but as Bennie asked a few pointed questions, with men at other tables listening, Chris realized that Bennie was a scout, sent to find out whether Chris was an agent from Immigration.

Chris laughed. "I'm just looking to make some money," he said casually. He talked about being a jazz drummer, just back from a long gig in Vegas, then steered the conversation back to the horses. After another coffee, he left, not wishing to press the new relationship too eagerly. With nothing else to do, and with the marked-up racing form sticking out of his jacket pocket, he went to the track. Acting on advice from Bennie, plus his new understanding of the art, he lost two hundred dollars.

The next day, Bennie greeted him warmly, and within half an hour, they had a deal. "You want to make some money?" Chris asked rhetorically. "I can get you all the cigarettes you want. You sell them for three dollars a carton, give me two." Chris called Harry, who drove out early the next morning, to a side street near Chris's apartment in a van filled with several hundred cartons of cigarettes that had been confiscated and were being stored with the property clerk at the NYPD. "Just be careful, they're untaxed," Chris warned Bennie. "No problem," Bennie said. Chris and Harry set up a regular tobacco transfer then. Sometimes the cigarettes were so stale, from their long shelf life with the property clerk, that the tobacco slid right out of the paper. But nobody seemed to mind, because everybody was making money, including the card shop owners and delicatessen owners who bought the cartons from Bennie at discount and sold them for full price.

When Bennie introduced Chris to his pal Gene, who wanted to make a few bucks, too, Chris added selected pieces of jewelry to his line, from the property clerk's inventory. He was authorized to sell anything except drugs and guns; he was authorized to buy anything, including drugs and guns, and as time went on, he did. Sometimes when he made such a buy, Harry would turn the information over to the feds, making sure to keep Chris out of the picture completely. Sometimes the information went round-robin, with so many in-betweens involved that the federal people didn't even know the information came from the NYPD. More often, Harry filed the intelligence for future use; their immediate goal went beyond drug busts.

As the eyes and ears of the department, Chris felt compelled to report everything he saw and heard. Everything seemed crucial. If he saw someone stick an envelope in his pocket, he would note the guy's name, the date, the exact time and location, without knowing whether the envelope contained payoff money or an electric bill. When he spotted Kostos's Cadillac, he made a note. "I got his plate number," he told Harry proudly. Harry sighed. "We already *know* his plate number," he said.

At the end of each day, which sometimes meant near dawn of the following day, as Chris began hanging around bars and clubs at night, he would write up pages of reports in longhand. "Type it up," Harry pleaded. "I can't read your writing." So Chris got a typewriter and set it up in the second bedroom at home, which he appropriated as a den. But he was a two-finger typist, and that method was so slow that he turned to a tape recorder. He filled cassettes with his reports, which he either delivered to Harry at one of their prearranged meeting places, or sent to him by registered mail, leaving it to Harry to do his own typing.

Liz came in as Chris was carrying the television set out of the room.

"What's happening?" she asked mildly. "Are we moving?"

Chris set the TV on the floor in the bedroom and came into the living room, a little out of breath.

"Hi, babe," he said, kissing her. "No, not moving, just reorganizing. I have to use that room for an office for a while, okay?"

"Okay," Liz said.

She changed into jeans and a T-shirt while Chris maneuvered the TV set onto an end table and got it working. He turned on the evening news, but when Liz went out to the kitchen, he followed her.

"The thing is, I'll be doing some work in there," he told her, feeling awkward about trying to explain what he couldn't explain.

"For your new job?" Liz asked.

"Right," Chris said. "But remember, I said I couldn't talk about it."

"I remember," Liz said. She reached into the cupboard and brought down some cans and a bag of noodles. "I'll make a casserole," she said. "Are you hungry?"

"Starving," Chris said. He wasn't thrilled at the prospect of another tuna casserole, but he wasn't going to object. He knew he wasn't the easiest person in the world to get along with, under any circumstances; especially now, he wasn't going to argue about a casserole. He thought that if he suggested going out to dinner, she'd agree. She let him have his own way, most of the time—they'd gone to the Caribbean on their honeymoon because Chris loved the beach. Liz didn't, and she'd spent the entire week under an umbrella, wearing a wide-brimmed straw hat.

Liz poured the mixture into a dish and put it in the oven. "About half an hour," she said.

Chris got a beer and they went back into the living room. He sat on the sofa and opened the newspaper while Liz went to the piano. She didn't play well, just enough to pick out the notes in a piece she was learning, but Chris liked the way she looked, sitting there. They'd had a good time shopping for the piano as soon as they got back from their honeymoon. Usually Liz didn't want him to go shopping with her—she always knew what she was looking for, and didn't need him.

"Did you have a good day?" he asked.

"So-so," she said, not looking up. "It could have been better."

"Well, hey, you're good, you're really good," Chris said. "So you'll have a better day tomorrow."

"I hope so," Liz said. She looked over at him. "How was your day?"

"Busy," Chris said. He paused. "Ah—one more thing, about my work. I'll be getting a new phone in the—in my office. If it rings when I'm not here, don't answer it. Just let it ring. Don't ever answer that phone."

"Will it interfere with our phone?" Liz asked. "I get business calls here, too."

"No, it won't interfere with our phone," Chris said.

"Are you sure?" Liz continued. "Is our phone going to be monitored?"

"No, no," Chris said impatiently. "It has absolutely nothing to do with our regular phone. It's on another wave length or something."

Liz didn't say anything more. She kept working on the piece, picking out the notes with two fingers. Chris hoped she was satisfied about the phone, and he assumed she was, but it wasn't always easy to tell what Liz was feeling. She wasn't a demonstrative person, probably because of her German background, he thought. It was hard to tell when she was angry. He thought she probably had never been really angry at him, just as he had never been really angry at her. They'd never had a serious argument. They got along fine.

The phone itself looked perfectly ordinary, a plain black telephone that he put on a small table next to an easy chair. But the workings of the phone were so complicated that Chris never knew how it worked, just that it was all electronic. It took the man from the phone company a whole day to install the equipment in a big box in the den closet. Harry came out that day and stayed to supervise the installation. All Chris knew for sure was that the phone was hooked up in such a devious way that if someone tried to trace the number—even someone from the phone company—they'd end up in Brooklyn. So Chris felt safe in giving the number to guys he was beginning to know, though he never told anyone where he lived. Most of the guys he met spent most of their lives in bars and clubs and restaurants, so the question had come up only casually, once or twice. He'd shrugged it off by mumbling that he lived in Valley Stream with his aunt, who was very sick and needed rest and quiet.

Gene seemed to like Chris, whom he called "Curley," and Chris liked Gene. He was a bad apple, no doubt about it. He'd spent time in the can, though he didn't say for what. But he seemed to Chris to be a good family man, too, at least in context. He was separated from his wife—only temporary, he said—and was living in an apartment in Astoria. He talked of his children with wistful pride, and showed Chris a wallet stuffed with their pictures.

Gene was low-level, too, but he was a step above Bennie. And Chris felt that the way to get to the higher-ups was through the lower guys, who always owed them money. Gene owed a lot of money to the shylocks, he told Chris. He needed to make a lot of money to pay them off, and to give to his wife, for the kids. Gene intended to solve his financial problems by winning big at the Greek dice game, *barbouti,* and when he invited Chris to come with him to The Grotto, a cocktail lounge in Astoria, where a high-stakes barbouti game ran, Chris was delighted to go.

The Grotto was Kostos's place. Chris wasn't introduced to him that first night, but he recognized him at once. Kostos wasn't very tall, about five ten, but he was very strong-looking, powerfully built, and muscular. He had a friendly yet commanding way about him. He looked very Greek, yet he looked what Chris called "Americanized" too. He acted the way Chris thought any capo in the Italian crime community would act, with the Cadillac, the pinky ring, the gambling, the women, the whole ball of wax.

Gene had told Chris something about Kostos, not realizing that Chris could have told him a lot more. Chris had heard at his Intel briefing that Kostos was thought to have had a role in the ten-million-dollar jewel robbery at the Pierre Hotel a few years earlier. Kostos's friend Sammy Nalo—"Sammy the Arab," who spoke Greek—had been convicted for that massive job and was doing time at Attica, where Kostos visited him. Kostos was suspected of having gotten a piece of that action; a lot of the loot was still missing. Nothing had been proven, though Chris had heard that when the police called on Kostos at that time, Kostos had greeted them at his front door wearing a bulletproof vest, carrying an automatic weapon.

Kostos was known as a kind of Robin Hood in Astoria. If a woman with, say, three children and no husband was about to have her rent raised, and word got to Kostos that she couldn't make it, Kostos was likely to arrange that her rent would stay the same or perhaps even be lowered. He gave generously to charities from one of his profitable businesses, which included a gas-skimming operation. Altogether, Kostos was most interesting, and as Chris became a regular at the Grotto, his life became more interesting, too. He met Kostos's brother Pete, whose violent tendencies seemed to border on the psychotic. One night Chris was sitting at the bar when Pete and Kostos got into a loud argument. Before anyone could stop him, Pete pulled a gun and shot the barmaid—Kostos's girlfriend—in the arm. Chris was stunned. He was dismayed that he couldn't react as a cop, even though he was carrying a gun. He wasn't carrying his service revolver, which he liked—that .38-caliber weapon was too big, too recognizable as the "detective special." He had a little .25 Titan automatic, which he could slip into his jacket pocket as easily as though it were a hard pack of cigarettes. He didn't have a bullet in the chamber because automatics were notoriously unreliable, likely to go off at any time, so if he'd had to use it, he'd have had to take time to load the chamber. Still, it was better than nothing. After so many years as a cop, carrying his weapon everywhere he went, he felt insecure without it, as most cops did. When his partner Phil got married, after only a year and a half on the force, he'd worn his gun under his tuxedo.

Chris hadn't anticipated a time when he'd want to pull his gun and not be able to. Still, the incident wasn't terribly serious—the girl had only a superficial wound. But Chris couldn't help thinking that the episode illustrated the widening gap between his regular life and instincts, and his undercover life. Perhaps because the gap was growing, he tried hard to maintain both lives as fully as possible. On nights when he stayed in Astoria, he tended to stay all night, both at the Grotto and at other neighborhood bars and clubs, when the mothers with toddlers and the fragile white-haired old women of daylight were replaced with what Chris termed "night crawlers." Many of them were Greek, but there was a sizable smattering of Italians, too. Chris met an Italian, Jimmy, whom he didn't like, but who became a good source. Sometimes Chris would end up at Jimmy's joint, help him close the place, then go out to breakfast with him, usually with Jimmy's gofer, Dominic, tagging along.

Then, on other nights, Chris would try to get home to Forest Hills reasonably early, to be able to spend at least part of the night in a normal way. He was wary of calling friends, who were sure to ask what he was doing. But if anybody called him, he almost always got on the phone and chatted, just to stay in touch.

When an old friend called him at home one night and asked him to drop by—he and his wife wanted some advice about adopting a child—Chris said sure, he'd drive out to Great Neck the next night. He spent part of that night at the Grotto with Gene and some other people, then drove out to visit his friends. When he got into their neighborhood, he stopped at an all-night diner to say he was running late but he was nearly there, did they want him to bring over some sandwiches, or a chunk of pie? He reached their house about midnight, and stayed about two hours before driving home to Forest Hills.

He saw Gene the next night, and the next. Then he took another night off. He and Liz were stretched out on their bed, watching a movie, eating popcorn, when the phone in the den rang.

"I need to see you," Gene said abruptly. "I'm in your neighborhood. C'mon over and meet me at the diner."

Chris stalled. "Well, where exactly are you?" he asked.

"I told you, out by your place," Gene said impatiently. "I'm calling from the diner on Little Neck Parkway. I was going to just come by your house, but I'm hungry, so I came here. Hey, I need to talk, Curley, c'mon over."

Chris made up the best excuse he could think of, instantly—he had a girl with him, they were drinking, having a good time—"You know how it is, pal? I just can't get away now, you know?" Gene laughed knowingly and accepted it. But when Chris hung up the phone, he was chilly with sweat. Thank God the night they followed me wasn't the night I went straight home, he thought. When he'd gone inside his friends' house, and hadn't come out right away, they'd apparently been satisfied that he lived there. He wasn't sorry that they thought so; it worked to his advantage that they thought he lived so far from his real place. But it scared him. What if Gene hadn't been hungry, and had just turned up on the doorstep?

"I need another place," he told Harry. "I'm jeopardizing my wife, and myself, and my friends, and this whole operation, by living at home." Harry was dubious. "That'll cost money," he said.

"Harry, I'm telling you, I've *got* to have another place," Chris insisted. "Besides, I've been to Gene's apartment, and Bennie's place—they're going to wonder why I don't ask them to stop by my place sometime."

Harry nodded. "Okay, I'll see what I can do."

Chris was annoyed at Harry for not giving the immediate go-ahead; hadn't the inspector said he'd have carte blanche? But he was even more annoyed at himself. He'd been careless for driving out to Great Neck without checking his rearview mirror. The casual days and friendly nights had lulled him into a sense of security that he now saw was unfounded and dangerous. If he was going to make any headway in this operation, he would have to disassociate himself more clearly from his former life. No more visiting old friends. No more spending so many nights at home, pretending life was normal when it wasn't.

But was he making any headway? He had to admit he

doubted it. The ninety days had come and gone, and although he felt he'd done his best, about all he had to show for it was evidence of some drug deals and the hustling of merchandise that guys thought was swag. The highlight of his life in deep cover had been meeting Kostos and, he recalled wryly, getting the Big G's plate number. Instead of spinning his wheels, maybe he should drop out now and head back to the 4-oh. No questions asked.

All this was running through his mind when he saw Gene again. Gene grabbed him by the arm, talking fast and enthusiastically. He had decided he could make the money he needed by opening an after-hours joint. But he didn't have the cash. He needed a partner.

Chris tried to look doubtful. "For that kind of joint to make it, you need to be able to pull in a lot of people," he pointed out. "You know the people?"

"I know a ton of people, but I haven't got the money," Gene said.

Chris grinned. "If you've got the people, I've got the money," he said.

He got twenty-five hundred dollars from Harry and went on a shopping spree down in the Bowery with Gene, buying bar stools, fixtures, glassware. Gene liked working with his hands, and built a beautiful curving bar of mahogany. They set up shop on the second floor of a nondescript little building, cream-colored stucco in front, red brick on the sides, on 23rd Road in Astoria, about four blocks from the Grotto. They had to give a percentage to the guy who owned the building and who operated a bar on the first floor, a dingy little place with a tacky awning over the sidewalk entrance. Their place upstairs could be reached either by going through the downstairs bar, or directly from the sidewalk, through a side door. Chris preferred using the outside entrance, because he didn't like the owner; Gene called him a weasel. The weasel didn't want them to open their place until two A.M., so as not to cut into his business. When Gene told Chris he'd persuaded him to let them open at one o'clock, Chris didn't ask how.

They called their place the C&G Club, using their initials,

which looked good on the cards they had printed, and sounded good when they said it: the Cee-Gee Club. They had a grand opening. Then, to drum up business, they spent a lot of time in the evenings "making a drop"—dropping cards and conversation, along with their money, at other bars and clubs.

Their work paid off, as their place became popular, sometimes filled with customers from opening time till daybreak, or even beyond. Some of the guys who came were small-time hustlers; some were waiters who just came by to relax after a night's work. Pretty girls came, drawn to places where men with money and power might be found, and some of those men came, too. "Johnny the Gent" always had his overcoat draped over his shoulder, continental style, when he sauntered in, always smoking a cigarette in a silver holder, always with a couple of flunkies trailing in his wake. Johnny was tall and pencil-thin, with long, straight, oily hair that he wore combed down to one side over his forehead, nearly into his eye. Chris felt especially good when he was able to finger Johnny as a major heroin dealer, because he hated the way the guy swaggered, boasting about the deals he was making, the money he was raking in through some diners he had going. Chris thought of his father and the coffee shops he'd worked so hard to buy and then keep going, without having time to enjoy his money.

"The Gent" became such a regular that Chris knew, sooner or later, the information Harry funneled to the DEA—Drug Enforcement Administration—would attract some federal people. From the way some strangers in the club walked and acted and looked around, he pegged them for feds. Chris and Gene had hired a bouncer to stand down at the door and screen people, but he wasn't very good at his job, perhaps because he usually had a girlfriend or two hanging around to keep him company. Chris couldn't blame the kid; he knew from experience that if the law wanted to get in a place, the law would find a way to get in. He assumed that he himself would turn up in surveillance photographs, and one night, when he left, he was sure the feds were on his tail.

Keeping an eye in the rearview mirror, he gunned the car past ninety and, just past an exit ramp, swerved sharply around as their car sped by. He drove almost sideways down the ramp, managing somehow to make it down without hurtling over. He pulled off the service road and parked under the ramp. Then he realized he should have kept going; if they got off the parkway now, they'd nab him readily. How ludicrous it would be to be hauled in for speeding. But no cars came down the ramp. He felt a little sorry for them, knowing how frustrated they must be feeling, having lost him. On the other hand, if he'd taken them home, he'd have had them parked outside his house forever. He hoped it would be a consolation to them when they got "The Gent," as he heard they eventually did. He heard that Johnny was on his way to Greece, which had no extradition treaty with the United States, when the DEA forced his private plane down over Switzerland, which did.

Gene had been right when he said he knew "a ton of people." He knew a short man who came in one night and motioned to Gene to move from behind the bar to their little office in back. Gene owed the guy's boss a lot of money.

Chris had been standing beyond the main door. When he saw the guy whip out a gun, Chris walked up behind him and stuck his little automatic in his back. "Put it away," Chris said calmly. "If you hurt him, you are going to get killed. My partner needs a little more time. You'll get your money. In the meantime, just get the hell out."

Except for being stared at by the occasional federal agent, Chris wasn't bothered by the law, as he had thought he might be. He'd always been a little worried about being recognized by a cop from the one-fourteen. He'd checked the precinct roster when he went under, and hadn't recognized any names. But you never knew when someone might be transferred there, someone who might know him. Harry was keeping an eye on transfers, but a guy might slip through without Harry noticing. Even if nobody from the precinct recognized him, Chris had expected some kind of crackdown, even a raid. With half a dozen Cadillacs sometimes double-parked on the narrow street at three, four o'clock in the morning, all the lights on upstairs, people coming and going, how could the cops not notice? He was always prepared for an official visit, but the only two visits he had from cops, as far as he knew, were on their own initiative.

The first time, he knew the man was undercover without knowing for sure how he knew. Maybe he'd seen him in the hall at Intel, slipping in or out of a windowless room. Or maybe it just takes one to know one, he thought, as the guy took a seat at the bar. He had a drink. As he ordered his second drink, he said quietly to Chris that he wanted to buy some stuff. "I don't deal in drugs," Chris said, as sternly as a scoutmaster. "But I can steer you to somebody who does."

The other two cops who came in were in uniform.

"Whose place is this?" one demanded.

"It's mine," Chris said. "What can I do for you, Officer?"

The cop didn't answer. He walked around the room, then came back to the bar, where his partner was standing with Chris. He pointed out some building-code violations, including the lack of a banister at the top of the stairs. "You'll have to take care of that," the cop said. "We'll be back to make sure you take care of it."

Chris knew then why they had come, and he tried to tip them off. "You're better off leaving this alone," he said. Looking a little confused, they left. Chris felt bad about it, but he had to report them to Harry. He never asked what had happened, and he really didn't want to know. He hoped they'd just gotten off with a warning. They were young, with their whole careers ahead of them. They needed a warning. Chris could never figure out why a cop would take a few bucks' bribe and then, maybe within the hour, bust into an apartment where he knew a killer with a shotgun was waiting, or venture out onto a tenth-story ledge to try to stop a suicide. And even now that he was on the other side of the fence, he still couldn't figure it out.

Not that he had much time for philosophical musing. Once the C&G Club got going, he rarely got home before sunrise. Sometimes he didn't get home at all, and just napped for a couple of hours on the sofa in the back office. His life was centered around the place. He came to know just about everybody who came and went, except for the two men who came in, just before dawn, when the place was nearly empty.

They looked as though they had stepped right off the screen, from the cast of every gangster movie Chris had ever seen on those Saturday afternoons when Mr. Zuckerman let him in free. They wore hats slouched down over their foreheads and long black overcoats. Chris could hardly believe his eyes. They were truly Damon Runyon characters.

The man who did the talking had a deep, gravelly voice. The other man had a punched-in face, like an old prizefighter's, with a wide, thick scar running down one cheek. He kept his right hand in his overcoat pocket, moving it around under the heavy clothes as though he were fingering a gun, which Chris assumed he was. The man who spoke seemed to have memorized a script, too.

"Who gave you permission to open this place?" he growled. "You guys must be crazy! You gotta have permission!"

Neither Chris nor Gene spoke.

"Who you with?" the man demanded. "The Big G wants to know who you're with. And if you're not with anybody, you're gonna be with us."

Gene shrugged. "Well, who are you with?" he countered.

"Listen, pal," the man said. "I know *I'm* with people, but I don't know about you. How much you make here?"

Chris spoke up. "Oh, a couple hundred a week."

The man frowned. "Lissen, we've clocked you, and we know you're doin' good. From now on, you gotta give us five hundred a week."

Chris grinned at them. "Five hundred a week? Tell you what. You give us five a week, and you take the joint."

"What are you, a smart guy?" the man growled. The other man moved his hand restlessly in his pocket, and for a moment Chris thought he'd gone too far.

"No, no, he's okay," Gene cut in hastily. "We have to think about it. Give us a little time to think about it, okay?"

"Okay," the man said. "You got time. You got one week."

The two men turned and strode out, shoulder to shoulder.

"Jesus, what is this?" Chris asked Gene. "Is it the jukebox?"

"Naw, I took care of the jukebox guys, and the vending," Gene said. "These belong to Kostos."

"But they didn't look Greek," Chris said.

"They're not. They're Italian," Gene said. "But they're from Kostos." He clapped Chris on the shoulder. "I'll take care of it, Curley. I'll call my pal Frankie."

"But they said they'd be back in a week," Chris said, trying to sound worried. In fact, he was delighted. He'd wanted to attract attention, to get to the higher-ups, and now they had attention, even though the one with his hand in his pocket had made Chris a little jittery.

"It'll be okay," Gene assured him. "I'll take care of it."

Chris's instincts had been right: The small-timers were the way to go. Gene's friend Frankie was the nephew of a Mafia figure who'd had an interesting, active career. His résumé included a position as chauffeur for the boss of the Luchese crime family at the famous crime convention in Apalachin, New York, when some five dozen high-ranking mobsters were rounded up by the law. Although he appeared to be semi-retired now—"My uncle's out on Long Island, feeding the pigeons," Frankie told Gene—he liked keeping a hand in, keeping up with things.

He told Frankie to tell the boys—Chris and Gene—that he'd set up a meeting for them with a man named Solly, at the restaurant and cocktail lounge of the Kew Motor Inn, farther out in Queens. "My uncle will take care of it," Frankie assured Gene, who passed the word to Chris, who couldn't help thinking that the operating principle in OC seemed like that in any business anywhere: It wasn't so much what you knew, as who.

"What if I need to reach you sometime?" Liz asked. "What if there's an emergency or something?"

She pushed her food around on her plate with the tip of

her fork. "I hardly ever see you, and I don't even know where to get in touch with you, if I need you." She sounded tired and cross.

Chris was tired, too. "Have you needed to get in touch with me?" he countered.

"That's not the point," Liz said. She paused. "No, as a matter of fact, I haven't needed to, and I haven't even *wanted* to. Because I know you wouldn't have anything to say to me."

She got up from the table and took her plate to the sink. She scraped the food into the trash, put the plate in the sink and turned on the tap.

"Well, sometimes I call you and you're not home," Chris snapped. "What if *I* need to reach *you?* I don't always know where you are, either."

"You're smoking again," Liz said, without turning around.

"That's right," Chris said. "I'm smoking again."

Liz turned off the water, dried her hands and walked out of the room.

Chris put down his fork. He wasn't hungry anymore, either. The happy evening he'd planned, a kind of reunion, was a disaster.

Liz had been delighted to find him home when she got in from the city, where she'd had a tryout for an industrial show. "I think I got it!" she said, hugging him. "I'm almost sure I got it! Oh, it's good to have you home. I'll take a quick shower and we'll go out to dinner."

Chris hugged her, then stepped back. He should have said, "Hey, it's so good to be home, and I'm so tired, let's stay home together." Instead, he told the exact truth. "I can't go out, and please don't ask me why. I just can't go out."

Liz's smile faded as he continued quickly. "But I picked up some steaks, and stuff for a salad, and a good burgundy. You go relax—I'm the cook here."

It hadn't worked. Now, Chris put away the food and roamed restlessly around the apartment. He heard Liz running a bath. He felt edgy and trapped. He wondered whether he might take a chance, patch things up with her, take her someplace to hear some jazz. If anybody saw them, Chris could introduce her as his girlfriend.

Of course he couldn't. He'd have to set her up with a story beforehand, without being able to explain why. That would make things worse. Better to stay home and try to coax her back into a good mood.

He poured two glasses of wine. When she came into the living room, he drew her down beside him on the sofa, and handed her a glass. "Let's not fight," he said. "Let's just enjoy being together, okay?" Liz didn't answer, but she took the glass and settled down next to him. "Let's go in the bedroom and watch a movie on TV," Chris said. "Stretch out and relax." Then he leaned closer. "I've got a better idea. Let's just go in the bedroom."

"I've missed you," Liz murmured, as they lay nestled together. "I've missed you too," Chris said.

"Are you coming at Christmas?" Liz asked softly.

"Hey, that's a long way off," Chris said. "Sure I'm coming at Christmas. I wouldn't miss Christmas."

Liz sighed contentedly. "Let's sleep late," she murmured. "I want you in the morning."

"Sounds good," Chris said. Then his eyes flew open. "Dammit, I can't. I have to leave early." He pulled himself out of bed and found the alarm clock. When he'd told Harry about the meeting coming up at the Kew, Harry had said to meet him at seven, at a post office in Manhattan, to talk about it.

He set the alarm for five-thirty, got back into bed and reached for Liz again. But she had turned her back to him. She seemed to be asleep, though Chris was sure she wasn't.

They should have gotten a bachelor for this job, he thought unhappily. A guy with no ties. He'd give her Harry's phone numbers in case she needed to reach him.

He should have thought of that before. He should have thought of a lot of things before. He should have remembered that in the real world, he was a married man. Liz must have noticed he wasn't wearing his wedding ring.

4

If anyone had ever told Chris that a time would come when he would appreciate Lieutenant Blanchard, he would have been speechless with disbelief.

Chris had hated only two people in his life. There were people he didn't like much, for one reason or another, and some he tried to avoid, but he'd actually hated, with a deep bitterness, only twice. As a child, he'd hated the woman who was godmother to one of his sisters. She was mean to him. She would hit him, for no reason that he could tell, whenever she had the chance. Chris's father had never hit him; his mother had given him a smack on the rear end, once in a while, if she felt he needed it. But this old woman had once slapped him across the face so hard, when his mother wasn't in the room, that his head spun to the side. He didn't cry; he just stared at her, hating her, thinking, you have no right to hit me, you old bitch. Even when he was grown, he would ask his mother to let him know when that woman was coming to visit, so he wouldn't be in the house.

Lieutenant Blanchard was his tactical officer in the army. When Chris enlisted, he was sent to Fort Dix, New Jersey, for his basic training. He found he liked the order and routine of military life. It seemed a rational, respectable way to live, and he decided to make the army his career. Since he didn't have a college degree, he had to take a test for Officers Candidate School. The test was hard, and Chris was pessimistic. The sergeant skimmed over the test papers as Chris stood by his desk, nervously.

The sergeant looked at him. "How much do you want to be an officer?" he asked.

"I just really do," Chris said. "All I want now is to be an officer in the United States Army."

The sergeant looked at the test papers, then back at Chris. He shoved the papers in a desk drawer. "There's a class starting in two weeks," he said gruffly. "You're in it, son. Good luck to you."

On the very first day at Fort Benning, Georgia, Lieutenant Blanchard singled Chris out, asking him to step forward from the rank.

"Candidate Anastos! You're from New York, isn't that right?" Lieutenant Blanchard asked.

"Sir! Candidate Anastos, sir!" Chris said, in the formal style required in addressing an officer. "Yes sir, that's right, I am from New York, sir."

The lieutenant smiled. "Well, I am a southerner, and I do not like New Yorkers," he said. "Are you carrying a knife, boy?"

"Sir! Candidate Anastos, sir! No sir, I am not carrying a knife," Chris replied.

"Now, I know you have got a knife on you, boy," Blanchard persisted. "I want you to hand over that knife to me right now." When Chris again denied it, the officer sneered. "I hate New Yorkers," he said. "And I am going to break you, boy! You are not leadership material. Now give me fifty pushups."

From that day on, Blanchard was on him constantly. Constantly! In the mess hall, where the men ate in total silence, staring straight ahead, without moving their heads, Chris would be eating, looking directly across the table, when Blanchard would loom over him. "Candidate Anastos! You're eyeballing again!" Whereupon Blanchard would pick up Chris's food tray and hurl it across the room. Chris would have to clean up the mess, then go outside and do pushups while the rest of the guys finished eating.

Once or twice a week, Blanchard would burst into Chris's room at two or three o'clock in the morning, turn on the light and bark, "Candidate Anastos! You're in the wrong room! You are being transferred to another room NOW!" Chris would lurch out of bed, gather all his bedding and gear, and move to another room on another floor, where he would make up the bed, hang up his clothing in the precise fashion, with uniform sleeves all pointing in the same direction in the closet, arrange underwear and socks folded in a certain way in the drawer, lay out his shaving gear just so. By the time he finished, it was time to get up. Once, Blanchard did that every night for five consecutive nights. Then he didn't come for a week. But by then, Chris was so edgy and tense, lying in bed awake, expecting him to come bursting into the room any minute, that he might as well have come.

Chris knew that some of the grueling routine was necessary and well-intended: the five-mile run before breakfast with full pack and rifle above the head, the chinning bar in the mess hall doorway—if you couldn't pull ten chins, you couldn't eat. "The word 'can't' is not in your vocabulary," Blanchard told the men. Chris understood that; an officer in the United States Army should be expected to do what ordinary men could not. He knew the purpose of keeping a guy mentally and physically off-balance was to keep him always at his peak, so when the time came to perform, he could handle it. When he was directing maybe forty or fifty men on a mission, the tac officer would scream in his ear, "What is your decision NOW?" He didn't have time to think about what he should do, or could or couldn't do; he just did it.

But Blanchard was going out of his way to harass him. Chris was not a star in the classroom, but his grades were passing. He tried to observe rules to the letter, mostly, though he did sneak cans of Sterno into his tent, on bivouac, because it was so damned cold. If it were set up properly, the heat would stay in the tent for about an hour and a half. His classmates elected him Code of Conduct officer. He took Blanchard's constant punishments: "You got a hair sticking out of your nose, boy! Give me one hundred pushups! How many pushups do you owe me now, boy?" "Sir! Candidate Anastos, sir! Four hundred and seventy-five, sir!" During the day, Blanchard would come into his room, scuff up the floor, smile and walk out, so that Chris would have to spit-shine the floor all over again.

The more Blanchard picked on him, the more Chris was determined to survive, and become an officer in the United States Army. He thought he was indeed leadership material. He mastered "Escape and Evasion," when the men were dropped into an unfamiliar zone at night, equipped only with a poncho and a compass, and instructed to get back to the compound before sunup. Even with trained army dogs loose in the area, and with officers acting as the enemy, Chris always made it back without being captured.

Near the end of his six months' training, he thought he'd made it. The candidates were already being addressed as "Lieutenant" when Chris met Blanchard in the hall outside a classroom one day.

"You think you're going to make it, don't you, boy?" Blanchard said, sticking his face right up under Chris's nose. "Well, I don't think you are going to make it, and I am not through with you yet." The man was breathing so heavily on him that Chris reached out and pushed him away. It was a very slight push, only one hand lightly on the lieutenant's shoulder, a please-move-back-a-little kind of push, but it was enough. Blanchard stepped back, stared for a moment, then grinned. "I broke you! I broke you, boy!" he said gleefully.

Two days later, Chris was paneled: brought before a military board. Blanchard appeared to testify against him. Just before they went in, the officer reached out and brushed a piece of lint from Chris's shoulder.

The hearing was short. The room was ice-cold, with the air conditioning turned too high. The verdict of the board was that Chris not be commissioned at that time; he was told to reapply for OCS and go through the training again. Chris said the heck with it and returned to his infantry unit for the rest of his military service, still owing Blanchard several hundred pushups.

Now, a decade later, Chris had to admit that all that training was coming in handy. He knew how to live with tension, constantly alert, making instant decisions, keeping people off-balance so they wouldn't have time to stop and wonder, who the hell *is* this guy?

He could scan a room or a restaurant and within thirty seconds know who was there and whether he should stay or not, by doing a map coordinate search: sectioning off small squares of the room and searching with his eyes in a grid pattern. One night when he stopped at Riccardo's, a restaurant and catering hall in Queens, he saw a DA sitting at a table with a major OC figure. They were drinking and talking; at one point, the mobster put his arm around the DA. "Don't give those guys any cases," Chris told Harry. "Stick all your cases in Manhattan." Harry turned it over to the feds, so Chris didn't have to deal with it, but the incident made him worry: Who's got a pipeline into the NYPD?

He lived with insecurity, on the edge. Every day he asked himself, "Am I going to make a mistake today? Did somebody see me? Did somebody find out something about me since yesterday?" He found himself analyzing every comment that was made to him, every glance. If someone looked at him in what seemed to be even a minutely different way, Chris would immediately become suspicious. The psychological fear was worse than the physical fear, though they usually went hand-in-hand, Chris discovered, when he and Gene drove out to the Lakeville Manor, a Long Island place, to make a drop.

Inside the front door, Chris made his grid search, but he hesitated a moment too long before turning back toward the door. "Hey, Chrissie, how are ya, how ya doing?" Dino called.

Dino was standing at the bar with Les and Arnie and a couple of others. That old gang of mine, Chris thought grimly as he walked over to them. To make it worse—a lot worse—they were drinking with Dominic, Gene's friend from Astoria, whom Chris had met at Jimmy's. Dominic knew Chris through Gene; Dino and those guys knew Chris from way back. They knew he was going to become a cop.

"Hey, Chrissie, long time no see," Dino said, studying Chris. Arnie was frowning at him. Chris wondered if they could tell he was hyperventilating, oozing sweat. Maybe they don't remember I went into the NYPD, he thought, knowing it was a futile thought.

Still, nobody said anything, as they all had a drink and talked about the C&G Club. Gene handed out cards. As soon as he felt he reasonably could, Chris nodded to Gene. "Let's go," he said. "We got more stops to make."

As Chris and Gene were walking away, Chris saw Arnie lean close to Dominic, saying something. Then they both turned and looked at Chris. From the way they looked, Chris just knew what Arnie had told Dom. Let me just get out of here, Chris thought. Just a few more steps and I am out this door.

"Hey Gene," Dom called. "Come back here a minute, will ya? I wanna talk to you."

Gene went back to talk to Dom. Chris went to the bathroom. He was in absolute panic. He had his automatic in his boot, and he even wondered for a crazy moment whether he ought to come out shooting.

Gene was waiting for him at the door, looking impassive. When they were back in the car and Gene still wasn't talking, Chris couldn't stand it. "What was that all about?" he asked. "What did Dom want?"

Gene didn't turn his head. He kept his eyes on the road. His hands gripped the steering wheel tightly. "Dom said that Arnie said, 'What's your friend doing with a fucking cop?' "

Chris felt a tight band across his chest. He took a deep breath, to loosen it and get some air.

"Arnie told Dom, 'I know that guy, and he's a cop, be careful,' " Gene continued.

Chris took another breath, then forced himself to laugh. "So, what's the big deal?" he said harshly. "Yeah, I was a cop, and I got fired. I got thrown off the job. So what?"

Gene turned and looked at Chris. "That's what I told him," Gene said in a level tone. "I said, 'Sure, I know that Curley used to be a cop. I thought everybody knew that.' " Gene turned his head and looked straight ahead at the road again. "I told him I've known you for twenty years, and you're doin' things with me now, and you're a good guy and I trust you."

Chris didn't know what to say. "Well, hey, thanks pal," he muttered. He felt limp with relief. Why had Gene bailed him out? Had Gene checked him out downtown and been told the bad-cop story? Or had Gene done it, regardless, because they were partners, because he had pulled his gun on the shylock who was hounding Gene? It was another question he'd have to think about, without being able to ask.

They checked in at their place, then ended up at Jimmy's. Dominic was at the bar, fresh from his conversation at the Lakeville Manor, talking to Jimmy. From the way they looked at him, Chris knew that Dominic was passing on what he'd been told. Neither of them said anything to him about it, and Gene's vouching for him had settled the matter, at least temporarily. But Chris felt that Dominic never trusted him after that. As for Jimmy, the question became academic.

One night Chris and Gene left Jimmy's place shortly after midnight, leaving Dom behind. Chris was behind the bar in the club when Dom came in, white as a ghost. "Gimme a drink," he muttered. He sat at the bar, his hands trembling as he clenched the glass. "They just whacked Jimmy," he said hoarsely. Jimmy had been gunned down in the Astoria municipal parking lot.

Chris realized sharply then what he'd always known: He was in more danger from those who thought he was a hood than from those who thought he was a cop. Guilt by association. Assassination by association. He felt reasonably safe in his own place, but outside, you never knew what was going to happen. You never knew what somebody you were with had going with somebody else. He left the Grotto one night about a half hour before Kostos. When Kostos got outside, a car pulled alongside the curb and a man with a gun leaned out and fired. Fortunately for Kostos, just as the car pulled up, he turned back toward the building and lowered his head slightly, as he unzipped his trousers to take a leak.

Still, he was in the hospital a while, where he told the questioning police that he didn't have any idea who had shot him—probably some black guys who'd intended to rob him. Chris never found out who had tried to whack him out, but it somehow got ironed out. Chris was glad, because he'd become rather fond of the old Greek. They sometimes sang Greek folk songs together, and listened to *rebetiko* music. "I like you," Kostos told Chris one night, clasping his shoulders, "but I don't do business with you unless I know you twenty years."

Chris wasn't terribly disappointed. He'd met Solly.

When Chris and Gene drove out to the Kew, they sat at the bar in the cocktail lounge until Solly motioned them to his corner table. They told him about the two men in overcoats who'd come to their club. "Did you give them money?" Solly asked. They said they hadn't. "Good," Solly said. "Once you give them money, you're committed to them." It was an insight for Chris into the curious code of honor among these thieves, a sense of obligation and commitment that existed along with a sense of fierce and sometimes deadly competition. "They won't come back," Solly told them. "You're with me now. I'll talk to Kostos tomorrow."

"Is that all there is to it?" Chris asked Gene, as they drove back to Astoria. "That's all there is to it," Gene said, laughing. "Those bums won't come back." And they did not. Once Solly talked to Kostos and gave the boys his blessing, the matter was closed. The two men respected one another and would do one another a favor whenever they could. It was Solly's pleasure to help out the young fellows who were friends of his friend's nephew. It was Kostos's pleasure not only to let them alone, once they had Solly's blessing; he would now patronize their place and send other customers around.

Harry was ecstatic when he saw Chris's report. "Holy shit!" Harry exclaimed. "We've never been able to get close to this bunch. Holy shit!"

At a morning meeting at a hotel on the Upper West Side of Manhattan, Harry gave Chris a rundown.

"They're out on Long Island, some of them," Harry said, "but they're operating downtown, all over the place. Trucking, construction, just for openers. We think your new pal Solly might be the connection."

Chris looked dubious. "What am I supposed to do now, exactly?"

"Exactly what you're doing," Harry said. "Keep your eyes and ears open. Only now you're in a spot where you can see and hear more. A *lot* more."

"So what about the Greeks?" Chris asked.

"Look, you've done nice work with the Greeks," Harry assured him. "And you'll still keep your hand in. What I'm telling you—and I'm not sure you're listening—is that now you are dealing with some heavyweights."

"Hey, I'm listening," Chris protested. "I'm just trying to get it straight. Who are these guys, anyway? You got pictures?"

"We don't have everybody on file," Harry said patiently. "I told you that. Look, if we knew what everybody was doing with everybody else, we wouldn't need you out there. You'll just have to stay on the lookout. Get yourself noticed. Stay close to Solly, he's got interesting associations." Harry paused. "You want to review photos, no problem. I can call it up here in ten minutes."

"No, that's okay," Chris said, a little annoyed that Harry might be doubting his memory. "I remember that stuff."

"Okay then," Harry said. He paused again. "You're getting in deeper, kid. You want a backup?"

"No way," Chris said.

Solly was a "made man"—initiated—in the Luchese crime family. He told Chris that his brother had had the contract to kill Joseph Valachi back in the early sixties, when both men were doing time in Atlanta. But Valachi, knowing he was marked, had not waited to be hit. Early one summer morning, in the prison yard, Valachi had taken a two-foot length of iron pipe and beat a prisoner to death. Only he'd killed the wrong man. Solly's brother was alive and well and living in Little Italy, operating a social club on Prince Street. He was a Luchese capo, believed by Intel to control a network through which other traditional OC families acquired much of their narcotics.

It was Joe Valachi who, after making that bloody error, had talked openly, at length, about the Mafia, giving law enforcement people and the general public a long look at the inner workings of "Cosa Nostra." Even before that, Senator Estes Kefauver had broken investigatory ground with his year-long examination of crime in America, including the infiltration of legitimate businesses by "known hoodlums." Kefauver had closed with a ringing statement: "I know it is hard to pin anything on the Costellos, Adonises, Anastasias, Zwillmans, Lanskys, and all the rest of that dirty crew [but] if it takes years or even decades, we should get them."

Chris was ten years old when the Kefauver hearings ended. Now, two and a half decades later, he was trying to pin something on them by becoming one of "that dirty crew." Still, what did he know about the Mafia?

He knew he'd liked *The Godfather*, especially the theme music, but he knew that much of the stuff written about the mob was romantic garbage. He knew they sometimes seemed like court jesters, with their nicknames and their slang, their pointy shoes, their black shirts with white ties, but from his perspective, it wasn't so funny.

He knew that his father had been right about their old neighborhood; Luchese, Frank Costello, and Joe Valachi had been among the regulars. Valachi had even owned the Aida restaurant, six blocks from Chris's home, until 1945, when he sold it for reasons not unlike George's: The neighborhood was going downhill.

He knew that the silly name he'd heard as a kid, "Three-Finger Brown," was Gaetaneo Luchese, a.k.a. Thomas Luchese and Tommy Brown. (He knew, but didn't know why, Italian mobsters favored Irish aliases: Aniello Dellacroce was Timothy O'Neil; Thomas Eboli, who'd been whacked out not long before Chris went under, was Tommy Ryan.)

And he knew that the term "wiseguy" was too intriguing and catchy to describe them. He preferred "asshole."

Solly chain-smoked Pall Malls. Chris never saw him—ever—without a cigarette. He was sixty-two years old, a little pudgy, short, with pouches under his eyes, a perpetually mournful expression and a mind, Chris found, like a calculator. Solly could calculate percentages in his head while Chris was still muddling through "times this" and "divide by this" on paper.

Partly because Chris was a friend of Frankie, via Gene, partly because Chris on his own was so likable and respectful and smart, Solly took Chris under his wing. Chris made a quick cigarette deal with Solly, who passed the instructions along to his crew, and made twelve hundred dollars for himself without moving from his chair at the Kew. When Chris learned that Solly did some deals with antiques, working through his son-in-law, who had a shop on Third Avenue in Manhattan, Chris wangled a vase and a few other objects from the property clerk. Solly was not impressed. "This isn't Ming dynasty," he informed Chris, who yelled at Harry to tell the property clerk to henceforth give him only authentic merchandise, not fakes.

Harry was hounding Chris to get inside Solly's brother's club on Prince Street. Chris explained to Harry what Harry already knew: You didn't just run down to Prince Street, drop in and snoop around. You waited to be taken there, and you wouldn't be taken there until you were trusted, until you'd proven yourself.

Chris was careful to let Solly think he could be trusted. When Chris began driving out to the Kew, he would hang around the bar until Solly invited him over to his table. In the meantime, Chris found that the barmaid's chatter could be very helpful. When other men arrived to talk business with Solly, Chris would get up and leave the table, so Solly would know he was a respectful guy. Chris knew that by winning Solly's trust at the outset, he'd hear those things and more, another day.

His technique worked so well that he seemed to gain not only Solly's trust, but a measure of concern. Knowing that Solly's family was heavily into heroin, he tried to make a deal with him. But Solly shook his head. "Keep out of that, Chrissie," he said in his slow, mournful voice. "I don't want you to do that. No babania. You're gonna keep out of that stuff." One night, at a gambling joint, Solly pointed his finger at Chris. "Are you carrying a piece?" Chris said yes. "Now you go right down and put it in your car," Solly said, as though he were correcting a wayward lad who'd been caught with a forbidden Hershey bar. Chris realized that Solly was protecting him; in case of a raid, Solly didn't want him to be collared for carrying a gun.

Other people noticed Solly's concern, especially one of his henchmen, a guy called Big Lou. "You know, Chrissie," Lou said to him one day, with thoughtful menace, "you're moving up awfully fast, and I keep wondering why. I spent two hours today thinking about you."

Chris grinned at him. Sometimes, he reflected ruefully, the style of the cop and the wiseguy were not so unlike: Each knew how to stay alert in a macho world, and had mastered the art of the snappy comeback. "That's funny," Chris shot back, "because I only spent ten minutes today thinking about you."

As a wisecrack, it was true enough. With managing the Astoria joint, and hanging out at the Kew, and dropping in occasionally at clubs in "Greek Town" along Eighth Avenue in Manhattan, Chris sometimes didn't know if he was coming or going. Trying to maintain a marriage was something that had to be squeezed in, somehow, sometime; it didn't help that even when he was at home, Chris felt he was at the mercy of the phone in the den.

He no longer remembered when payday was; he knew his check, four hundred dollars and change, was being deposited for him every two weeks; he'd written out rent checks in advance, and that aspect of his life began to seem less and less real, part of another world. Sometimes he didn't know what was going on in that world, and he didn't particularly try to know. He picked up a newspaper most days, so he wouldn't lose touch entirely, which is how he knew that two cops had been killed.

Chris stood frozen, right there on the sidewalk by the newsstand as he read the story through. The cops had been gunned down in the street, where they'd stopped a car—a red convertible. The reason for the killing wasn't yet known, but the cops had been on "routine patrol." They lay dying in the street, one a fifty-year-old veteran, Sergeant Frederick Reddy, one a thirty-four-year-old, Police Officer Andrew Glover.

Now, in the traffic noises all around him, all Chris could hear was the woman in the doorway of her shop screaming, "Holdup! He gimme holdup!" He remembered his partner tackling the guy, and Chris tumbling down on both of them. He remembered the medal—his first medal, and the first for Andy Glover, too. He remembered Andy's grin, that sensational grin that split his face in half. Andy had always seen the bright side of life.

When he went to the country with Liz that Christmas, he felt he needed the trip more than ever.

They walked in the woods. They made a snowman. They roasted marshmallows in the fireplace. They lay on the floor together, near the Christmas tree, looking into the fire. Chris hadn't realized, until he was out of New York, how tense he'd become. Now he could feel the tension drain away. For a day and a half, he had absolutely nothing to worry about. He didn't have to be on edge, constantly on guard. Liz noticed the difference. "You're a different person when you're out of the city," she said. "You're not so tense. You're more like yourself."

Yet he wasn't sorry when it was time to return to his other life, which he had to admit he was enjoying. He didn't think of it as lying. He was acting; playing a role. It never occurred to him to feel guilty or bad in any way about what he was doing. All the wrong things he was doing were being done for all the right reasons. How many people ever got the chance to do what he was doing and never have to pay the price?

He liked the feeling of cash in his pocket. He liked being able to go to a restaurant with a group and pick up the check. He didn't do that often, lest he be considered a lob, a popcorn—in laymen's language, a pushover—but he did it often enough to please Solly and, he had to admit, to please himself. He liked tossing a ten-dollar bill to the kid who parked his car, leaving a twenty-dollar tip for the barmaid after a night at the Kew, or at the Grotto. He liked eating well, at places where OC guys ate. The restaurants were not always fancy, though some were, but the food was invariably first-rate. These customers demanded the whitest veal, the best imported pasta, the most carefully garlicked sauces, the freshest fish. Chris learned to be specific when he ordered: not just bourbon, but Jack Daniels. He learned to drink sambuca—not unlike the ouzo his father had sometimes brought out, on holidays at home—with three coffee beans in it. The waiter always brought the bottle to the table, along with a dish of coffee beans. You poured your own, and you had to take three beans—not four, not two, always three—for good luck.

He liked being recognized and catered to. At Lucho's, on Third Avenue in Manhattan, the chef would come out from the kitchen, when he heard that Chris had arrived, to take his order personally, to assure Chris that he'd make the sauce just the way he liked it, extra garlic. Chris liked summoning the chef, then, after the meal, to give compliments and a large greenback to go with it. He liked being able to peel off, say, six hundred dollars from his bankroll, when he was buying, leave a two-hundred-dollar cash tip, and he liked knowing that, after that, he'd never have to call for a reservation.

He liked bouncing around. The restlessness that had led him, in earlier years, to pick up club dates here and there, never planning ahead, to live for the day, now had a justified outlet. When Frankie said, "Hey, Chrissie, let's go to Vegas for the weekend," he liked being able to say, "Why not?" and hop on the plane without a second thought. Gene went along. They had no business to conduct, though they ran into a bunch of people Gene and Frankie knew; they just went to eat and drink and have some laughs. Chris didn't have to justify the trip on his expense account, because Frankie insisted it was his treat, thanks to one of the credit cards in various names he carried.

Like most of his colleagues, Frankie considered spending his own money a mark of dishonor, though he had enough of his own from his no-show job in construction. Or almost no-show; for his thousand dollars a week, Frankie was supposed to show up at the building site and blow the whistle at starting time, and again at quitting time. As far as Chris could tell, Frankie never let that responsibility weigh too heavily. Chris liked going to the track with Frankie, especially as he was beginning to win more often than he lost. He liked buying a hot Brioni suit, a seven-hundred-dollar job, for a hundred-fifty. He liked being able to buy hot gifts; when the barmaid at the Kew said to him one night, admiringly, "Chris, you are class personified," he reached in his pocket and handed her a gold chain. He liked the freedom of motion in this job—and he didn't have to try to sell anybody insurance.

And he liked the apartment Harry set up for him, in the Waterside complex, just off East 25th Street in Manhattan. In the dark-red high-rise, jutting out into the East River, he had an apartment above the twenty-fifth floor, with a glorious nighttime view of twinkling lights, sparkling dark water, jeweled bridges.

Harry outfitted two apartments, one above the other, with an amazing array of monitoring devices. When Chris came into his apartment and turned on the wall switch at the door, all systems flicked ON; the recorder, the camera inserted behind a picture on the wall, facing the sofa. The phone was rigged, but simply, not in the sophisticated method they'd used in Forest Hills: There was a carbon mike in the mouthpiece, which meant that Chris could unscrew the mouthpiece and take out the mike, if he wanted to, and somebody who unscrewed the mouthpiece would see the mike, too. Since they didn't know how long Chris would be needing the place, Harry said—probably not very long—they didn't want to go through the complicated, expensive electronic business again. When Chris was alone, with no need for gadgets, he wouldn't use the wall switch; he would turn on the table lamps in the living room and in the bedroom.

The kitchen was small, not even a separate room, with only a divider between the kitchen space and the living room. Since Chris didn't intend to do much kitchen duty, it didn't matter. Once in a while he had a yen for Greek food, after years of thinking he'd had his fill. At school, when other kids had peanut butter and jelly sandwiches or baloney sandwiches, in their lunchboxes, he'd find that Katrina had sent him off with eggplant parmigiana, olives, artichokes. When he had feta cheese in his lunch, other kids would hold their noses and say, "What the heck is *that*?" Chris would sometimes throw his lunch away, on the way to school, and either go without, or buy a handful of candy bars and call it lunch.

The apartment was unfurnished. "Don't get carried away," Harry warned, when Chris set out to furnish the place. "You're not supposed to be living like a sheik." Chris said he wouldn't. An hour later, Harry called back. "I've arranged a loan from the Salvation Army," he told Chris. "I thought you might get carried away."

So Chris went to the Salvation Army where, somewhat to his surprise, it worked out fine. The Salvation Army people, having been told that two rooms of furniture were needed for an important NYPD project, had sorted out some very good pieces, including a sofa in a dark-green fabric and an upholstered chair, lightly used, just enough so the pieces didn't look too new. The dining table and chairs were ordinary-looking, but Chris knew that the guys who would be coming around to play cards would play on an overturned orange crate, if necessary. The queen-sized bed had a new mattress. Chris bought satin sheets, in a whimsical mood, to give the place some flash.

At the Salvation Army, he bought a small suitcase full of women's clothes, using a mental picture of Liz to guide him in choosing the clothes, which the clerk told him was size eight. He bought three pairs of high-heeled shoes and went to a drugstore where he asked the salesgirl to pick out a collection of cosmetics for him to give to a young lady as a gift. All these things scattered around the apartment would give visitors the impression that Chris had a woman in his life. In fact, he had suggested to Harry that a policewoman be sent under, to be his occasional girlfriend. When Harry vetoed that idea, Chris had begun picking out girls from the flock at his place to take to dinner from time to time, or to a club. If he'd never been seen with a female, he thought he'd be looked at with suspicion. Although he thought there was a good deal of latent homosexuality among mob guys, they had women—lots of women—in their lives. In these circles, Friday night was "*gummare*" night—girlfriend night—at clubs and restaurants, Saturday night was wife night, usually at the same clubs and restaurants. Chris figured the wives must have thought, What the heck? The man's a killer, a shylock, an extortionist—what difference does it make if he has a girlfriend?

Chris had lived with his mother until he was married, so this was the first place of his own, all his own, that he didn't have to share even with a wife. He put up a *Rigoletto* poster and shelved his opera records. He put up bookshelves and stacked some of his books, including *Bulfinch's Mythology*. He hung a framed print of his favorite painting, Edward Hopper's "Early Sunday Morning."

Once, it was said, you proved yourself in the mob by making a hit: killing somebody. Harry had a plan, in case that ever came up—he'd have arranged to have the potential victim kidnapped by the law and held in faraway protective custody while Chris took all the credit. They didn't expect it would come up, though, and it didn't. In the modern mob, Chris found, you proved yourself by showing that you were an earner. Anybody could be connected, whether Greek, Jew, even black, if he could prove himself an earner. He wouldn't be cut in on a flourishing enterprise, but he would be given a chance to prove he could turn around an operation that wasn't doing well. Chris knew he was being tested when Solly commissioned him to take over the management of an OC spot on West 38th Street in Manhattan. "The guy who's running it for me is slacking off," Solly told Chris. "He's out, I'm putting you in."

As much as he wanted to get next to Solly and his crew, Chris was dismayed at the prospect because, beside the gambling operation, there was a prostitute section. He took a chance, and told Solly of his qualms. "I don't want you to be a pimp," Solly assured him. "I just want you to manage the place."

Chris recruited a guy from Astoria to oversee the pross operation and, altogether, it wasn't so bad. The old loft building was clean and well-kept, with a directory in the small lobby that listed the place as The Daily Planet. The girls were mostly young and pretty, recruited from ads for "Hostess" in the *Village Voice;* many of them were college students. And the customers were mostly clean-cut, upright citizens; businessmen with briefcases, making a quick detour between their offices and the nearby Port Authority Bus Terminal, where they caught buses home to the suburbs. Still, Chris felt cheap as he worked on the bookkeeping: thirty-five dollars a pop, with twenty-five for the house, eight for the girl, two for towels.

By 8 P.M. the pross business had died out, and Chris could concentrate on the gambling side, which he enjoyed. He decided to set up a barbouti game. He thought he could pick up the cups for rolling the dice at any store, maybe even Woolworth's. When he couldn't find them anywhere, he had to ask a guy at the Grotto. "You're still a Greek greenhorn," the guy jeered. "There's only one place you can get them, and they have to be hand-stitched, with a special kind of leather." When he wouldn't tell Chris where that one place was, Chris turned to Kostos, who sent him to a cobbler in Astoria. Chris had to pay two hundred fifty dollars for the pair of cups. Harry hit the ceiling when Chris showed him that item on his expenses, but he calmed down when Chris handed over a large bundle of bills. On a good night, The Daily Planet grossed eight to ten thousand dollars. Even on a slow night, two to four thousand. The place in Astoria wasn't doing so well—Chris suspected that Gene was skimming, to pay the shys—but it didn't seem to matter so much. Even after Chris turned over Solly's share—sometimes to Solly himself, sometimes to Big Lou—Chris had a lot of cash to turn over to Harry, while still keeping several thousand in his pocket for day-to-day expenses. He couldn't help thinking, hey, maybe crime *does* pay!

"See that guy?" a club owner said to Chris one night at the Skyway, a joint near LaGuardia. "He's one of the youngest captains in the police department. He pulls yellow sheets for me."

Chris didn't know the guy, but he felt a little sick. He still felt bad when he learned that cops, even captains, had their price. As a child, he'd been walking with his mother along a street in East Harlem, when he'd caught a glimpse of a scene that, even now, all these years later, stood out in his mind in a dreadful freeze-frame.

They'd been passing a tenement building, Chris clinging

to his mother's hand, when he'd turned his head slightly and had seen, in the doorway of a building, a man beating up a cop in uniform. The man was hitting the policeman hard, holding him up against the wall with one hand and punching him in the stomach with the other hand.

Katrina hadn't seen it, and in a moment they'd passed by. It had bothered Chris then, though he hadn't said anything about it; he wouldn't have known what to say. Later, he realized he'd seen a cop on the take being beaten up by a guy he'd doublecrossed, or hadn't paid off sufficiently, or whatever.

Even when he became a cop, Chris had had only one encounter that illustrated to him the relationship of some cops with some OC people. He and Phil had never worked with the public morals unit, whose job it was to keep tabs on after-hours places, the KG's—known gamblers—and the clubs in their South Bronx neighborhood. But one day, about eleven o'clock in the morning, they'd spotted a guy on a street corner who seemed to them to be making all the right wrong moves. When they parked their car around the corner and got out, intending to talk to him, the guy took off. They ran him down at Emilio's, where he was sitting at the bar with a drink in his hand.

"Why were you running away from us?" Phil demanded.

"Who, me?" the man mumbled. "I don't know what you're talking about." While Phil was getting the guy to his feet, patting him down, Chris noticed a tiny slip of white sticking out from the thick vinyl padding along the bartop. When Chris pulled on it, other bits of paper came up, too.

"Digits," Chris told Phil. "Numbers. The guy's a bookie."

He jabbed a finger at him. "We're taking you in for gambling," he said, as a voice called softly, from the semidarkness at the end of the bar. "Officer, can I talk to you?"

Phil stayed with the numbers runner while Chris walked the length of the bar, to the man who'd spoken. He was older, with gray hair, well-dressed. "Can we work this out?" he asked Chris.

Chris stared at him.

"Let my guy go," the man repeated, "and you and I can adjudicate this right here."

Chris felt as though he had been smacked in the face. "If you are offering me a bribe," he said loudly, "this is what I am going to do. First: I am going to kick you in the balls. Second: I am then going to lock you up also."

The man just smiled and shrugged, a small, half-sad, half-sanguine smile that said, have it your way, but you're wrong.

Chris put the slips in his helmet bag—they always carried helmets in the car, for riot situations—and they drove with their prisoner back to the station. Chris was astonished to find that they were not congratulated on making the bookmaker collar; in fact, they got a lot of flak. They were criticized for having overstepped their role and some cops suggested they just drop it, even though it was felony weight. When they went ahead with the procedures, vouchered all the evidence, they were given the silent treatment, made to feel like outcasts. When the court date came, all the evidence—the betting slips—had mysteriously disappeared. Chris thought again of the man's quiet arrogance, the smug sense of power reflected in that look on his face.

Now he was seeing that same look on the faces around him. In their world of rules and power plays and respect, these men—at least the older men—spoke quietly. Solly had an especially slow, deliberate way of speaking, as though nothing in the world could upset him.

The deeper Chris got with the Italians, the more he felt that this route was more productive. He had pretty much concluded that there was no organized crime structure among the Greeks. Obviously they had connections, roots within the Italian families, but as far as the Greek crime community went, it was not organized. Only Kostos and a guy from Canada seemed to have real influence; below them, the mob was on the loose. The Greeks were so unstructured, in fact, that Gene suggested to Chris that they set up a crime family.

Chris knew that Gene and most of the others felt he was

more intelligent than they. He didn't necessarily think so; he felt a novice in their world, while they knew all the angles. Still, they were coming to him for advice. Chris was fascinated by one guy who made about ten grand a month in fraudulent insurance claims, who came to Chris for advice in filling out the forms. Chris was fascinated by his MO: He would buy cars in various states, change the VIN—the Vehicle Identification Number—get a duplicate car, stage a wreck, and eventually collect. The operation was so complicated that it went over Chris's head, and he was impressed. The scheme was so profitable that the man moved from Astoria to a luxury building on the east side of Manhattan, where he organized a tenant's association. When he collected a five-hundred-dollar membership fee from most of the sixty tenants, he moved out.

"Why don't we start our own thing, and you be the top guy?" Gene asked Chris, who thought it was an excellent suggestion, as he explained to Harry. "I'll draw more attention, I'll get more information."

Harry turned purple. "Are you *nuts*? Are you *bananas*? Have you gone totally *berserk*?" Harry yelled. "Do you have any idea what could happen to you? Forget it! I am telling you, forget it!" So Chris had to explain to Gene regretfully that it was too bad, he just didn't have time to be a godfather.

It was true that his time was limited in Queens, now that he was paying so much attention to Solly and the Italians. When Solly invited him to a christening party one Sunday in late spring, Chris was glad to go. He was always on the lookout for new names and faces.

The house was big and rambling—not a mansion, but a house that spoke of money and all the consolations money could buy. More than the house, it was the wide sweep of lawn that impressed Chris. He knew the price of acreage on Long Island. A circular driveway led to the main entrance, where Doric columns—a little too grand for the house—flanked the doorway.

Chris didn't go inside that day. The party was outdoors,

on the expanse of freshly trimmed lawn, where a blue-and-yellow-striped tent had been set up. A long table was laden with food: watermelons scooped out holding melon balls, strawberries, gleaming black grapes. A chef in a tall white hat carved slices of baked ham; there were enormous bowls of pasta and seafood. White-jacketed waiters walked around, pouring what seemed to be oceans of champagne. An accordion player and a violinist strolled among the guests.

Chris waited until he was sure he was being observed before he approached the gift table. Some of the women had brought crib blankets and booties, but the gift of choice was cash. He took a new hundred-dollar bill from his pocket and dropped it into the crystal bowl in the center of the table, with bouquets of blue-tinged carnations on either side of the bowl.

He turned and almost bumped into her. She was slim and lovely, wearing a pretty summer dress, silky and kind of floating, with a beautiful Florentine cross, blue enamel overlaid with gold, around her neck. Chris's first thought was that she looked more Irish than Italian. She reminded him of the actress, Katharine Ross.

Smiling, she moved past him. Chris found Solly and pointed her out. Solly nodded. "A nice girl," he said solemnly. "And that's her papa, over there on the side. Know him?"

In fact, Chris did. He hadn't yet heard the name, but he'd heard Harry: "You'll know him when you see him."

5

She was a tool, a device. It was a lucky break that she was so pretty and so much fun to be with, but Chris viewed Marty only as a means of gaining access to her father.

John had been a killer. He'd handled a shotgun on trucks that were ambushed, in the violent days of Prohibition. Then, Harry told Chris, John had come up through the ranks. Chris didn't like that phrase applied to OC people. He thought it was too clean, too wholesome, and should be reserved for the military, and for paramilitary outfits such as the NYPD. But he knew what Harry meant. John had moved up from armed robberies into a form of white-collar work, dealing with labor unions, settling problems. By the early 1960s, he was a mediator, and had helped settle the Gallo-Profaci gang war. Now John seemed safely detached from the bloodshed. He was involved in legitimate and some semilegitimate businesses, including a real estate firm. He was as successful as he was elusive.

It was precisely because of his status as an experienced, knowledgeable elder that he was so significant a target. A man like John knew more—and could tell more—about the workings of organized crime than a dozen wiseguys whose names splashed across the newspapers regularly. He had layered so many buffers between himself and the soldiers on the street that he'd managed to stay out of the reach of the law.

Now he was just one beautiful arm's-length away.

Chris didn't talk long with her at the christening party. As a hostess that day, along with her mother, she had to circulate. But he got her phone number at work, and when he called, they made a dinner date. He met her in the lobby of the building where she worked, in Manhattan, in the graphics department of an advertising agency. Chris took her to Tre Scalini, which he'd learned was a place her father liked; being seen there with her would bolster his reputation.

He felt they were noticed when they walked in, though that may have been, at least in part, because she was such a good-looking girl. While the sterotype mob daughter wore thick makeup, raccoon eyes, and spike heels, Marty didn't even look Italian, Chris thought. She had fair skin, not olive, and her brown eyes were lighter than his. She was fairly tall, about five seven, with a great figure—not big in the bosom; wiseguys who judged women by their measurements might have called her skinny. Chris thought she was elegant—lean and graceful. She wore a pale-blue dress with a darker-blue jacket, and the Florentine cross she'd been wearing on the day of the party, blue enamel with a thin gold overlay. It occurred to him that they made a nice-looking couple.

Marty was easy to talk to, though Chris was careful not to talk much at first. He said he was a jazz drummer, realizing as he said it that jazz drummers were a dime a dozen; because he wanted her to think well of him, he added that he was a vibes player, too. He'd done some cruises, and was just back from a long time in Vegas, not sure what he'd be doing next. Maybe another cruise. Marty said she loved music, any and all kinds, so Chris picked up on that. They discovered they shared a love for opera—a real passion, and they thought they'd go to the opera sometime soon. "I hope it's not *Aida,*" Chris said. "I don't care much for that one. *Rigoletto*'s my favorite. But even if it's *Aida,* I'll go."

"How did you come to like opera so much?" Marty asked. Chris talked about a neighbor who was an opera fanatic, an old man who used to call Chris, across their backyards in Queens, to come over and listen to the radio broadcasts on Saturday afternoons from the old Met. Even before that, Chris said, his parents had encouraged his interest in music, from the time he was a kid. Then he stopped, not wanting to go too much into his background. "Well, I guess mostly because my father liked it," he said lamely.

"Mine too," Marty said. "I guess all Italian fathers like opera."

Chris was annoyed. It wasn't her fault, but he didn't like hearing her father linked with his, even in the most innocent way. "My father isn't Italian," he said, more sharply than necessary. "I mean, he wasn't Italian, he was Greek. He passed away."

"Oh, I'm sorry," Marty said. She looked embarrassed, and Chris was a little ashamed at the way he'd spoken. "But my mother is Italian, sort of," he went on. "She was born in Greece, but she lived in Italy for a while. So maybe she's half-and-half."

Marty's full name was Martina, but the only person who'd called her that was her grandmother, for whom she was named. The Florentine cross had belonged to her grandmother, who'd been a very special person, and Marty treasured the cross. "When I was little, everybody called me Tina," she said. "But as soon as I was old enough to have something to say about it, I changed it." She looked curiously at him. "Christian is a beautiful name. Do you have a nickname?"

So much for the jazz drummer story, Chris thought; most mob guys had nicknames. He wanted to say no, but he also wanted her father to consider him someone he could do business with. "Well, sometimes," he said. "Some people call me 'Curley.' "

She nodded. "I won't call you that. I'll call you Christy."

The evening was pleasant, with casual small talk. Marty was an only child, though she had lots of cousins; the christening party was for the son of her cousin Rosemarie. She lived at home with her parents on Long Island. Chris mumbled that he lived with his aunt out in Valley Stream, and she wasn't at all well. "Oh, I'm sorry," Marty said again.

Chris offered to drive her home, but she said she had her own car in a garage near her office. They walked over to Park Avenue, then down, enjoying the warm spring evening. Chris waited until the garage attendant drove her car up the ramp, then waved a casual good-bye.

He called her the next day. "I had a really good time last night," he said. "When can I see you again?"

"I had a good time, too," Marty said. She sounded as though she really had had a good time. They made another dinner date. "Let's not go to Tre Scalini again," Marty said quickly. "I'll show you a little place I love."

The restaurant was on the far east side, near the river, almost under the bridge—a tiny place, only nine tables, run by a Frenchwoman and her two grown children. "I thought Italian girls only liked spaghetti," Chris teased, as they settled at a table. Marty smiled. "Maybe you're not such an expert on Italian girls, then."

Chris frowned at the small menu, hand-written in a curly script. "All I ever learned to say in French was 'Ouvrez la porte' and 'Fermez la porte,' " he admitted. Marty laughed, and read through the menu, translating as she read. Chris was impressed. "Where did you learn such good French?" he asked.

"In Paris," Marty said. "I studied art there for a year." Chris liked the way she said it, in a simple, matter-of-fact way, without sounding snobbish.

He was dubious about French food, though, and ordered a lamb chop, the most familiar item on the menu. The sauce was unusual, but he liked it, and he felt comfortable in this little place. It was so far off the beaten track that he didn't worry about being seen by somebody he knew, or by somebody who knew Liz.

He didn't press Marty with questions about her father,

because he didn't want to make her suspicious. Take it easy, he told himself; slow and easy. The luxury of working in intelligence was that he had no deadline. Some cops spent years infiltrating various groups—the Black Panthers, the FLAN. Considering that the Mafia had been around for at least half a century in the United States, and in Italy a lot longer, what was the rush?

It seemed to him that the best way to develop this friendship was to do it as normally as he could, getting to know this girl and letting her get to know him, at least as far as he could allow her to get to know him. So they talked of ordinary things—the opera, movies, where they'd gone to school. Chris talked of his elementary school, where he'd enjoyed the art classes best. "We didn't wear uniforms in my public school," he said, "but once a week, when we had assembly, the boys had to wear a white shirt and a red tie. I don't know if the girls had to wear anything special. I wasn't paying much attention to girls in those days."

Marty grinned. "I'm glad you know better now," she said.

Marty said she'd gone to parochial school, then to a convent school—all girls—for high school, with uniforms every step of the way. Then her father insisted she go to Marymount for college—more women—where she studied art. When she graduated, her parents rewarded her with the year in Paris. "I guess they spoiled me," she admitted. "But I didn't mind. They even gave me a car for high school graduation."

"Hey, me too." Chris said. "Bright red. Boy, did I love that car!

"I had a great childhood," he went on, enthusiastically. "I wouldn't trade my neighborhood, the one I grew up in, for anybody's neighborhood in the whole world. It was such a mixed bag, where I grew up and I learned so much."

Marty seemed genuinely interested. "What did you learn?"

"Well, I learned how to box, and how to play stickball, and how to make wallets from leather scraps," Chris recalled. He felt a little foolish, then, having just heard about her privileged background. "I guess that doesn't sound like a lot, probably. But it was terrific. What I really learned, I guess, was that there are all kinds of people in this world, you know, and I think I learned a lot of things you don't get in school. I really didn't like school, after the early grades."

"I think it sounds like a lot," Marty said. "Some people get very good educations and never learn anything they ought to know. Why didn't you like school?"

"I just found it boring," Chris said. "My Pop thought I was just lazy. I liked it all right, up to a point." He grinned. "Up to the point where I got thrown out."

Marty looked surprised. "You don't sound like somebody who got thrown out of school. You must read a lot."

"I do," Chris said. "Not as much as I used to, though." That was certainly true. It was all he could do, on this job, to scan the headlines; it was hard to concentrate on anything else. He couldn't remember when he'd last read a book.

They talked about books. Marty liked history, though she admitted she'd never come across one of Chris's favorite publications, *The Civil War Times*. "*Bulfinch's Mythology* is my favorite book of all time," Chris said. "There's always a lesson there. And I liked biographies, especially stories about inventors. I could tell you the names of the guys who invented the X ray, and the paper clip, and the zipper."

"Who *did* invent the zipper?" Marty wondered.

"Well, to tell you the truth, I don't remember," Chris said. "Maybe Edison. He was the greatest inventor of all time. A little eccentric, but a brilliant man. Maybe even Thomas Jefferson, because he got involved in everything. Especially architecture—he was great at that. Someday I'm going to drive down and take a look at Monticello. He was so knowledgeable—I mean, his train of thought was unreal. He opened up the whole wide USA, you know, with the Louisiana Purchase, and Lewis and Clark. He wasn't afraid to take chances!"

Marty was smiling, and Chris realized he'd been rambling. "Hey, sorry, I didn't mean to get carried away," he said. "I just really enjoyed reading about those people."

"I've enjoyed hearing about them," Marty said. "You must have started reading when you were very young."

"I don't remember exactly when I started," Chris said, "But once I learned, I didn't want to stop reading. I know I was reading the newspapers when I was seven or eight. I liked stories about the military, and war heroes, and for a while I wanted to go to West Point. I guess that's why . . ." He was about to point out the link between the military and the department, then caught himself. "I guess that's why I like movies about the military."

"Why would you have wanted to go to West Point?" Marty asked. She seemed fascinated by the idea. Chris guessed she didn't run into many guys in her father's world who'd wanted to go to West Point.

"Oh, I don't know," he mumbled. "I guess I'd been seeing pictures of soldiers or something. Or maybe because I'd been reading about the Korean War. I can remember sitting on the curb on Columbus Avenue and seeing a big headline in the paper about a place called Pork Chop Hill. I remember that really clearly, I guess because the name was so funny. Pork Chop Hill. When the movie came out, I think I was the first person in line, I was so anxious to see it. I couldn't wait." He laughed. "I'm just thinking, you probably weren't even born yet when I was reading about Pork Chop Hill. You're just a kid."

"I'm not a kid," Marty protested. "I may be a little younger than you are, but I'm not a kid. I'll be twenty-five this summer."

"Twenty-five!" Chris exclaimed. "An old lady! Twenty-five and not married yet! I'll bet your mother's lighting candles all over the church for you."

Marty laughed. "Well, how about you?" she countered. "How old are you?"

"Thirty-six," Chris said.

"Thirty-six and not married yet!" Marty said. She looked at him thoughtfully. "Were you ever married?"

"No," Chris said.

"Well, then, maybe somebody ought to go around and

light some candles for *you*," Marty teased. "It's just that my father insisted I go to college, so I went, and then I wanted to work. I really love graphics, and I'd like to do my own designing someday. My father wanted me to go to college because he didn't have much education."

"That's kind of how it was with my family," Chris said. " 'Get an education,' my Pop always said, 'because that's the one thing nobody can ever take away from you.' It meant an awful lot to him, because he never went to school at all, not even one day."

He paused, choosing his words carefully.

"He made money, though. He started with nothing. When he first came over, he said he worked seven days for seven dollars. But he worked hard and had a good business." He paused. "I hear your father's in the trucking business."

Marty said nothing.

"Has he been in that business long?" Chris asked.

"As long as I can remember," Marty said.

"That's what I heard," Chris said. "I've heard some things about your father."

"So have a lot of people, Christy," Marty said quietly. "But no matter what you've heard, he's still my father."

Chris enjoyed the evening so much that he thought he wouldn't take Marty back to Tre Scalini or any other high-profile place. Let it happen slowly, he told himself. When she gets to trust you, she's more likely to volunteer things about her father. They began to meet once a week, always openly, never in a clandestine or sneaky way. Chris got opera tickets. *Rigoletto* had closed, so he had to sit through *Aida*, but he had a good time anyway, both at the opera and at the Plaza, where they stopped for a nightcap and spent a merry hour arguing about the effectiveness of certain high notes.

He didn't feel it was really necessary to use Marty for display purposes, anyway. He was becoming noticed on his own. One night he went alone to a restaurant in mid-Manhattan where Lou had taken him. It was a relief to go to dinner alone without having to wear the damned wire, without maneuvering a seat at the end of a table, where it wouldn't be so easy for a guy to bump up against him or throw an arm around him; those guys did a lot of hugging and grabbing and touching one another.

He was enjoying a good dinner when Artie, a regular there, approached him.

"I think you're a cop," Artie said bluntly.

Chris didn't stop eating, and he didn't deny it, which he thought would have been suspicious.

"You're entitled to your opinion, Art," he said casually.

Artie put his hand on Chris's shoulder. "I said, I think you're a cop," he repeated darkly.

Chris put down his fork. He stood up. Maybe it's time for the best defense, he thought. He picked up the fork and pressed the tines against Artie's shirt lightly.

"Do me a favor," Chris said harshly. "You think I'm a cop, Art? Okay, so you think I'm a cop. That's okay with me, pal. I don't give a shit what you think. But you keep it to yourself, okay? Because I'm doing good, I'm making money, and if you fuck things up for me with other people, you're going to get hurt, understand?"

He pressed the fork a little harder. "I don't care what you think," he went on, talking gruffly. "It doesn't bother me at all what you think. But if you start badmouthing me to other people, you're in trouble, pal. Because you don't really know who I am or what I do, do you? DO YOU?"

Artie backed away. "Hey, okay," he mumbled. "Hey, don't get so upset."

"I spend my money here," Chris went on fiercely, "and I'm telling you, just keep your fucking opinions to yourself, okay?"

"Okay, okay," Artie muttered. "Hey, I'm sorry. Dinner's on me, okay?"

Chris put down the fork. "Okay, then, no problem."

He went back to his dinner, feeling good about his act. But just as he was finishing, Artie returned. "I feel like moving around tonight," he said. "Let's have a drink around the corner."

Chris thought this was Artie's way of apologizing, admitting he'd been wrong. "Sure, why not?" he said.

The place around the corner had a reputation as a good place to fence merchandise. Chris had met a prosperous fence there. He knew that in the long run, fencing was important, because it eventually affected the general public: When goods are stolen from warehouses, trucks hijacked, everybody ends up paying for it down the road. But it wasn't a priority with him, so he didn't pay much attention to other conversations. He just sat at the bar with Artie.

They were on their second drink when Artie reached into his pocket and brought out a folded tinfoil packet. "This is a present," he declared. "Even if you *are* a cop, I can give it to you. It isn't a crime unless I sell it to you."

Wrong, pal, Chris thought. Giving it to me is a criminal act, too. But he was less concerned with the legal point than with the realization that Artie still wasn't satisfied. So he took the stuff and put it in his pocket. "I'll blow later," he said. But Artie shook his head. "No, *now*," he said. "Let's go in the bathroom."

There, Artie was insistent. "C'mon, c'mon, let's blow." Chris knew the guy wouldn't let up until he was convinced; he must be thinking a cop would never go that far.

Chris thought he could fake it. He'd done it before. At his club, when guys he was with had passed around a joint, he'd taken it; he'd learned that if he blew out instead of in, he got the same glow. If the other guys started laughing, then, Chris started laughing, too, and they wouldn't know the difference.

Even with heroin, it had worked once. He'd gone into an apartment building to make a buy. Four big guys, really huge, were in the apartment, and when he'd bought the stuff, they'd stopped him as he was about to leave. "We want you to get off here," one guy said.

Chris had tried to talk his way out of it. "I'll do it later. I ain't got my toys with me."

The biggest guy smiled tightly. "We got all that shit right here."

Chris gave it one more shot. "Naw, I don't like using anybody else's shit." But the guy just handed him the needle. When Chris looked around the room, he saw two guys blocking the door, another at the window.

He took the needle and went into a corner, near the bathroom door. With his head bowed and his back turned, he put the needle through the skin on his arm, and out the other side. He stayed in that position for a minute or two. What do I do now? he thought. It occurred to him that maybe they'd given him pure flour, and that this was a test.

"How do you feel, brother?" one guy said, peering at him. Chris straightened and shrugged, his heart pounding. "I've had better,' he said arrogantly. The guy smiled. "Okay man, you're cool," he said, motioning to the others to let Chris out.

Now, in the bathroom, Chris hoped he could duplicate that scene.

He handed the packet from his pocket to Artie, who took a large dash between his fingers and put it up his nose, keeping his eyes on Chris. Chris took some, bent his head, smeared it on his upper lip, and made such a general fuss about it that Artie was apparently satisfied.

They went back to the bar, then Art wanted to blow again. They went through the same routine twice more, until most of the stuff was used. Chris kept the small residue in the packet with him.

"I'm going to call it a night now, Art," he said. But Artie draped his arm around Chris's shoulder. "No, not yet," he said. "Now we're going over to Spartacus and get laid. For a hundred, you get the works."

He was watching Chris closely, for his immediate reaction. He wants to see me undress, Chris thought, to see if I'm wired or armed. Since he wasn't wired, thank God, he decided to string him along, maybe settle this once and for all.

Spartacus was called a health club, though Chris had never

seen any exercise machines there, let alone aerobics classes. But it had showers and lockers and private rooms for its select clients; there was a fifty-dollar admission charge just to get in the front door. Chris gave it one more try. "Some other time, Art," he said. "I don't feel like paying tonight." Artie grinned. "Don't worry about it," he said. "I'm paying the freight."

At the bar at Spartacus, done up like a Roman fantasy, Artie beckoned to a girl to join them. She brought a friend with her. The men went up to the locker room, where Chris took off all his clothes, put them in a locker and put the key on the elastic band around his wrist. Just like the YMCA, he thought wryly. As screwed up as Artie was, with all the booze and the coke, he was watching intently as Chris came out of the shower. So Chris dropped the towel he'd wrapped around his waist and stood, facing Artie.

"Well, whaddaya think, Art?" he asked lightly. "Am I okay?"

"Yeah, okay," Artie muttered, blinking. He shook his head. "After this, we'll meet downstairs and then we'll go for a ride," he said.

Chris didn't like the sound of that. A ride might mean going to a diner for scrambled eggs. Or it might mean a different kind of ride. He waited until Art had disappeared into a room with his girl, then Chris went into one of the rooms. It was small, plain, clean, like a serviceable but not luxurious hotel room.

"Hello, how are you tonight?" said the girl who followed him in.

"Not so good," Chris told her. "Listen, honey, I'm a little too drunk right now, you know?" He knew from his occasional experience with these girls, back at the 4-oh, and more often at The Daily Planet, that they wanted nothing to do with drunks. A drunk would take all night, wear the girl out.

"I gotta go, sweetheart," Chris told her. "Here, this is for your time."

He handed her twenty-five dollars, dressed quickly and

got out fast. He was so tense that when he got down to his Waterside place, which was so conveniently close, he couldn't fall asleep. He lay on the bed, his eyes wide open, thinking that this was one hell of a stressful way to make a living.

"Why the opera?" Harry wanted to know. "And why the best seats?" When Chris explained, Harry was not only satisfied, but pleased. "Don't let her get away," he said. Chris said he didn't intend to.

But he continued to have arguments with Harry, who'd yelled at him for going to Vegas with Frankie. "It's too dangerous," Harry told him. "I didn't know where you were going. What if you hadn't come back? I might never have known what happened to you."

"Listen, I made a commitment," Chris said. But Harry kept on. "Well, you should have asked me, or at least you should have told me, where you were going, before you made the commitment."

"Look, Harry," Chris said. "I have to make instant decisions here. I can't say to a guy, 'Wait a minute, I don't know if I can go to Vegas with you, I have to ask my mother.' "

Harry sighed. "I'm getting old before my time with you," he said. "I feel responsible for you." Chris could see that Harry was under a strain. The guy smoked four packs a day, and sometimes, after their meetings, Harry would say he needed a drink. Chris usually could use a drink, too, because he knew Harry had a point. If he were taken for a ride, dumped somewhere, he might never be found. And even if he were found, he had false ID. How would my mother know, Chris wondered. How would my wife know?

If worse came to worst, if somebody put a gun to his head, he always intended to say, "I'm a cop. I'm a detective with the New York Police Department." He had nothing on him to prove that—no shield, no "detective special"—but he would give them Harry's phone number and say, "Check it out, call this number." If he could convince them that he was a cop, he felt it would be okay, at least with the older guys, who still respected cops and would feel that as a cop, he was just doing his job. Besides, hitting a cop would draw so much heat that they would feel it wasn't worth it.

He wasn't so sure about the younger guys, though. One of Carmine Persico's sons had breezed into an after-hours place on the upper east side of Manhattan one night, where Chris was making a drop. He'd looked Chris straight in the eye and said, "I've always wanted to kill a cop." Even though Chris felt that the kid was just shooting off his mouth, he knew that the old rules of this game, such as they were, were less important to the generation coming up. He also knew that, in such a situation, there probably would not be time for discussion, giving out phone numbers; people who considered him an informer would be likely to shoot first and ask questions later. As an informer, Chris would meet an informer's fate; shot offguard, then dumped, and if the shooter felt melodramatic, with a canary stuffed in his mouth.

Yet Harry never suggested that he drop the project. He just renewed it automatically. Even if Harry had suggested that they curtail it, Chris would have objected. He didn't want to stop. He felt like an actor in a developing drama. And if you were reading a script, say, would you want to stop in the middle? Wouldn't you want to know how it all came out?

And the plot seemed to be thickening. The longer Chris stayed under, the more there was to do. It wasn't just one-way intelligence, from Chris to Harry to the vault or wherever. Sometimes Harry had questions for him, names to target, cases that Chris might be able to help with. When Homicide talked to Harry about a body that had been found floating in the East River, Harry passed it to Chris. It wasn't a body actually, just a torso; the head and legs were missing, along with most of the arms. But the arms had been cut off below the elbow, and one elbow had gotten stuck in a drainpipe, which is how the body came to be found. Slowly, painstakingly, the ID had been made, partly through spinal X rays, partly by checking back with a woman who'd reported her father missing, months earlier. The dead man turned out to be a shylock from Astoria. When his daughter turned over his papers to Homicide, the name of Kostos and his brother were found in his account book. Apparently Pete the Greek had still owed the dead guy seventy thousand dollars. "See what you can find out on this homicide," Harry told Chris, who thought he had a good chance of picking up something, now that he was meeting so many people. He'd met lots of guys in Astoria, more at the Kew, a crew in Manhattan.

And he met John.

When Marty first asked him to pick her up at her house, on Saturday when she wasn't working, Chris didn't go inside. He drove up the circular driveway, parked in front of the columns marking the front door, got out, rang the doorbell, then went back to the car and waited. By the time she invited him to dinner, he was familiar enough with the place that he was able to park his car, ring the bell and stand there without his hands sweating. Still, he was nervous when the door opened.

"Hello," the woman said, smiling at him. "Come in, please. I'm Marty's mother. She'll be down in a minute." Chris stepped in. She closed the door and then, to his surprise, she kissed him lightly on the cheek. "I'm very glad you could come," she said.

The interior of the house was just as he'd imagined it. The foyer was dim but fairly large, with a wing chair opposite the door. Several rooms opened off the foyer. The living room was stiff and formal, with heavy furniture, a dark-red carpet and an unused look. In the dining room there was a mahogany table seating twelve; the room was lighted with an elaborate chandelier. An ornate sideboard stood along one wall, a china closet with leaded-glass panels along the wall opposite. The door between the dining room and the kitchen was not a swinging door, but one that closed tightly.

Marty came down the stairs just as John came in the front door. He took off his coat, handed it to his wife and stood looking at Chris, not smiling.

"Daddy, this is Christian," Marty said. Chris put out his

hand which, to his dismay, felt damp again. John shook his hand, looking at Chris with a steady, cool expression. Chris wasn't nervous now; he was terrified. He felt that the man could see right through him. He wanted only to turn and run out of the house as fast as his legs could carry him. John kissed his wife on the cheek, then his daughter. Still, he didn't smile.

John was a stocky man, a trifle overweight, but immaculately dressed. He moved and acted just as Chris had known he would. Underlings in the criminal world made swift gestures and talked fast, hustling to gain a listener's attention. John didn't. Like members of the British ruling class, who move and speak with deliberate pacing, hands behind their backs, John didn't need to capture a listener's attention. He knew he already had it.

Certainly he had Chris's, as they moved without further ceremony into the dining room. John took his place at the head of the long table, as Anna came from the kitchen with a steaming platter of chicken cacciatore. When she saw that Chris was standing at his chair, waiting to sit until she was seated, she gave him a beautiful smile.

He liked Anna at once. She reminded him of his mother, though they didn't look at all alike. Anna was slim and animated, not the stereotypical Italian mama; she had a great figure, Chris noted, if a little heavy on the backside. Her salt-and-pepper hair was carefully waved. She looked cared-for, the kind of woman who gets not only a regular manicure, but a pedicure too. But she had Katrina's manner of making a man feel comfortable, of making him feel that he was the most important man in the world, that nothing mattered except what he said.

John didn't say much, though. He didn't strike Chris as being a talkative man. Marty talked about a layout she was working on. Anna was watching Chris, apparently trying to make him feel at ease.

"We're all music lovers," Anna said. "We started Marty's music lessons when she was just a little girl."

Chris was about to speak when John broke in.

"What instrument you play?" John asked abruptly.

"Ah, drums, vibes," Chris said. "Drums, mostly."

"Where in Vegas?" John asked. His tone was sharp, just short of accusing. Chris thought quickly. Marty must have told her parents about his background. He recalled what he'd told her, without naming a specific place, thank God. John could have checked him out with one phone call.

"Small lounges, mostly," Chris said. "Some of the hotels, but just a couple of nights in each place. A week at most."

John seemed about to continue when the phone rang. Anna looked questioningly at her husband.

"I'll take it, Mama," John said. He threw down his napkin and got up. He went into the kitchen to take the call, closing the door tightly behind him.

Chris couldn't hear anything John was saying, so he tried to relax. He wasn't wired. He never wore the wire the first time he was going to meet someone, because he didn't know the guy's habits. The guy might be a grabber, and Chris couldn't risk being caught in a bear hug when he was full of lumps and bumps. John certainly wasn't a grabber—more like an iceberg—but Chris was not sorry he hadn't worn the Nagra. Without it, he could concentrate on other things. He was enjoying the food, especially the potato salad. The potato salad he remembered had always seemed kind of mushy, with everything mixed together. Anna's had wedges of potato, with chunks of cucumbers and tomatoes and sliced black olives, all in a spicy oil-and-vinegar dressing. "This is the best potato salad I've ever had," he told Anna, who beamed at him.

John came back to the table and had just picked up his fork when the phone rang again. Some OC guys didn't even have phones in their homes, Chris knew, but John got up again, sighed heavily, and threw down his napkin. This time John went into the den to pick up the phone. Chris could hear his voice, but he couldn't make out anything John was saying. He stopped straining to hear, because he found himself in the odd situation—actually, he should have expected this, he told himself—of being more concerned about not giving something away than of getting something on John.

As the women cleared the table, John sat perfectly still,

saying nothing, just looking at Chris. Chris was relieved when Anna brought coffee. After coffee, John stood up. "Good night," he said to Chris, somewhat formally. As John left the room, Anna smiled at her daughter. "Why don't you and Chris go out now?" she said. "I'll take care of things."

It was still daylight, not yet eight o'clock, as Marty and Chris drove into the village for ice cream. "My mother likes you," Marty informed him as they drove.

"Well, I like your mother," Chris said. "She reminds me of my mother." He paused. "What about your father? Does he like me?"

"Oh, I think so," Marty said. "He wouldn't say so, at least not yet. But I was watching him, and he was watching you, and I think he likes you." She smiled. "Because he knows I like you."

It was still early when they got back. "Will you come in for coffee?" Marty asked. Chris said he wouldn't, but he'd call her tomorrow. He walked her to the door, where she kissed him on the cheek, smiled, and went inside.

As he drove away, Chris smiled too. He felt good. In this undercover life, he'd adopted different styles, depending on who he was bouncing around with. When he was with Gene and Bennie, he was a hustler, a fast talker. With Frankie he was that way, too, only more relaxed. He had a good time with Frankie. With Solly he was more respectful, a guy who took orders. This evening, except for his nervousness when he met John, he'd felt comfortable. He felt almost lighthearted, rather like a young guy who'd just met his girl's parents for the first time and felt he'd passed inspection. As he approached Queens, he was feeling so good about feeling that way that he decided to stop and see his mother.

But when he drove by, the house was dark. There was a light in the wing where one of his sisters lived, but Chris didn't want to see his sister. So he drove the short distance to the Grotto, had a drink, then went over to his own place shortly after midnight.

Gene was getting ready to open. "You look good," Gene said. "What have you been up to?"

"I feel good," Chris said. "What have I been up to? None of your business, pal." They both laughed, and they had a drink together.

Chris was still feeling good when Bing arrived.

Bing didn't say hello. "What are you doing in this place?" Bing demanded.

"Hey, Bing," Chris said brightly. "How ya doing'? It's been a long time, Bing." One hell of a long time, Chris thought. A lot of years since he'd seen Bing, though Bing had called him to congratulate him when the "Hero Cops" story came out.

"I heard this was your place," Bing said flatly. "So, is it? Is this your place?"

"Yeah, Bing, that's right, it's my place," Chris said.

Bing made a fist and slammed it down on the bar. "Son of a bitch!" he said.

People were looking at Bing. Chris hurried out from behind the bar and steered him down to the far end. "Sit down, have a drink," Chris urged. Bing sat down heavily on a stool, keeping his eyes fixed on Chris. "Good to see you again, Bingo," Chris said heartily. "What'll it be?"

Bing just stared at him. Chris walked back around the bar, poured a scotch and set it in front of Bing, with a glass of ice and a glass of water. He poured one for himself and lifted his glass. "Here's to you," Chris said.

Bing stared at Chris. "Son of a bitch! Lowlife! Thank God my father isn't here to see you." He picked up the glass and drained it.

"Have another, Bing," Chris said cheerfully. He poured another, then set the bottle on the bar. "Help yourself," he said. "It's on me. I've got to make a phone call. Be right back."

He could feel Bing watching him as he walked the length of the bar and went into the little office. I've got to get him out of here, Chris thought. Maybe if he drinks enough, he'll forget what's bothering him.

Chris was standing there, trying to figure out what to do, when Gene came in. "What's with that guy at the bar?" Gene asked. "The guy you were talking to. Know him? He's giving me the creeps."

"Yeah, I know him," Chris said. "He's got problems. Problems with his wife."

Gene looked more sympathetic, then. "Okay, but take care of him, will you?" Gene asked. "Go out and do something about the guy."

Bing was crying. He was crying noisily, sloppily, putting his head down on the bar, then lifting his head, still sobbing, and fumbling for his glass.

Chris grabbed his coat and walked down to the end of the bar. "C'mon, Bing," he said. "Let's go home."

Chris steered him out onto the street and put him in the car. He hoped Bing still lived at the same place, the house where he'd lived with Sal, when the old man was in the rackets and Bing was on the fringes. If he had moved, Chris didn't know what the hell he'd do with him. Chris drove to the house on the side street in Astoria where he knew Bing had lived, and was relieved when he began digging in his pocket for the key.

Inside, Bing took off his coat and let it drop on the floor.

"C'mon, I'll get you to bed," Chris said. He pushed Bing gently down the hall to the back bedroom. He intended to just sit him down on the bed, take off his shoes, then leave. But when they got into the bedroom, Bing started yelling. "Son of a bitch! I was so proud of you, and my Pop was so proud of you, 'cause you were makin' something of yourself. You were a cop! What happened, hey, what happened with the job?"

"I just blew it, Bing," Chris said. "I needed some cash—what can I tell you? C'mon, babe, sit down on the bed."

Bing wouldn't sit down. "Proud of you, proud of you," he moaned. "You're a loser. And I'm a loser. And you're a loser." He was weaving back and forth. Then he fell to his knees, heavily. He bent down and reached under the bed. He dragged out a box and opened it. He dug into the box and brought out fistfuls of bills.

"Is this what you need?" Bing screamed. "Money? You need money? Then why didn't you come to me for money? I got money! Here, take the money, take it, take it!" He threw wads of money into the air. Chris ducked, involuntarily, as though the bills fluttering down had sharp edges.

"Oh, Bing, you don't understand," Chris said bleakly. "I don't want your money."

"Don't understand, don't understand," Bing repeated, in a kind of chant. "But you were a cop and now you're a loser. I'm a loser and my Pop was proud of you." He kept throwing bills in the air. "Take it, loser, take it!"

"Hey," Chris said. "Everything's going to be all right, babe. I gotta go now."

"Yeah, go!" Bing shouted. "Go on, get out, just get outta here, you make me sick! Get the hell out!"

He was still flinging money around as Chris left. Even at the front door, he could hear Bing crying. He didn't know what to do, so he just picked up the coat Bing had dropped and hung it on the rack behind the door.

For Marty's birthday, Chris went to a florist on Madison Avenue and ordered a dozen roses sent to her office. As he peered through the glass doors of the refrigerator case at the glistening, long-stemmed beauties, he decided that one dozen looked skimpy. He changed it to two, then shook his head. "Make it three dozen," he told the florist. "I want three dozen roses, different colors—red, white, blue, whatever. Mix 'em up."

The florist looked startled, then slightly suspicious. "And how will you be paying for these, sir?"

Chris was irritated at the clerk's tone, which he thought sounded very snooty. So he made a show of bringing out a wad of hundred-dollar bills. "With money," Chris said airily.

He knew Harry would need convincing that three dozen roses had been necessary, but he knew he could convince him. Chris wasn't using the department's money, anymore; all this spending was done with money earned from his various enterprises. Technically, he wasn't supposed to use that money, which was labeled "ill-gotten proceeds" or some such bureaucratic term—and which was supposed to be turned in, according to the rules. But the rules were made by guys who never got out of the sight of their desks, Chris reasoned; guys who, when it came to knowing what was going on out in the field, sometimes didn't know shit from Shinola.

Chris and Harry had had some loud, long discussions about money and what Chris could and couldn't do with his excess profits. Chris's view was that such money was like money you won at the track, and was more disposable than money you worked for. Chris and Gene had taken five hundred dollars from their club profits, early on, and had gone to play barbouti at the Grotto. Together they ran their thousand up to fifteen thousand. "Let's go," Chris said then. "Let's get outta here with this win."

Gene wanted to stay. "We can run it up to fifty thou, I'm sure, I'm positive," Gene said.

"Then give me my half," Chris said.

But Gene didn't want to. "I need it all, if I'm going to run it up to fifty." Gene said.

Chris couldn't stand to watch, anymore, so he went back to the club and slept on the sofa in the office, waiting for Gene, who didn't return until ten o'clock in the morning.

"Where's the fifty?" Chris asked.

"We owe them two grand," Gene said.

When a couple of guys came around, looking for that sum, Chris gave them two hundred dollars and told them to come back the following week for the rest. He reported all this to Harry, who didn't think much of the episode, at all. Harry didn't approve when Chris loaned money to guys both at the club and at The Daily Planet, either, but Chris felt it was a way to get in good with all these people.

In the end, Harry had told Chris that as long as he didn't tuck any away for himself—he sounded embarrassed when he said that, but Chris didn't mind, knowing that Harry had to say it for the record—and as long as he kept reasonably good track of what he spent, he could do what he felt he needed to do. Harry would fix it up with anybody downtown who might question three dozen roses or anything else. "Tell them it's an investment," Chris said breezily.

Harry gave him a little lecture then. Chris's attitude was beginning to bother him. He felt Chris was getting too cocky and tough, running around as though he didn't have to answer to anybody for anything. "If you need a day off, you have to fill out a twenty-eight, just like anybody else," Harry told him. "You remember what a form twenty-eight is, don't you? Maybe I better bring over your old uniform and you put it on, wear it for an hour or two. You're a cop, don't forget. Remember who you are."

Chris thought Harry was being a prick. Chris had to act the way he did, spend the way he did, to make the right impression. Marty was used to having money, to being with people who had money. He never wanted her to think of him as being short of cash or hard up, in any way. Not that she always expected to be wined and dined lavishly, he knew; her favorite little restaurant near the bridge was a homespun bargain, and some of their happiest times cost little or nothing that summer as they began spending Saturdays at the beach.

Chris had always loved hot summer days as much as he hated winter. The only time he'd welcomed the cold was early in his career at the 4-oh when he was still in uniform. In the summertime, people swarmed through the streets all night, many of them drinking, then brawling or shooting. The neighborhood quieted down when the temperature dropped; cops always said the weather was the best policeman. Even in the bitterest cold, Chris had always done straight eights—working his full shift without hiding out in some warm space—except his first Christmas Eve. He'd been standing on Willis Avenue in what seemed like zero-degree weather, near an Irish tavern. A loudspeaker above the door was playing a record of a dog barking to the tune of "Jingle Bells." People kept knocking on the window of the place, beckoning to him.

Finally he gave in. He walked inside, said "Merry Christmas," and when the bartender set a bottle of V.O. in front of him, Chris poured a long one. Everybody cheered.

He felt better when he was at a beach, stretched out, thinking, reading, listening to his radio. He knew guys who said if they had money, they'd buy a yacht or a fancy foreign car. All Chris would buy if he had money, he always said, was a beach house. Nothing big or elaborate, just a cabin of some kind, a little place where he could hear and see and smell the ocean. Water had a calming effect on him, and he felt wonderfully calm and relaxed when he and Marty went to the beach. Because he'd spent so many days at the beach, both as a teenager and later, when he was supposed to be selling insurance, he didn't take her to one of the busy, heavily populated Long Island beaches, where he might have been spotted, but to Gilgo, an inlet beach beyond Jones Beach.

The first Saturday they went, he rented a speedboat and they went for a spin. Chris was hardly an expert at the wheel, but he did okay. He felt terrific, and Marty seemed to be having a good time, too. He thought she looked gorgeous, with the spray flinging up around her face, her long dark hair streaming in the wind. She looked happy and healthy, wholesome and sexy, all at once. "You look like a commercial for suntan lotion," he said, but with the noises of the motor, she didn't hear him.

She'd brought a picnic supper: wedges of cheese, rounds of rye bread with prosciutto, grapes and nectarines and two slices of angelfood cake. Chris had brought a bottle of white wine that was warm by the time they opened it, but it tasted fine, anyway, as they spread a blanket on the sand, ate, and drank and talked.

Chris found a lot to talk about, going back to his childhood. He recalled how his family had gone to Orchard Beach, on summer Sundays when he was little. The subway trip had seemed very long, but it was exciting, too, everybody laden with bags and towels. Once they got there, they stayed all day and evening, until almost dark. His father worked on

Sundays, but a couple of uncles went; his uncle Mike had taught him to swim, at Orchard Beach, when Chris was five years old. "We were doing shishkebab at our picnics twenty years before the world discovered it," Chris said.

It occurred to Chris that one reason he could relax and talk and enjoy being with Marty so much was that he didn't have to think about any sexual involvement. He could get to know her as a person, without clouding the issue with romance, which of course was out of the question. First of all, he was a married man, even though he rarely saw his wife. Second, he was getting to know Marty for purposes of the job, not for personal reasons. The department frowned, to put it mildly, on a cop getting romantically involved in a case. If the case ever came to trial, and a witness could testify that she'd been intimate with the investigating officer, it would probably be over, both for the case and for the cop.

He didn't want Marty to think he didn't find her attractive, though. In fact, he was struck by how lovely she looked in her one-piece bathing suit, a black-and-white print, with a big white cotton shirt draped around her shoulders. She hadn't made a fuss about combing her hair or putting on lipstick or anything, which he understood women did in order to look good. Liz always spent a long time on her makeup, it seemed to him, and was forever pulling out a mirror when they were out someplace, to check and see what she looked like.

So he kissed Marty warmly but not lingeringly, and she kissed him back. He put his arm around her as they sat side by side, watching the sun begin to set. As good as it felt to have her close to him, he didn't have to think ahead, as he might otherwise have thought, about sex entering the picture. He had the luxury of just getting to know her. He had the wonderful freedom to just become her friend.

That summer, 1977, was Chris's third summer undercover and in some ways the most interesting. He'd met Marty. And in mid-July, he was at Waterside when all the lights went out. He heard news of the city-wide blackout on his battery-powered radio, and heard that all off-duty policemen were to report to work immediately.

Using his flashlight, he dialed Liz and got her answering machine. "It's me," he said. "I just called to make sure you're all right." He paused awkwardly. "Well, uh, since you're not home, I guess you're out with somebody, so that's good." He paused again, not knowing what to say on the tape. "Uh, I'm working now," he said. "Bye now."

He called Marty. "How are you doing?"

"We're fine," she said, laughing. "We must have about fifty candles, at least, all over the house. It's like some enormous birthday party. I wish you could see this."

"Hey, I wish so too," Chris said. "See you soon."

He turned the radio back on and heard again that off-duty officers were ordered back to work. He felt a slight pang that he was missing the action; the 4-oh would be a hot spot tonight. Of course he wasn't off-duty; he was never off-duty. Still, he couldn't be sure he wouldn't hear from Harry. Sometimes Harry hung around in the upstairs apartment; he just might pop down and suggest that Chris go out and make himself useful. Of course Harry wouldn't, and even if Harry were just arriving at the building, say, he'd never make it up nearly thirty flights of stairs, not with his four-pack-a-day habit.

He called his mother, who said she was fine, the girls were with her, and the children, everybody was fine. "I'm fine too," Chris said. He groped in the refrigerator for a beer that was still nice and cold, sat down on the sofa and called Phil.

Now that Phil and his family were back from St. Louis, transferred to New York, Chris called him often. It was against the rules, of course, to talk to anybody about the job, but Phil was such a straight arrow, and Chris's closest friend. Chris trusted Phil beyond the point where he'd ever expected to be able to trust anyone. If Phil had ever said, "Hey Butch, I'm coming over to do a lobotomy on you," Chris would have said, "Okay, what time are you coming?" He felt he could tell Phil anything. Yet he hadn't told him everything he was doing, just that his undercover job involved organized crime, and he was bouncing around, making good progress.

Now, sitting in the dark, with his beer, Chris told Phil how good he was feeling. He told him he'd met a girl who could be helpful in the work he was doing, and he was finding out that he actually liked her a lot, wasn't that terrific?

He was surprised that Phil didn't seem to think it was so terrific. "Be careful," Phil said. "Watch out that you don't dig yourself a hole so deep that you won't be able to climb out."

Chris was disappointed in Phil's reaction, and a little annoyed. "Hey, don't worry about it, Partner," he said. "I'm doing fine." Afterward he realized he'd used a phrase he hated, a phrase common in the mob. There were several phrases that bothered him, that they used all the time; "good people," as in "He's good people," usually said in a muttered growl; it was meant to be a compliment, but to Chris it always sounded like a slangy curse. "Doin' the right thing." When somebody picked up a restaurant check quietly, without making a grandstand show, somebody would mutter approvingly, "He's doin' the right thing." He especially hated it when they said, "Don't worry about it," because that meant there was something to worry about.

"Do we know a captain in the Bronx?" Solly asked Chris one night at the Kew.

As Chris stared at him, Solly rephrased the question. "Do *you* know a captain in the Bronx?"

"Hey, who . . ." Chris stammered. "Hey, no, I mean, why would I know a captain in the Bronx?" It wasn't hard for him to sound astonished; the question had come out of the blue.

"Hey, Solly, why do you think I'd know a captain in the Bronx?" Chris asked again. Solly just shrugged and said nothing more. He never brought it up again, and he continued to treat Chris as he always did, in his soft-spoken, amiable, even affectionate way.

Chris worried endlessly about it. It was another example of a ball being tossed in the air, bouncing around, without knowing where or when or even if it would ever come down. Another reason to worry and wonder: What does he know? What has he found out about me since yesterday? He almost wished Solly had said something definite, accusing him of knowing a captain in the Bronx. At least that would have been something concrete to deal with, something he could pin down. Uncertainty was the worst. He was at the bar at the Kew when a woman who was sitting alone, drinking, smiled at him, then moved from her place to the barstool next to his. She was attractive—not a great beauty, but a nice-looking woman, in her late thirties. He thought she was just a lonely lady, looking for company—the Kew Motor Inn attracted an ordinary, middle-class clientele—until she spoke.

"I need a gun," she said quietly.

"What do you need a gun for?" Chris asked, startled.

"I just need a gun to take care of things," she said.

"Well, go on up to Harlem," Chris advised. "You can buy a hundred guns." She shook her head. "No, I can't go up there."

She said her name was Darlene, and she kept pressuring. It was obvious that she had targeted him, picked him out of the crowd at the Kew. Then she got up abruptly, without finishing her drink. "I'll call you later," she said.

Fifteen minutes later, the phone behind the bar rang. "It's for you," the barmaid said. She knew Chris well by now, and she gave him a sly wink as she handed him the phone.

Darlene told him her room number and urged him to come up. "Bring a bottle with you," she murmured. She kept talking vaguely about "taking care of things." As curious as he was, Chris had no intention of going up to her room—God knows what he'd be walking into—so he said he'd call her later from another phone. When he called back, he taped the conversation, in which she said not only that she needed a gun, but she wanted to give him the contract to kill her husband. Chris stalled and said he'd be in touch. He passed the report to Harry, but as far as he knew, nobody ever solved the riddle of Darlene. He never heard from her again, and she never reappeared at the Kew. Maybe she was a mob woman, setting him up. Maybe she was legit, in the sense that she was an unhappy wife who really did want her husband removed. Maybe she was crazy. Maybe she was a federal agent, perhaps with Alcohol, Tobacco and Firearms, looking for a weapons bust; he knew that at one point the Kew had been targeted by the feds.

She might even have been another undercover cop. Between the feds and the NYPD, with its various task forces and branches and projects, sometimes the right hand didn't know, couldn't know, what the left hand was doing. Chris was with Solly and an associate of Solly's, a guy named Slater—one of the few guys known only by his last name, instead of the reverse—when a fellow whom Slater knew walked in. "Hi, how are you doin', come on over," Slater called to the newcomer, who joined them at the table.

Chris knew him too. He didn't know the name, but he recognized the face. The guy was from Narcotics.

Slater and the nark were talking when Solly interrupted "Where you from?" he asked.

"Brooklyn," the guy said.

"From Brooklyn," Solly repeated. "Then you know the Nineteenth Hole?"

The guy shook his head.

"You don't know the Nineteenth Hole?" Solly repeated.

"No," the guy said. Solly didn't say anything else. When the guy left, Slater went with him.

Solly looked at Chris. "That guy's a cop," he said simply. "Every fucking wiseguy in Brooklyn knows the Nineteenth Hole."

As soon as Chris left, he called Harry. "Reach out, whoever this guy is, and pull him up," Chris said. "He's burned, and he's going to get himself hurt." Stupid! Chris fumed. Idiot! A guy who couldn't deal with the unexpected shouldn't be in the game.

Not that you could always anticipate, Chris admitted. Things happened quickly. He was at the bar at Lucho's one night, minding his own business, when a guy sitting next to him left to go to the toilet. While he was gone, the guy's girlfriend said hello to Chris. Chris said hello, and they were chatting casually about nothing at all when the guy returned. He placed his hand heavily on Chris's shoulder. "I'm telling you, you leave my girl alone," he growled.

Chris reached up and brushed the hand away. "You've

got it all wrong, buddy," he said in annoyance. He'd come to Lucho's just to have a drink and a good meal from the chef who catered to his whims, for no other reason. This guy didn't even look like OC; Lucho's wasn't a heavy place. Ordinary people from the neighborhood stopped in at the bar on their way home from work, and the mob guys who came were mostly low-level. The place had a gloomy feeling, though sometimes a woman played the piano that was squeezed at an angle in the narrow archway between the bar and the dining room. There was dark paneling along the walls, and plastic geraniums in hanging baskets.

But the food was first-rate, and in this low-key neighborhood spot, Chris felt he could unwind a little. At most bars and clubs, he had to be constantly on guard, so he relished a chance to be by himself and have a good dinner. And now this bum was messing up his evening.

As Chris stood up, ready to move into the dining room, the guy picked up the girl's glass and hurled it at the wall. When the glass shattered, one tiny sliver flew into Chris's eye. It hurt like hell. Muttering, holding his hand over his eye, he made his way out to Third Avenue and hailed a cab. "Take me to a hospital," he said.

"Which hospital, mister?" the cabbie said, turning in his seat to peer curiously at Chris.

"Oh Jesus, Bellevue," Chris said. "Hurry up." But as the taxi headed down Second Avenue, Chris thought the Emergency Room at Bellevue—always a hotspot for accidents, stabbings, shootings—might be swarming with cops. "No, make it Beth Israel," he said. That was the next place he could think of in the neighborhood close to Waterside.

The young doctor on duty used a machine pressed right up against Chris's forehead. "You've got a piece of glass in your eye," the doctor said.

"I know that, Doc," Chris said peevishly. "So what can you do about it?"

"So I can take it out," the doctor snapped, putting Chris in his place. Chris kept quiet as the doctor worked, then.

Fortunately, the cornea wasn't damaged, though Chris had to wear a bandage for a few days. He lost all visual perspective, and found himself raising a foot to take a step when he was on level ground. Stepping off a curb seemed like stepping off a cliff. He stumbled a lot. He was thoroughly aggravated at the whole stupid incident, though he took a wry interest in the knowledge that the hospital bill would be sent to the address he'd given from one of his fake IDs. The Valley Stream address was an abandoned warehouse, so the bill from Emergency was destined to float around the city forever.

So many guys were coming to his Friday night poker games that Chris recruited a man from Astoria to make drinks, and a couple of pretty girls to serve sandwiches. That wasn't difficult, because the help, especially the girls, could easily pick up a couple hundred dollars a night in tips. Chris cut the games to pay his expenses, taking a percentage of the pot, usually 10 percent, and sometimes he even sat in. Guys who ran the games usually didn't do that, but he got bored, just watching, and he thought sitting in would convince anybody who needed convincing that the games weren't fixed. Experienced players didn't need convincing; most mob games weren't crooked, just cut-throat.

Often the games went on so long, with people coming and going all night, that Chris was surprised that his neighbors didn't complain. The Waterside complex seemed so wholesome and middle-class. Healthy-looking people streamed in and out of the athletic club on the balcony level, with its exercise machines and heated pool. In the outdoor plaza, spacious and agreeably aranged for people-watching, like a European plaza, he saw people strolling, old people with their faces tilted to the sunshine, their eyes closed; young people with babies in carriages, teenagers on skateboards, and he wondered: How can you not know? He couldn't figure out how he could get by with what he was doing, right under all these respectable noses.

Not that his clients came noisily. They just slipped out of

the elevator and tapped on his door, almost unheard. But there were so many coming! He began to run two games simultaneously, one game around the nondescript Salvation Army table, another half-on and half-off the sofa, partly on the end table, leaving a couple of people with no place to sit—they had to kneel. Sometimes Harry stood watch in the apartment above, but more often, it was left to Chris to report on who came. It got to the point where guys Chris knew were bringing so many players he didn't know that when he met Harry, and Harry showed him pictures, Chris sometimes couldn't match any of the new ones with the faces in Harry's portfolio. Whenever he was able to identify a photo, without any doubt, he did, but when he wan't absolutely sure, he said so, even though Harry got frustrated. Chris was bending over backward not to make a false ID, because he'd never forgotten how terrible it was to be told he'd fingered the wrong person.

He'd been sitting at the front desk at the 4-oh, because it was his turn to catch a case, when a woman came in, with a boy about eight or nine years old clutching her hand. The woman carried a black tote bag in her other hand; she wore a kerchief and a black coat. She was not so much leading the boy as dragging him, because he looked as though he just wanted to be somewhere else. Anywhere else.

"Can I speak to a detective?" the woman asked.

"You can speak to me," Chris said. "I'm in charge here. What's the problem?"

"Well, my son tells me," she began, then she stopped. She looked closely into Chris's face, apparently trying to decide whether she should tell him what her son had told her. Then she went on. "My name is Mrs. Lopez, and this here is my son Miguel. My son Miguel is telling me that there is a man in the projects who is doing bad things with my son. Not with my son Miguel, with my other son."

Chris looked at the boy. "What happened?"

Miguel suddenly seemed anxious to talk. "Well, I play in the street with my brother, and this man comes down . . ." Miguel went on to tell about the man who came to the school playground, talked to them, then invited them up to his apartment. The man told the boys he had some new bicycles to show them, that they could use.

"What happened when you got upstairs?" Chris asked.

"Then the man, we went into the bedroom, and he stuck his dick in my brother's ass," Miguel said.

Mrs. Lopez began to cry.

"Did he do that to you, Miguel?" Chris asked gently.

"No," Miguel said. "Just to my brother."

"Where is your other son, Mrs. Lopez?" Chris asked

"I am sick at my heart," she said. "He is at school."

Chris went to the school, spoke to the teacher and got the thirteen-year-old boy out of class. "Your brother is telling me things that have happened to you," Chris said. "Are they true?"

"No!" the boy said angrily. "No, they are not true!"

"You can tell me the truth," Chris said. "I'm your friend, and you don't have to be ashamed to tell me."

"It's not true!" the boy insisted. "Nothing happened."

Well, maybe the little guy is making it up, Chris thought. Maybe he's trying to get attention or something, who knows? Still, he had to be sure. "Let's just go get some ice cream then, as long as we're out here," Chris said. "I could use some ice cream." They walked to a new place that had just opened, near the station, where the owner served homemade ice cream. Chris ordered a scoop of vanilla, and the boy got a banana split.

"You know, if anything bad did happen, it's not your fault," Chris said. He paused, but the boy said nothing. He kept his eyes on the dish. "As painful as it seems now," Chris said, "you'll feel better if you tell me. I know that for sure. And if something happened and you don't tell me about it, it's going to bother you for the rest of your life."

The boy jabbed at his ice cream, and began to cry. Chris handed him a napkin. "Finish your ice cream," he said. "Then you can tell me."

When the boy finished, he put his spoon in the dish and with his eyes down, staring at the spoon, he told Chris where they'd gone to see the bicycles, and what happened there. He looked up at Chris with such a bleak expression that Chris reached over and hugged him, almost knocking the dish off the table. "It's okay," Chris kept telling him. "It's not your fault. It's okay."

He took the boy to the station, to wait there with his mother, then went to the man's apartment. He was sure he had the guy cold, but when the door opened, Chris just stared. The guy was in a wheelchair.

"I'm investigating something," Chris said. "Can I come in?"

As he walked in, Chris could see kids' drawings taped around the archway into the kitchen, and on the refrigerator door. He crossed to the window, which looked directly across the street into the schoolyard. Pictures of children were taped around the window frame. Through the open bedroom door, he saw two shiny blue bicycles. Still, the guy was in a wheelchair.

"What am I being accused of?" the man asked in a calm voice.

"We can discuss it at the precinct," Chris told him. "I want you to come with me now."

The man smiled slightly. "Of course I'll come with you."

Chris wheeled him downstairs, lifted him into the car, and folded the chair into the backseat. At the precinct, he put the man into a small room. "Wait here," Chris said. "I'll be right back."

Chris went down the hall to the room where Mrs. Lopez was sitting with her sons. "I want you to tell me again what happened," he said to the older boy. "And you must be very, very sure."

The boy repeated the story in detail, with his younger brother chiming in. Mrs. Lopez twisted her hands in her lap, nervously. "It'll be all right," Chris told the family. "You did the right thing to come here."

Chris went back to the old man. "I'm placing you under arrest," he told him. The old man stared at him. "What for?" he asked in a strained voice.

"For child molesting and sodomy," Chris said.

The man clutched his chest and fell forward in his chair. "I'm getting a heart attack," he gasped. Chris thought he was faking, but he wasn't. Chris called the Emergency squad and rode in the ambulance with the old man to the hospital.

By the time Chris got back to the station, about three hours later, a priest was talking to the captain. Chris wasn't surprised that the priest knew about the case; in that neighborhood, everybody knew everything that was going on.

"Chris, this is Father Conlin," the captain said.

"Hello, Father Conlin," Chris said.

"I want you to know that this man you are accusing is a pillar of society!" the priest declared. "He is a very religious man, and you are wrong to accuse him."

"Well," Chris said, "I have two kids saying this is what he did."

"Kids make up stories," the priest said.

"I know kids make up stories," Chris said. "But I believe these boys, and based on what we know, I had to arrest him."

When the priest had gone, the captain pointed his finger at Chris. "If you're wrong about this, you're going to be pounding a beat in the most Godforsaken part of the Bronx," he warned.

"I'm not wrong," Chris insisted, thinking, please God, please don't let me be wrong.

Back at the hospital, he found the man's condition had stabilized, so he took prints and sent them to Albany. At the bedside arraignment next day, Father Conlin had just arrived when the report came back. Chris showed him the yellow sheets, the guy's previous record: twenty-one counts of lascivious conduct, going back to the 1940s, from different places: Boston, Washington, Chicago.

"From now on," Chris told the priest, "you stick to your work and I'll stick to mine."

Father Conlin smiled sadly. "We're both doing God's work," he said.

* * *

One Saturday in September, when Chris drove Marty home from the beach, her mother came to greet him in the front hall. "We'd like you to come for dinner tomorrow," she said, smiling at him. "Sunday is our macaroni day."

"Thank you very much, I'd like that," Chris said. "Thank you."

Marty walked out to the car with him. "I forgot to ask what time," Chris said. "What time should I come?"

"Oh, you know what time families eat on Sundays, don't you?" Marty said casually. "What time does your family eat?"

Chris thought back quickly to Sunday dinners with his parents and his sisters. After the long Greek liturgy, they were home in early afternoon. Katrina and the girls immediately disappeared into the kitchen to work on the lamb dinner, the main event of the day, while George settled down with the Sunday newspaper, passing Chris the comic section. "About the middle of the afternoon," Chris said. "Three o'clock, three-thirty."

"That's right," Marty said. "See you tomorrow."

A little after noon on Sunday, Chris drove down to Prince Street with a thick envelope for Solly, his share of the week's take. On the way back to his car, he stopped at a fruit and vegetable stand and bought a big bunch of chrysanthemums, a mix of rust-colored and dazzling yellow. As he headed out to Long Island, he thought that Sunday dinner at his girl's house sounded like an old-fashioned movie, with Van Johnson, maybe, and June Allyson. He was dressed in his Sunday best, too, a dark suit with a light-blue shirt and striped tie, although his mop of curls, and the dark glasses, always added a slightly raffish look, no matter what he wore.

Traffic was light, and he reached the house early, before two o'clock. He was surprised to see a couple of cars already parked along the curving driveway. Almost as a reflex, he noted the plate numbers and repeated them in his head, over and over, as he walked to the door and rang the bell. He wasn't wired, and he could hardly whip out a notebook and jot them down. He knew he'd remember them; the sharp memory that had gotten him through high school with hardly any studying came in handy in this job.

"Don't get the wrong idea," he warned Marty, when she opened the door. "You don't think these flowers are for you, do you?"

Marty laughed. "Then you should give them to her yourself. She's in the kitchen." Chris followed her as far as the doorway into the dining room, then he stopped. John was sitting at the dining room table with three men. There was a platter of fruit and cheese on the table, and a jug of red wine.

The men stopped talking when they saw Chris. John waved a hand toward him. "This is Chris," he said. He did not give the names of the men, who nodded curtly, not smiling. They did not seem pleased to see him. Same here, guys, Chris thought; walking into a roomful of strangers isn't my favorite thing. He hoped that from the way he looked—awkward and nervous, standing in the doorway clutching a bouquet of flowers—they would take him at face value. Anna came from the kitchen, and as she smiled, kissed him, and took the flowers, he heard John murmur, "My daughter's boyfriend."

Chris had been interested that it was Anna who'd invited him for Sunday dinner, and now he understood. Marty may have wanted to ask him, and maybe she'd suggested it to her mother, but the invitation had to be cleared with a higher authority, because Sunday was more than macaroni day. John was holding court at his table; the men were not casual dinner guests. Anna must have asked permission from her husband, and gotten the nod to have Chris join them.

John beckoned Chris to sit down and poured a glass of wine for him. Anna brought out the mums in a glass bowl. "I chopped the stems down so we could have them on the table," she said. "They're beautiful. They're my favorite flower." She placed her hand lightly on Chris's shoulder for a moment. "Make yourself at home," she said. "Have something to eat. Marty's helping me in the kitchen." She went back into the kitchen, closing the door tightly behind her.

Chris drank his wine and cut a wedge of cheese. After a

short silence, one of the men began talking again. But Chris was too edgy to pay close attention at first. He was on pins and needles, expecting one of the men to turn to him and ask him a direct question. A half hour, Chris thought. If a half hour passes and nobody asks me anything, I'm okay. Whether that was an accurate barometer or not, it was the barometer he used. He didn't want to keep looking at his watch, but he had a good sense of time, and as a half hour passed, he began to relax. He caught the names of only two of the three men: Angelo and Ed.

The men didn't always stay seated. One or two would get up and drift into the hallway or the den. John would talk with one of them in the alcove near the window, then another man would join them. There were all kinds of corners and spaces where people could mingle and talk, in a sort of open-house atmosphere. Chris got up from the table, too, taking a piece of cheese, and sat for a while in the wing chair in the front hall, where he could see into the dining room, the living room, and the den. The den looked impersonal and uninteresting, like a doctor's waiting room. But the conversation he was hearing was not uninteresting. At least one of the men was from the garment center, looking for a loan from John. Somebody mentioned "a hundred large"—one hundred thousand dollars.

Chris knew the garment industry was vulnerable. If a guy had a bad year and was in debt, no bank was just going to hand over a hundred thousand dollars for his fall line. Yet without the money there would be no fall line. He was a legitimate businessman, but if he couldn't get the loan from a legitimate bank, he had to look somewhere else, quickly. And so, loansharks didn't have to advertise; they didn't go around drumming up business, grabbing somebody's lapels and saying, "Hey, you gotta borrow money from me." Somebody in the garment center would steer the client to John, and somebody would probably come along to vouch for him.

Chris had done that, though with considerably smaller digits. He'd taken guys to the Elmhurst Diner, where Big Lou did business in the last booth. "Lou, this is Jake. He needs five large."

Lou would peer at Chris, not at Jake. "Are you vouching for him, Chrissie?"

"Yeah, I'm vouching for him, he's okay." Chris became what the banks would call a cosigner, responsible not just for the guy's debt but for the interest—the vigorish, the juice, the payment that had to be made regularly, usually weekly, without ever reducing the original amount. If a guy borrowed, say, a thousand dollars, the vig might be two hundred a week, every week, until the thousand could be repaid in a lump. The only way to beat the shy was to repay the debt quickly, but that rarely happened; a guy who needed a grand so desperately one week was unlikely to have it in hand the following week, unless he scored at the track, which was also unlikely. More often, the borrower couldn't even come up with the vig, week after week. In the old days, such an unfortunate might have been hurled down a flight of stairs or dragged into an alley. Dead men never came up with the vig, though, while men who were threatened, possibly roughed up a bit, but left alive, could be bled forever. Thus, contemporary shylocking involved the art of negotiation. "Okay, we'll bring the vig down from five hundred a week to two hundred, and here's what you're gonna do: You're gonna get rid of the girlfriend, no more cards, no more new cars, and okay, no problem. But if we find out you're bouncing around, you got a new Caddy, then it goes back to five and then you got a problem." Thus things were worked out, most of the time: When one guy whom Chris vouched for didn't cooperate, his laundromat burned down.

From the transactions Chris had watched, or had been involved in at the Kew and the Elmhurst Diner and other spots, he knew the looks on the faces of all the players: the shy, the client, the voucher. He knew the language: "Hey Chrissie, I promise, next week, I promise, on my mother's eyes!" John's friends were not talking street slang; they were well-dressed, and John's dining room was not the end booth at a diner. But the nods and gestures, the body language, were unmistakable. A shy was a shy was a shy, and thus did he prosper and worm his way into legitimate businesses. If the guy borrowing from John couldn't pay on time, he wouldn't be whacked out. He would just have a new partner.

Precisely at three o'clock, the kitchen door opened, and Anna appeared with a platter of steaming pasta. Marty was behind her, with a tureen of red sauce. John sat at the head of the table, and Chris took his usual place in the middle of the table, next to Marty. Since that was the place he'd been given the first night he came to dinner, he always sat there afterward. Anna sat at the opposite end of the table from her husband, nearest the kitchen; the three men sat across from Marty and Chris.

When talking stopped and serious eating began, Chris could immediately tell who was Italian and who wasn't by their language. An Italian guy called pasta "macaroni," no matter what kind it was, except for special dishes—ravioli, lasagna—while a guy who wasn't Italian would say "Pass the linguine." To an Italian, sauce wasn't sauce: it was "Pass the gravy." Table manners were a giveaway, too. Almost all the OC men Chris had met, including John, bent low over their plates and ate greedily, almost to the point of slurping their food. Chris thought this harked back to the days when they'd been poor and hungry, when food on the table was not necessarily a given. Or maybe they just had lousy manners. In any case, Chris kept his head up, his elbows off the table, as he'd been taught; it occurred to him that even though eating properly—"Eat nice," Katrina would say—came naturally to him, it was making a good impression on Anna, and he was pleased about that.

Dinner was a lengthy affair, about three hours. Between courses, people got up and wandered around; one of the men left, after the pasta, and didn't return. There was an enormous amount of food—the mums had to be removed from the table to make room for all the dishes. Bountiful meals had been the custom at Chris's house, too, even after he was grown up. Whenever Phil came by the house, Katrina would greet him with affection and would immediately disappear into the kitchen. Phil would hear dishes rattling, the refrigerator door opening, pots and pans being brought out. "I'm just going to be here a minute, m'am," Phil would call out. "Thank you very much, but I really can't eat anything." Then Katrina would emerge with a tray laden with food. "I'll just set it down here and you can just take what you want," she would say.

Of all the dishes on the table, John seemed fondest of the *braciole,* the pork cutlets. "Good, from Brooklyn," he pointed out. Chris knew that OC people went out of their way—or, more precisely, sent someone else out of their way—to get what they considered the best available food in any category: pork cutlets from a shop in Brooklyn, fresh fish from Fulton Street, long loaves of bread from Zito's, cannoli from Ferrara's on Grand Street in Little Italy. Chris's favorite was the chunky potato salad, and he remarked on it. Anna was pleased. "I knew you liked it the first time you came to us," she said.

Marty and Anna cleared the table, finally. John got a bottle of sambuca from the sideboard, while Anna brought coffee and the required dish of coffee beans. John and Angelo drank espresso, the others drank American coffee. Shortly after the men left, John got to his feet, stretched and yawned. "Good night," he said. Then he looked pointedly at Chris. "Are you going out tonight?"

When Chris hesitated, Marty replied, "Yes, Daddy. We're going to a movie."

John looked at Chris a while longer, then nodded. "Well, good night," John said. Chris got up as John left the table.

"Come again soon," Anna said to Chris. She kissed him on the cheek.

"Thank you, I will," Chris said. "Thank you for inviting me." He felt a twinge of guilt when she kissed him, considering he still had the plate numbers in his head.

"Well, I see the way to your heart is through my mother's potato salad," Marty said, as they drove off.

"You got it," Chris said. "Why else do you think I come all the way out here? Just to see you? It's the potato salad that does it, kid."

Happily, there was no line at the movie house. Even though Chris felt better in Marty's neighborhood than in Manhattan, he didn't like standing in a ticket line anywhere. He remembered that John Dillinger had been not only recognized but gunned down outside the Biograph Theatre in Chicago, after seeing *Manhattan Melodrama*. Once he was inside the darkened theater, Chris felt okay.

"I'm really glad you came today," Marty said, when they got back to her house.

"Me too," Chris said. "I'll call you tomorrow."

"And don't forget Saturday," she said. She kissed him quickly and went inside.

He'd told the truth, he reflected as he drove away. He was very glad he'd come. Talk about mixing business with pleasure! He was very pleased with himself. He had a good report to give Harry on the men who'd come to dinner, and he was looking forward to Saturday at the Metropolitan Museum of Art. When Marty had suggested a day at the museum, he knew he shouldn't; it was too public, not the wisest place to hang around. But people he didn't want to see were more likely to be at the beach, or at bars and restaurants, than at a museum.

Except for Liz. He'd gone to museums with Liz, and to weekend brunches in the city. Liz liked spending a day in Greenwich Village, browsing through the shops, enjoying the street life. He made sure always to know Liz's schedule, whether she was going to be in the city or on the road and, if in the city, whether she was working and where. If she wasn't out of town, and didn't have a booking, he steered clear of museums and midtown stores, especially Bloomingdale's.

Sometimes he knew Liz's schedule when he telephoned her, and sometimes he heard it from her answering machine.

"I'm in Indianapolis for three weeks. Please call back later." Sometimes he wasn't sure she was in Indianapolis when she said she was. He didn't quiz her closely, because she didn't have the right to quiz him. He'd made that very clear. If she said she was going out for three weeks with an industrial, he made it a point to call, at the end of that time, and if she had returned, he tried to get out to Forest Hills within the next couple of days. But even then, he felt a strain. She wasn't as talkative as she had been, and he couldn't blame her.

He'd noticed the strain during the holiday period of the second year he was undercover, in 1976, even before he'd met Marty. He and Liz had spent Thanksgiving Day with friends in Forest Hills; he'd spent a lot of time playing with the friends' children, in order to avoid conversation about himself. At Christmas, the trip to the country seemed different, somehow. He'd felt lonely, even in the welcoming warmth of her parents' house. In a way he couldn't quite pinpoint, Liz seemed different. He knew he seemed different to her, too—uncommunicative, distant. He had a lot he wanted to tell her, but nothing he could say.

He couldn't even be sure she felt the same toward him. It crossed his mind that maybe she was making new friends, too—people she didn't want to talk about. "Are you seeing other men?" was a question he wanted to ask, more than once, to bring it out in the open. But since he couldn't bring his life into the open, he didn't ask. That unspoken agreement—don't ask me and I won't ask you—was keeping the balance. He had never expected his marriage to become a balancing act, but when he saw his wife, about once every three weeks, it seemed to him that that's what it had become.

Chris had enjoyed art since Mrs. Fletcher had given him his first colored pencils, in kindergarten, and art was Marty's talent. They'd already made a visit to the Museum of Modern Art, and had had a fine, satisfying argument. Chris had never liked Picasso. In fact, he hated Picasso. "He draws noses over here and eyes over there," he complained to Marty. "If there's a message there, I don't get it."

"Oh, you're just old-fashioned," Marty teased.

At the Met, Chris argued, there were pictures worth spending time on, pictures by people like Caravaggio and Tintoretto. "But I'm not just old-fashioned," he protested. "I like Edward Hopper, he's modern. And I don't care that much for Rembrandt, there's too much of a haze in his stuff."

The day at the Met was so pleasant, with late brunch after, that when beach weather tapered off, Saturdays in the city became a habit. In the crisp autumn sunshine they walked down Fifth Avenue, window-shopping, talking. Marty liked going all the way down to Greenwich Village. On autumn Saturdays, it seemed as though everybody in New York headed down to the Village to stroll around, and shop, and then wander on a little farther, where the Village streets spilled over into Little Italy, with its many good restaurants. But Marty never wanted to go that far.

She seemed more relaxed with him now than she had been in the beginning. She'd seemed cautious about him at first, a little leery, which Chris could understand. But the more they were together, the freer she seemed. It occurred to Chris that they had something basic in common that they couldn't talk about: Each lived in two different worlds. Marty was an intelligent woman who had to know who her father was and what he did. Mafia children might be satisfied, when they were young, with some made-up story about their fathers —they were in Europe, or away on a long business trip, when they were in fact doing time. But when children grew up, they had to know. Even if a father had not done time, they had to know. What did Marty think her father was, a used-car salesman?

But then Marty had gone to college. She'd lived in Paris, and now she had a promising career as a graphics artist. When she was away from her house, from her father, she moved into that world. Chris met her there. He was no scholar, but he was interested in things that interested her: movies, art, history. Most wiseguys didn't know anything about these things, and didn't want to know. Chris felt that if you hung around wiseguys for any appreciable length of time, you could lower your IQ by fifty points, easily.

When Marty asked questions, he tried to stick as close to the truth as possible, to make it easier to remember what he'd said in case the subject came up again. So when she asked about brothers and sisters, he said he had two sisters. But he added that one lived in California, and the other was married to a man in the military, stationed in West Germany, so that Marty wouldn't ask to meet them. He couldn't bring himself to say his mother was dead, so he said his mother was a nut about travel, and was always going someplace; right now she was on a long cruise, all the way around the world. He was aware of the irony, as he said it; Katrina had been in only two states in her entire life, New York and New Jersey. She never wanted to go anywhere else, and when he and his sisters had urged her, after George's death, to get out more, take a trip, see something of the world, she had looked bewildered and had asked them why. Why would a person ever want to leave home?

Chris tried to divert questions back to Marty, or to ask them first. So she talked about her friends, some from college, a couple from her office, and one very close girlfriend who had just gotten engaged and had asked Marty to be in her wedding. That was a long way off, Marty said, but she invited Chris to come, and Chris said he would.

"Who are *your* friends?" Marty asked. "I'd like to meet some of them."

Chris shrugged it off. "My friends are mostly alcoholic musicians," he said. "My friends you wouldn't want to meet, believe me."

The safest topic was his father. He could talk truthfully and at length about George, and he found himself telling Marty things about his father, and remembering things as he told her, that he'd almost forgotten. In grammar school, each child had had a bank account; once a week, the child would bring in money—twenty-five cents, fifty cents, possibly a dollar—and give it to the teacher, who would record it in the child's bankbook and deposit it at a branch of the Bowery

Savings Bank on 86th Street. George had been so pleased at this method of teaching thrift to the children that he had given Chris five or ten dollars a week to deposit. A few times, Chris remembered, he had twenty dollars to hand the teacher. Chris recalled how the other kids stared when he brought in such amounts; even the teacher looked surprised. On Saturday afternoons, when Chris went to the movies, he usually had a couple of dollars in his pocket, but in order to be one of the gang, he did as the other kids did and bought just one thing—a "sugar daddy," a box of Milk Duds—and made it last all afternoon.

"What did your father look like?" Marty asked.

"He was a good-looking man," Chris said. He could see the wedding picture that his mother kept on the living-room table: Katrina in a long, straight-skirted dress that she'd made herself, with a high collar and puffy sleeves, George standing stiffly at her side, his hair slicked back, his dark eyes looking squarely into the camera. "My father looked something like a younger Clark Gable, only without the mustache," Chris said. "But he had the same hairline, and the same eyes, kind of the same expression."

"Do you look like him?" Marty asked.

"Maybe a little," Chris said. "Only his hair was straight. Everybody in my family has straight hair but me. I think the reason I always hated having my picture taken was because I hated my curly hair when I was a kid."

"I'd like to have a picture of you," Marty said.

"Hey, why would you want a picture of me?" Chris asked. His voice was light, but the question made him edgy.

"People give each other pictures," Marty said. "I could show it around the office and say, 'This is the millionaire who sent me the roses.' Or maybe I could make it into a dart-board." Chris laughed, but Marty kept on. "No, really, do you have a picture I could have?"

"No, actually, I don't," Chris said. "I really always did try to get out of having my picture taken. I got a box camera for Christmas when I was eleven or twelve, and I took it apart to see how it worked, then I couldn't put the thing back together." That was mostly all true. The only recent picture he had, besides his police ID, had been taken in the driveway of Phil's house in Rockland County. Chris had been visiting and he was in the driveway, about to get in his car, when Phil's wife came out with their little boy, Chris's namesake. "We want a picture of the two of you together," Judy said. So Chris stood there, holding the child's hand, feeling foolish, not knowing whether he should look into the camera or down at the boy. He didn't know where the picture was, now; he supposed Phil and Judy had it.

"Well, we'll have to do something about that," Marty said. "I really do want a picture."

Chris started to say something snappy, but he stopped. He was uncomfortable now with smart-ass remarks when he was with Marty. In the beginning, he'd done that easily. One night, Marty had looked at him curiously. "I'm trying to figure you out," she said. "You're different from the other men who know my father, and I can't put my finger on what it is."

Chris had lifted his glass and winked.

"I'm one of a kind, baby," he said.

Now he talked normally. He was aware that the more he talked with her in his usual way—not a wiseguy, not a philosopher, just in between, like a regular person—the more she would see he was different. And he was glad of that. He didn't want her to think of him as just another hood.

She didn't seem to think that. She seemed comfortable with him, too. Chris noticed that she laughed more when she was away from her house. She didn't seem intimidated by her father, but she was noticeably freer and more at ease when she was with Chris, more apt to express her own opinions, more her own person. Chris didn't spend a lot of time trying to analyze her relationship with her father; he told himself not to be a bargain-basement Freud. But he could see the difference in her, as she came to know Chris better.

She had the freedom to become his friend, too.

* * *

Harry ran the plates and told Chris that Angelo, one of the men at the Sunday dinner, was an informer. Angelo had known John for thirty years, and had just recently been flipped. He'd been nabbed for something and was facing heavy time. Angelo was about John's age, pushing sixty; he didn't have time to do heavy time.

Sometimes Chris suspected that guys he met were informers. He would call Harry and say, "Check this guy out," and give the plate number. If word came back that the guy had been locked up, then suddenly was out on bail, Chris could put two and two together. This time the information was definite: Angelo was an informer.

Chris didn't like informers. He and Phil had used them, working street crimes. But when it came to major stuff, Chris felt they couldn't be trusted, that they would lie as readily to the NYPD or whoever they were working for as to the guys they were informing on. Informers were likely to tell you anything you wanted to hear. Harry had told Chris at the outset that somebody higher up had suggested that Chris use an informer on this job, the way the Bureau used informers with their undercover people. Harry passed on the idea a little reluctantly; the rivalry between the department and the FBI was no secret, even to the general public. But Harry had to point out that using an informer in the mob to vouch for Chris would make it easier. "This is my pal Chrissie from Vegas, he's good, he's okay."

Chris had refused. He didn't want anybody out there to have any kind of control over him; you never knew what that guy might do, what kind of pressure he might be under, what he might end up saying about Chris.

Anyway, the fewer people who knew about him, the better. Too many people on a project meant too many possible leaks. There'd been an undercover project in the Bronx, during Chris's time at the 4-oh, though in another neighborhood, with an informer involved. Chris thought the project, a kind of sting operation, had gone sour because there were just too many guys in on it, both federal people and city detectives. Their plan was to buy a discotheque where OC guys hung out. An ex-con who was an informer for the Justice Department had teamed up with a city detective who spoke fluent Italian. The joint was interesting, patronized by Carlo Gambino, among other heavyweights, and the whole thing seemed carefully planned, with the informer paid five hundred dollars a week for his efforts. Yet within five months the plan had collapsed, partly because of ridiculous blundering—they'd nestled a camera in a tree directly in front of the joint, which a guy would have had to be blind not to notice—but also, Chris thought, because there were just too many players. It turned into an expensive fiasco. The patrons fingered the potential new owners as the law, and stopped coming. Once they stopped coming, there was no point in buying the place. "People ceased to appear," one federal agent reported dryly. "We realized we could get stuck with a white elephant."

Harry brought up the idea once more, but Chris was adamant. "No way, Harry," he declared. "I don't care what the Bureau does. I'm a street kid, and I'll do this on my own."

Now, Harry agreed that Chris was doing very well on his own. He'd moved up, from hustling untaxed cigarettes, to the higher levels of organized crime, first with the Greeks, then with the Italians. He fit in perfectly. He wouldn't have fit in with other crime outfits. Everybody knew that organized crime was not limited to Italians. Chris heard conversations about deals going down with the Chinese, where Chinatown overlapped Little Italy. Russian mobsters had Brighton Beach, and there was a kind of Irish Mafia in the Hell's Kitchen area, on the west side of Manhattan. In fact, when Chris reported that one of Kostos's flunkies did a few things with the Westies, Harry was interested. He told Chris he'd heard that the Westies were doing hits for the Castellano people, and he suggested that Chris go over and look into it.

"*You* go, Harry," Chris said. "Forget it. The way I look and dress, they'd throw me out the window, if I was lucky."

The Westies were violent and unpredictable, inclined to chop up a guy for no rhyme or reason. You couldn't play around with them.

With the Greeks and the Italians, Chris could play around.

He was doing well with them because he was accepted. He was accepted because he was believable. And he was believable because he had become the person they thought he was. Beyond the dress and the mannerisms, the language and the gestures, the way of walking and talking and scheming, he felt like Chrissie the jazz drummer, the smart guy on his way up. That wasn't what he *did;* it was what he *was*. Undercover work was referred to, in the department, as being "out there," but in truth, it was "in there."

On television and in the movies, undercover work seemed to consist of constant confrontations, at least one major shootout a day, two or three murders per week. In his undercover life, Chris dealt with what could be considered critical stuff maybe five or six days a month. The rest of the time he lived with these people in their everyday lives, doing everyday things: He was driving Frankie to a place in New Jersey regularly for Frankie's dental work. They didn't show that stuff on TV because it wasn't dramatic, just as they didn't show the loneliness.

Not that he had time on his hands to sit around feeling lonely. Solly had sent him out to Zero's, a discotheque on Long Island, as part-time manager. Chris was so busy, in fact, that he had to start turning Solly down. When Solly wanted him to take over the loanshark operation at one of the city's major newspapers, Chris and Harry had discussed it and had decided that that would take too much of Chris's time and wouldn't be productive.

He was too busy to be aware, except intermittently, of the loneliness. Sometimes the isolation of his life was obvious: When he reported to the police firing range for periodic practice and testing, he wore a bag over his head. The emotional isolation was, of course, less obvious. He was conscious of it only when he was by himself, once in a while at Waterside, and when he was with Liz.

Even when he was with Liz, now, he felt almost as lonely as when they were not together. The warm sharing of their first two years of marriage was dissolving, replaced by silence. Not hostility, just silence.

Chris still didn't want to drop the project, though. He liked living on the edge. He was getting by, living by his wits. He liked knowing that he could step right up to the edge and stay there, keeping himself balanced. But the more time he spent on the edge, the more he needed, sometimes, to step back to firmer ground.

His time with Marty had become that safer ground. In the six months he'd known her, he'd begun to think less about her father than about how good it was to be with her. And, as to her father, Chris was beginning to think Marty probably didn't know all that much, or if she did, maybe it wasn't such a good idea to try to get it out of her. Maybe that would put her in a precarious position. So he put that on the back burner, in a way, and just relaxed with her. She had become the only person whom he saw regularly with whom he could talk. From enjoying her company, he came to need it.

He'd lost track of both the clock and the calendar. On a day-to-day basis, the time of day or night meant nothing. Sometimes he grabbed a couple hours sleep on the sofa at the Astoria club before going to meet Harry, or going somewhere with Frankie, or down to Prince Street, or out to the Kew, or over to The Daily Planet to spend the day, or part of it, and so on, into another night.

Seasons blended into one another; mostly he knew only whether it was hot or cold outside. It was always snowing when he went to the country at Christmas with Liz, and it was snowing on the night he and Marty went to the opera, then to the Oak Bar. When they left, some horse-drawn carriages were still lined up, as late as it was, at the edge of Central Park. "Let's take a ride," Chris said.

The driver tucked the thick robe over their laps and smiled at them. The tiny lights twinkling in the trees along the road in the park, with the thick snow drifting past the lights, turned the scene into a blurry wonderland. Chris reached for Marty, to kiss her, just as the carriage door on his side flew open. He reached for it with one hand and held the door shut all the rest of the way, while trying to keep his other arm around her, trying to hold her and kiss her at the same time. They couldn't stop laughing. When Chris took her hand to help her down, they couldn't let go.

At Waterside, he unlocked the door and headed quickly for the table lamp, bypassing the wall switch. Marty looked around. "Oh, this is nice," she said. She walked to the window and looked at the snow falling on the dark water. "What a beautiful view," she said.

"It's a nice place," Chris agreed. He took her coat and opened the closet door. "It's my niece's place," he said hurriedly, in case she'd glimpsed the woman's clothing there. "I usually stay at my aunt's, but my niece is in Paris—no, London—studying art. So I'm using her place. She left a lot of her stuff here."

Marty sat on the sofa while Chris opened a new bottle of brandy. "I see your niece likes Hopper, too," Marty said. "I guess so," Chris said. They talked a little about painting, as they sipped brandy, but it wasn't long before they kissed. They kissed again.

In the bedroom, Chris wished he hadn't gotten those damned satin sheets.

7

Chris went for a walk. As much as he detested the cold, he had to get out of the apartment, beyond the reach of Harry and the telephone. He had a lot of thinking to do.

He thought he shouldn't see Marty again. Look at what you've done! He berated himself. You are a married man, and a cop doing a job, and you have broken the rules. You made a dumb mistake, and you better just drop it, now.

He thought that Marty would be hurt and bewildered if he didn't see her again. She'd think she was a one-night stand, and he couldn't bear for her to think that. He'd never wanted any woman to think that. In all his years of bouncing around, he'd had a one-night stand only once, possibly twice. He remembered drinking at a bar one night with one of the go-go girls, both of them smashed; he remembered going home with her, though he didn't remember her name. But he'd never been out for easy conquests, and he'd taken a lot of kidding about that when he was in the army, when guys seemed to consider women as notches in their belts, the more the manlier. Sometimes, when he'd gone out with a girl and they hadn't ended up in bed, she was annoyed. "What's the matter, are you a fag or something?" one girl had snapped. He'd always felt that a woman made more of an emotional commitment when she slept with a man than the man did, so he should feel some sense of obligation to her. When he had begun staying over with Liz at her apartment on the upper east side, he had felt a commitment that had led him to the altar.

He thought he had made a major mistake in getting to know Marty so well. How could he not have seen this coming? How could he have imagined that he could become her close friend without sex coming into it, not as a hasty, meaningless tumble but as a natural development in a friendship between two healthy, passionate people? He thought they'd had a fantastic time in bed.

He thought about the worst-case scenario. If it ever came to court, he thought it wouldn't be a tremendous problem. He could simply say that he'd done it because his life was threatened. "My life was in danger. I had to make the decision, and I didn't have time to confer with anybody." That was the catch-all, saving phrase in undercover work: My life was in danger.

He thought it wouldn't come to that, though. He thought that if it came to that, Harry would save him, somehow. He thought he couldn't possibly tell Harry about this.

He thought he had a solid reason to be with Marty. It wasn't as though he were having a love affair sponsored by the city of New York. He had a job to do.

He had trudged several blocks up First Avenue in the thick snow, then down again. His feet were stiff with cold, so he ducked into a coffee shop on 23rd Street. Sitting at the counter with a mug of coffee, he thought it out rationally.

He thought it made perfect sense. He was two different men. Chris the cop had a wife and in-laws, nieces and nephews, bills to pay, an apartment in Forest Hills. Chrissie lived at Waterside, a life that was totally, completely, entirely, separate from the other life. And no bills to pay, either.

He thought that because he was two different men, living in two different worlds, he could love two different women in different ways for different reasons.

He thought it was as simple as that.

* * *

Liz was pleased about her New Year's Eve booking at a club in Westchester. The place was small, she said, but it had a good reputation among agents and show-business people, a kind of insider's place. For her combined Christmas-and-birthday present, Chris gave her an amplifier she wanted, a big, boxy thing with plug-in mike for projecting voice tones and nuance. He'd bought it in Manhattan, wrapped it himself in shiny red paper, and wedged it in the back seat of the car for the trip to the country. In a way, it seemed pointless to take it all the way to Massachusetts and bring it back again the next day, but he wanted her to open it on Christmas day, in the country, the way they always did. They always had several presents for one another—some small things, such as a scarf, gloves, a book, and one major gift. Chris liked directing the action: "Open this one first, now that one, now the flat box," leading up to the main event. Liz loved the amplifier and got it working right away. That evening, after Christmas dinner, she sang for Chris and her parents and a couple of neighbors who'd dropped in. When she sang "Ave Maria," you could have heard a pin drop. As soon as they got back home, she started practicing for New Year's Eve.

"I'll be there," Chris promised.

He'd always enjoyed the week between Christmas and New Year's, when people were in unusually good moods. Even at the 4-oh, cops had seemed less grumpy and cynical then. Marty was working, but she said there was a holiday mood around her office, and one afternoon she took a three-hour lunch. They walked around Rockefeller Center, watching the skaters against the glittering backdrop of the Christmas tree. Ordinarily Chris wouldn't have felt comfortable doing that, just standing around, but with the holiday crowds so thick, elbow-to-elbow, he felt reasonably secure. As they stood at the edge of the upper promenade, leaning over to look down at the bright figures flashing by, Marty asked him to come to a New Year's party at a club on Long Island.

"Well, there's something else," Chris began. But Marty looked so disappointed that he relented.

"I'll be there," he promised.

By New Year's Eve, though, he didn't want to go anyplace. He was wiped out from an especially busy week, from all the bouncing around. How many bars can you visit, how many nights can you stay up all night, fall asleep at dawn, then start all over again at noon, he wondered, without it catching up with you? Solly had asked him to keep a sharp eye on Zero's during the holidays, when extra money flowed in and people had to be watched extra closely, so Chris had had to run out there every night.

He'd been to Zero's years earlier, when the place was called The Golden Slipper, serving up rock music and Chinese food. It was a big, noisy place, popular with young people then. One New Year's Eve, before he became a cop, he'd gone there with his date and two other couples. The place was jammed, with tables squeezed in so tightly people could hardly move. The food was cold and greasy when it finally came late, and everybody got irritable. One of the girls in a group at the next table made a snide remark to Dottie, a girl in Chris's party.

"What did you say?" Dottie demanded.

The other girl laughed in a sneering way. "You heard me," she said.

Dottie's boyfriend Richie got up and pushed his way through the chairs, around to the other girl's boyfriend. "You better watch your girlfriend," Richie warned. "Tell her to watch her mouth." That young man jumped up. "And just who the hell are you?" he hollered.

In reply, Richie swung at the guy. Blood gushed from the guy's nose; a friend of his jumped up and within seconds, it was a free-for-all. Chairs were being overturned, glasses thrown, people were yelling and punching. Chris couldn't believe it. The music kept blaring. Next thing he knew, a couple of state troopers strode in. When one of them spoke to Richie at the direction of the guy with the nosebleed—

"He started it! He started it!" the guy was yelling—Richie reached down to the table, picked up somebody's plate of chow mein and pushed it right into the trooper's face. Chris watched in horrified fascination as the trooper stood there, frozen, looking at the orange-y and brown chow mein sliding down the front of his uniform. Miraculously, Chris and the others talked the trooper out of locking Richie up. They all got out as quickly as they could. The Golden Slipper closed down for a long while, then. Chris hadn't gone back, and he'd lost all taste for Chinese food.

In its reincarnation as Zero's, the place was jumping. It wasn't just a mob spot; as he looked around, Chris saw that it was obviously still considered the place to go by young couples. Two bands played, alternating, so there was never a time out. There was valet parking, good food, non-Chinese —steaks, shrimp, chicken—and an air of flash that Chris enjoyed. As an emissary of Solly's, who owned a piece of the place, Chris got the red-carpet treatment, being admitted by bouncers and escorted to a ringside table ahead of all the people standing in line shivering.

On New Year's Eve, he dressed slowly in a dark suit—he'd never worn a tuxedo—while looking longingly at the sofa. He just wanted to flop down, stretch out, and watch the new year come in on television, from Times Square. Around 10 o'clock he drove to Westchester.

Liz looked absolutely terrific in a long dress with a black skirt and a silvery top. She wore a big black bow in her blond hair. Chris thought she looked like a young Patti Page. She sounded great too, he thought, feeling pleased about the amplifier. He looked around the room and saw a table to one side of the small stage, where he recognized two of her friends and their husbands. He joined them, and when Liz glanced over and saw him, she smiled, without dropping a note.

At midnight, everybody counted down, ten to one. "Happy New Year!" people cried, as the band played "Auld Lang Syne." Liz stepped down and came over to him.

"Happy New Year," she said.

"Hey, Happy New Year," Chris said, and kissed her.

She sat at the table and they had a glass of champagne. "I hope it will be a happy year," Liz said.

"Me too," Chris said. "I want this to be a very good year." He finished his champagne and stood up. "I have to go now," he said. "I gotta run."

Liz looked wistful. "Do you really have to?"

"Yeah, I really have to, something came up," Chris said. He leaned down and kissed her again.

"You look fantastic," he said. As he got to the door, he heard her singing again. He turned for one more look, then left quickly.

What a time for a guy to walk out on his wife, he thought uneasily, as he pulled out of the parking lot. He told himself that he'd been with her at the most important moment, the stroke of midnight. But he didn't feel good about it, and for a minute, as he waited at a red light, he thought of turning back.

Marty's face lighted up when she saw him. "Oh, I was afraid you weren't coming," she said. "I've been watching the door."

"I said I'd come," he reminded her. "I had a long drive, but I'm here. Happy New Year."

She led him to her table and introduced him to her friends. It was a private party, no wiseguys, and after a couple of drinks, Chris relaxed. But he wouldn't dance, no matter how much she pleaded.

"Musicians don't know how to dance," he explained. "I'd step all over your feet. You wouldn't have any toes left." He smiled. "You look beautiful," he said, "but I still won't dance."

She was wearing a bright-yellow dress, high in the front but with no back to it; her hair was piled on top of her head, fastened with a gold clip. She was wearing the Florentine cross.

"Are you sure you won't dance?" she asked again.

"I'm sure," Chris said. "But I'm fine, you go dance with somebody else."

She shook her head. "I don't want to dance with somebody else," she said. "I want to be with you." She reached out and laid her hand over his on the table.

With his wavy white hair and chubby face, Aniello Dellacroce looked kindly, even benevolent; some of his soldiers called him "Uncle." He was sometimes called George Rizzo and Timothy O'Neil, among other aliases. A United States Senate Committee had called him "the most powerful boss in New York." In fact, Dellacroce was not the boss but the underboss, second in command of the Gambino crime family. At Intel, where they had the advantage of closer perspective than the people in Washington, he was called, with terse simplicity, "an extremely powerful individual" in the Gambino group.

Chris called him Neil. He'd been a gunman for Albert Anastasia, in the wild days of "Murder Incorporated." When Anastasia died—in such dramatic gangland fashion that it qualified as a rub-out—Carlo Gambino took over as boss, for nearly twenty years. When Gambino died in the fall of 1976, Dellacroce was considered the likely successor, until a conference in a Brooklyn kitchen anointed Paul Castellano, Gambino's brother-in-law. But if Dellacroce was always the underboss, he was never underestimated. His name meant "Little Lamb of the Cross."

Chris was a teenager, hanging around the tranquil streets of Queens, when Anastasia was slaughtered in the barbershop of the Park Sheraton Hotel. Now Chris was hanging around clubs and restaurants with Dellacroce and his crew, drinking with them, singing Italian songs. Although Dellacroce seemed to like Chris, the old man was traditionally closemouthed. In the early seventies, he'd been jailed for contempt, when he refused to answer a grand jury's questions about organized crime, even when offered immunity. He'd served time for tax evasion—specifically, for evading taxes on a six-figure stock payment he'd received for arranging labor peace for a Long Island manufacturer. But those were relatively minor convictions, considering.

Not all Dellacroce's crew members were as discreet. One chunky guy with a cigar liked to drink, and the more he drank, the more he talked. One night at a club he draped his arm around Chris and explained the heroin routes from Palermo to Milan to New York. He stopped talking when Dellacroce arrived, but Chris had heard a lot by then.

"What does he look like?" Harry asked Chris, as they set about backgrounding the guy.

"He reminds me of a penguin with a cigar," Chris said.

Chris turned up at several places the Penguin frequented after that, including a rendezvous with some Colombians in Jackson Heights, but the Penguin was drinking, so he didn't seem suspicious at the sight of Chris, just pleased.

Dellacroce and the Penguin worked out of the Ravenite Social Club on Mulberry Street, between Prince and Spring, where Chris was taken by Solly. The Ravenite was Gambino land, and Solly was Luchese, but Chris found that family lines blurred when there was work to be done, deals to be made. Some endeavors were so lucrative that there was no need for anybody to get possessive or grabby; both families were conspicuous in the garment center. Chris sometimes couldn't tell family members apart, because in fact they were often not apart. If one family tried to move in on another's territory, without negotiating a split, of course there would be trouble, and often there had been. A Luchese couldn't just waltz into Gambino territory and open an after-hours place, but he could get the okay, then give the Gambinos a cut.

In general, it didn't seem to matter so much what family a man belonged to, or was connected with, as what he could accomplish. It was earning power that mattered: manpower. Intel filed Solly's brother as Luchese, yet he'd been given the contract to kill Joe Valachi by Vito Genovese. But it was not just individual crimes that mattered, under the RICO law; it was the activity of a "criminal enterprise," a group that engaged in racketeering. And so it was the interaction and the associations that mattered. RICO was a kind of web; Chris was a spider. He didn't know who might be caught in the web; he might never know. His job was to keep spinning.

At sixty-three, Neil Dellacroce had a big house on Staten Island—though he spent most of his time at the Ravenite and a nearby apartment—and a flock of young girlfriends. Chris figured it was the power, the money, and the aura that attracted the girls, because in most cases it wasn't the guy's looks. True, Dellacroce was nice-looking, in a craggy way, but most of the others were not. Solly was short, baggy-eyed, kind of cramped-looking, yet he had a *gummare* twenty-five years younger than he. As for Solly's brother, Chris thought he was the scariest-looking SOB he ever hoped to meet. The guy looked as though he'd just stepped out of his coffin. His eyes were small and sunken; his skin was the color of wet cement. And he had a deadly temper to match. One day, shortly after Chris arrived, the guy leaped up from his chair, knocked it over, and screamed that the place was filthy. He grabbed a broom and swept the floor of the Prince Street Social Club with a zest that would have been funny if it hadn't been so terrifying. He had plenty of girlfriends, too.

Chris couldn't figure out why these guys, with all their money, wanted to spend their days sitting backward in a chair, their arms folded, watching and listening. Chris thought that if he had their money, he'd be long gone from Mulberry Street, basking on some beach. He thought it was just that they didn't want to miss anything; they wanted to be part of every score, every decision, every sitdown. They had spent their lives creating an intimidating reputation, and they didn't want to waste it. They encouraged the mystique, the stories that were built up around them.

Some of the stories told about Dellacroce were believable to Chris, some weren't. A *Time* magazine cover story that came out not long before Chris met him reported that Dellacroce had once arranged to have the bodies of two murder victims dumped behind a police station. That was plausible as a kind of sinister prank, Chris thought. But Chris couldn't buy another incident reported in that article, which had Dellacroce discovering cops tapping his phone and then forcing them at gunpoint to chew and swallow the tapes. If anything, Chris felt the guy was extra-nice to cops. One day Chris and a couple of other guys were standing on the sidewalk in front of the Ravenite with Neil and his son Armond, nicknamed Buddy, a hefty, strong, if not overly bright, twenty-three-year-old. A patrol car pulled up, and a uniformed cop got out and began writing summonses for the double-parked cars.

Buddy swaggered over to the cop.

"Whassa matta, you got nothin' better to do?" he jeered. "Why doncha just get the hell outta here?"

The cop put his hands on his hips and glared, but before he could do anything, Neil stepped in. "I'm sorry, Officer," he said. Then he turned and slapped Buddy across the face, right there in public.

"Don't you ever talk to a police officer that way!" he yelled at his son.

Chris knew that Dellacroce was itchy about phones, though. The first time Chris walked into the Ravenite, he noted the phone on the wall to the right of the door. It was a pay phone. On a subsequent visit, Chris saw that the phone was gone. When he made casual inquiry—"Hey, where's the fucking phone? I gotta make a call"—he was informed that Dellacroce, apparently feeling that even pay phones were tappable, had ripped the phone right off the wall and hurled it out onto Mulberry Street. Eventually a new phone was installed; Chris got the number and called both Solly and the Penguin there.

More often, Chris reached Solly at the Prince Street club, though at first he couldn't even find the phone there.

"There's got to be a phone," Harry kept insisting.

"I know, I know," Chris kept saying. "I just can't locate the damned thing."

Chris kept hearing a phone ring, as he sat playing cards, and finally tracked down an extension phone in the dark alcove behind the bathroom, listed to the pizza parlor next door.

Until he went undercover, Chris had never been inside an OC social club. But he found that in decor, at least, they were not unlike neighborhood clubs he'd known. Social clubs were an honorable European tradition, transplanted from the streets of Naples and Athens to the sidewalks of New York. As a teenager, Chris had joined the Astoria Social Club, where there was a pool table, a refrigerator stocked with beer, and a neat sense of belonging.

As a child, he'd gone to the Democratic Club in East Harlem, where men smoked cigars and discussed politics. His father never missed voting in an election, and he'd insisted that Chris register to vote as soon as he was eligible. George was not an argumentative man, but Chris had heard him raise his voice indignantly when someone said that one person's vote didn't matter. "I tell you, it *does* matter," George declared. "It's an honor and a privilege to vote. It's the biggest freedom we have in this country."

Chris grew up thinking his father was the proudest American who ever lived. Once George became a naturalized citizen, he never wanted to set foot out of the country. Franklin D. Roosevelt was his idol; George called him the savior of the people. Chris also remembered vividly the election of 1948, when he went to the club with his father and listened to him preach eloquently on the virtues of Harry Truman. He remembered George's delight, next morning. "We have a wonderful President," George told the family. "He will be a fine President for all people." George was so passionate about politics and citizenship that Chris was surprised his mother never became a citizen. But she lived her life through her husband and her children; maybe she thought she was American enough, through them. Certainly George had patriotism to spare, and though Chris didn't always follow his father's political leanings, once he was grown, he'd always voted in every election, local and national, until he went under. Then he didn't vote at all.

Chris never heard politics discussed, at least not in any depth, at the clubs he visited. People still talked occasionally about the assassination of President Kennedy, but national politics didn't seem to interest them nearly as much as politics on the local level, the level on which they lived and operated.

They seemed to respect some politicians, and not others, and they seemed to know exactly who was who. Often Chris did too, and he had to be careful not to say too much when they talked of their relationships with certain politicians in the Bronx and in Queens. Some of it was familiar to him, some wasn't; in either case, he passed it along to Harry. The periodic investigations of organized crime, and the accompanying publicity, along with crime in general, seemed of little interest to the men Chris knew. Certain local crimes caught their attention: After a television news report on a child molesting case, Chris heard one guy yell, "That bum should have his nuts cut off!"

Chris didn't hang around for hours at the clubs. He tried to time his visits, in and out, learning their routine. There was always a TV set going, always a card game or two in progress: poker, gin, ziganette. There was an assortment of chairs and tables, mismatched; a couch that had seen better days, a bank calendar tacked to the wall. Chris never saw a kitchen, just a refrigerator; hot food was sometimes delivered from the Taormina or the Luna or another neighborhood restaurant. At the Ravenite, the bar was sometimes tended by Gene Gotti, brother of John Gotti, who paid his respects to Dellacroce faithfully on each visit. Johnny G. was considered a flashy dresser, and seemed to be on his way to becoming a media celebrity. Chris was unimpressed. He thought that anybody who hijacked as consistently as Gotti could be a Dapper Dan, too.

The Gambino family was considered, by the Intelligence Division, to be the strongest of the five crime families in New York, followed by the Luchese and the Genovese clans. Chris was involved, to one degree or another, with all three. His association with Solly gave him the entrée, but as he became known, he was able to bounce on his own. He preferred being taken someplace by a guy who was already known, though, because that made it easier to fit in, and to pick up on ongoing conversations. Sometimes he knew who he would be meeting, and sometimes he didn't. He had a simple rule for himself: Wherever somebody led him, he went.

He felt he was accepted by everybody without being completely trusted by anybody, except, probably, Solly and Frankie. But that was not surprising. In this world, trust was elusive at best, terminal folly at worst. Carlo Gambino, stoop-shouldered and mousy-looking, had helped plan the barber-shop slaying of his boss, Anastasia. Two decades later, when Gambinos gathered in that Brooklyn kitchen to choose Don Carlo's successor, one of them took the precaution of taping an automatic under the table.

Chris could never be a "made" guy, because he wasn't Italian, but he could be connected, as long as he was an earner. Chris was proving himself a strong earner, if not as productive as another non-Italian, Jimmy Burke. Chris met Burke at Robert's Lounge, one of the many Queens joints Chris was led to. Under the leadership of Paul Vario, a Luchese capo, Burke handled the day-to-day operations at Kennedy Airport, where a six-million-dollar robbery was carried out at Lufthansa Airlines in December, 1978. Chris was always aggravated that the heist was probably being planned at Robert's and other places, earlier that year, without him catching on.

He knew guns were moving, though, and he bought a couple from a big guy named Rudy, once at Chris's own club and once at a topless bar Rudy had just opened in Astoria. Rudy didn't seem to like Chris when they first met, but as Chris moved up, some of the respect given to Solly, John, and other men Chris knew rubbed off on him. When Rudy offered to sell him a couple of guns, Chris was a willing customer. He wasn't interested, at that point, in making a bust for illegal arms dealing; that was no more a priority than making a drug buy. If he knew beforehand of a crime going down—a hijacking, a killing—of course he couldn't just sit on that information. But in case of a routine gun deal, it was just something that might be useful. Harry would have the documentation, names, dates, and serial numbers, and it might even turn out to be some kind of leverage, someday.

Chris just wanted to buy the weapon, while Rudy insisted on telling him more than he really wished to know. What

Chris mostly knew about guns was that he didn't like them. Thanks to movies and TV, people thought cops pulled their guns several times a day, and shot somebody once or twice a week. In fact, even in his early days in the NYPD, when the rules on the use of deadly force were not as stringent as they later became, Chris had been reluctant to wield the weapon. He'd seen a woman who was leaning out a window get shot in the head, from a cop's gun, during a riot in the 4-oh neighborhood, and although he knew it had been an accident, he'd also known there were too many such accidents. That's why cops were not allowed to cock their guns: The trigger on a cocked gun needed to be pulled very slightly, only about one eighth of an inch, with very little pressure.

In the old days, a cop could shoot at a guy in a stolen car: "A fleeing felon." But why would you want to shoot at a stolen car? There might be kids in that car. Besides, using the gun led to a lot of headaches. You were questioned by the duty captain, who evaluated the situation and filled out stacks of forms. Then they kept you inside, doing desk work, until the whole episode had been investigated. There was the psychological effect, too: Some guys, once they shot somebody, got trigger-happy, others got trigger-shy. Either way, it was traumatic.

Chris wouldn't have minded if he hadn't had to carry a weapon at all, but of course he'd had no choice. He'd even had to buy his gun. His original gun, the blue-black service revolver, had cost him fifty-five dollars. He'd had his choice of the Smith & Wesson or the Colt. Both were .38 caliber, about the same size, but the mechanisms were different.

To open up the cylinder of a Smith & Wesson, you had to press forward, and you loaded the cylinder by turning it counterclockwise. On a Colt, it was reversed: You pushed the cylinder backward, and rotated it clockwise for loading. The difference was small but significant: If a cop had to reload while somebody was shooting at him, it was helpful to know which way to turn the cylinder.

Rudy, on the other hand, was a gun collector and connoisseur, knowledgeable about capability, velocity, and the intricate mechanism of the 9 mm. Walther PPK that he sold to Chris for a hundred and fifty dollars, about half-price. Rudy threw in a box of ammo, too. He was one of Big Lou's side-kicks; Lou had known Chris since Chris first met Solly, and Lou told Chris that both he and Rudy had taken care of a lot of people with machine guns. Although Chris could not pin Lou down to specifics, and could not even be sure if Lou was telling the truth—after all, Chris could have said that about himself, too—he knew from other sources that Rudy was a dangerous guy. So when Lou told Chris, "Rudy's good with a gun," Chris thought he might just as well believe him.

Some of the men Chris met were just casual acquaintances, no more than an introduction: Anthony Corallo, nicknamed "Ducks" for his skill at ducking indictments, and Paul Castellano—"This is Chris. This is Paul C." Some he came to know much better, including another of Lou's cronies, Nick Gregoris. Nick lived in Howard Beach, not far from the Bergin, the Gambino satellite club supervised by John Gotti. Nick bragged a lot to Chris, too—"I put away a lot of people in Brooklyn"—and while Chris couldn't be sure of that, either, he knew that Gregoris had done time and that he had indeed been active in Brooklyn until something went wrong. "They chased him out of Brooklyn and gave him to me," Solly told Chris mournfully. Nick had been involved in the bloody Gallo-Profaci feud. He was the only man Chris knew who carried a stiletto—a push-button knife with an eight-inch blade. Nick showed it to Chris one night at the Kew.

The Kew came to seem like a second home to Chris. He got phone calls there; he was a regular at the corner table, which was always reserved, whether anybody showed up or not. The Kew was an especially secure place for Chris to be, after the night he went with Frankie to a new place Frankie knew.

Only it didn't look new to Chris, as Frankie pulled into the parking lot. It looked vaguely familiar. Chris remembered the bowling alley connected to the cocktail lounge, and when

Frankie introduced Chris to the owner, who then called to his wife to come over and meet these people, Chris remembered everything only too well.

The ten years since he'd been here telescoped; as Josie smiled at him now, it felt like yesterday. He and his buddy, both of them in partial uniform, raincoats over uniform pants and shirts . . . jumping out the window, feeling like Errol Flynn. Here was Josie smiling, holding out her hand, looking at him with an unmistakable look that told him she remembered, too.

Chris hoped he wasn't swaying on his feet as he took her hand. She can't say anything, he told himself. There's no *way* she can say anything! She would implicate herself with her husband. She wouldn't take that chance, would she? How can she possibly say anything?

Josie said hello. She said it was nice to meet him. She said he should sit down and have a drink. But she didn't say anything.

Marty felt good about what was happening between them, Chris knew. She was warm and receptive and loving. Chris was vaguely uneasy when they were at Waterside; he always had a lurking feeling that there was some kind of device in the place that he didn't know about, and that Harry might have been picking up more than Chris thought. Harry had a key to the place, too. Then he told himself he was just being overly nervous, a little paranoid. Still, he felt better when he and Marty went away. She got a few days off from work, and they met at the Eastern Shuttle gate, at LaGuardia, for a flight to Boston. Chris was so anxious to get away that he didn't even mind it, though he disliked flying. Before they knew it, they were settled in at an elegant old hotel, downtown.

Chris was in absolute heaven. He felt liberated. No grid search when he walked into a restaurant; no mumbling to Marty at the sight of a long ticket line, "I don't feel like going here." No dark glasses, although he was so accustomed to wearing them by now that he wore them anyway.

They spent an entire day at the Museum of Fine Arts, and when they felt their feet were about to drop off, they went back to the hotel and kicked off their shoes and ordered from room service.

They went to a concert and had a long, late supper afterward, as they analyzed the music they'd heard. Chris talked so enthusiastically about music that Marty suddenly smiled brightly, as though she'd just thought of something.

"Did you ever think about opening a music store?" she asked. "You like music so much—you'd be so good at it."

"Well, no," Chris said truthfully. "I never did."

"Or an art shop," she continued. "Maybe you should go back to school—or art school—and develop that. Have you thought about that?"

"Well, no," Chris said, again truthfully.

She put her hand over his on the table, as she had a habit of doing.

"Look at me, Christy," she commanded.

Chris looked.

"You're not like the other men who know my father," she said quietly. "You can do better."

On the flight back to New York, Chris was as tense as he'd been lighthearted on the way up. He was withdrawn, so silent that Marty noticed it. "You're a different person when you're out of New York," she said. Liz had noticed that, too, only Liz had added, "You're more like yourself."

Except for Zero's, there was no place he could take Marty that was connected with his work, to maintain the notion that even when he was with her, he was doing his job. He didn't even like taking her to Zero's, because guys kept coming over to talk to him, and he had to act at least somewhat like Solly's man. He could tell Marty didn't like it, either.

Every other place was out of the question, either because there was too much going on, as at the Kew, or because they were such dumps. One place on the lower east side, The Still, was a hole. Solly's brother owned a piece of the place, so when Solly asked Chris to drop by and pick up some money, Chris felt he had to go. A cop who'd gone bad hung out in there, Chris heard; he didn't know whether that cop would recognize him, and he hated to take the chance. He made the stop quickly, taking the envelope from behind the bar and scooting out without having the drink he was offered. He didn't look at any of the guys huddled at the bar, though he did admire the old painting of Rudolph Valentino over the bar. He was thinking he'd have to come up with a good reason for Solly why he couldn't make stops for him there, when the problem was solved. The FBI rolled in with vacuum cleaners and hit the basement, where a man had been murdered. They were looking for evidence—hairs and the like—and after they vacuumed, they shut the place down.

A joint on West 22nd Street—far west, in the warehouse section—was a dangerous place, he'd heard. He didn't realize how dangerous until he got just inside the door, past the bouncer, a big black guy.

"You got a piece?" he was asked.

"Yeah, I got a gun, what's the problem?" Chris asked.

"You got a piece, you gotta leave it here," he was told.

If you said no, they didn't take your word for it; they patted you down. Chris had seen a lot of strange sights in his time, but he still marveled at the sight of a couple of dozen guns stashed in little cubicles, row on row. People checked their guns as routinely as though they were coats or hats. You didn't get a claim check; if you didn't know which gun was yours, you were in such a bad way that a claim check wasn't going to help.

Anytime you have so many guns around, Chris thought, there's going to be a shooting, sooner or later. He didn't stay long, the first time. When he went back, he went prepared. He'd removed the firing pin from the gun he checked—if he got shot, he'd rather not be shot with his own gun—and he tucked another gun in his boot. That gun had the firing pin in place.

The joint didn't have a name, but Chris thought it could have qualified for the quaint old label, "den of iniquity."

Mounds of coke were piled along the bar, with people leaning over, snorting through straws as casually as people lined up at other bars to drink. Unlike other mob joints he'd known, this one was patronized by as many blacks as whites. One black guy with snow-white hair and bright blue eyes had a stable of both black and white women and was of particular interest to Chris.

Blue-eyes wasn't snorting, but he was smoking a joint, and he handed it to Chris, who pretended to smoke it—he was excellent at faking that, by now. Chris had just finished a drink when he heard a commotion at the end of the bar.

A woman was being pushed up against the wall. She was nude. She was crying hysterically, as two men began stubbing out cigarettes on her breasts and on her stomach. One man grabbed a long stick, like a broomstick, and shoved it up her vagina. She gave a piercing scream, but people along the bar, blowing their coke, just looked over at her, as though it were the evening's entertainment. Blue-eyes shook his head mournfully and told Chris the whore was being taught a lesson—she was a junkie who'd lifted somebody's wallet.

Chris felt helpless. He couldn't stop it. Yet he had to stop it. He'd have to pull his spare gun and whatever happened, happened. He got up from the bar stool and felt dizzy. He began to sweat. The man who had been torturing the woman yelled something. Through a sweaty blur, Chris saw him throw her clothes at her. Clutching her clothes, crying, she ran into a back room and the door closed behind her.

Chris weaved his way outside, retrieving his gun on the way, past the bouncer. He was thinking fuzzily that she hadn't come out—maybe he should call the cops—when everything started spinning round and round.

He fell to the sidewalk and vomited. He lay flat on the pavement, thinking: the car—I've got to make it to the car. He never parked directly in front of a place, always two blocks away, at least. If anybody was watching the place, law enforcement or otherwise, he didn't want them to run his plate and cause unnecessary complications.

What the hell is wrong with me? he thought groggily. He couldn't get up. His stomach was on fire, being stuck with knives. He vomited again, pulling himself along the sidewalk. He'd only pretended to smoke the joint; it had to be the drink. Now what? Was somebody going to come up behind him and rob him, or worse? Inch by inch, he dragged himself along the sidewalk. I've got to make it to the car.

By the time he got to the curb, he was able to raise himself slightly. He crossed the street on his hands and knees. Down another block, still listening for footsteps, waiting for the crash of a weapon on the back of his head, the hot slash of a knife in his back. Or maybe one gunshot. Maybe he wouldn't feel a thing.

He reached for the door handle on the car, pulled himself up, found his keys and pulled the door open. I made it, I'm okay, I'm safe, he thought, as he fell into the backseat.

He awoke with bright sunlight streaming across his face. He still felt sweaty and sick, but he was okay. He never knew what had happened, or why. He just knew it was a dangerous place.

A while later, he got a call from the doorman. Chris had been right: With so many guns around, sooner or later somebody was going to start shooting. The guy had been shot and was calling from the hospital.

"I know who did it, Chrissie," he said, "and I want you to get him. I don't care what it costs!"

Chris said he'd talk to him about it, the next time he saw him. But when Chris and Harry discussed it, they decided Chris shouldn't follow it up. The doorman was only a source, not an OC figure. There were too many other things going on. What happened on West 22nd Street was just all in a day's work.

For their fifth wedding anniversary, Chris and Liz went to dinner at a little Italian place in the neighborhood. Forest Hills was only a ten-minute drive from the Kew, but the restaurant was run by Yugoslavs, so Chris was sure it wasn't on the Kew guys' list. Chris and Liz had been there often, when they were first married. The owner greeted them cheerily and took them to a nice table in the back, but not so near the kitchen that it was hard to talk.

Chris was determined to make this a pleasant evening. He had a lot of time to make up for, with his wife. It had been so long since they'd been out together that it seemed unreal. Hey, this is my *wife,* he thought, as he looked at her over the top of his menu. This girl is my *wife.* I owe her something. I owe her a lot.

Liz didn't want champagne, so they let the owner persuade them to try his favorite wine, a white, from Yugoslavia. Chris didn't know they made wine in Yugoslavia, but he liked it. He ordered fish; Liz had veal marsala, because she didn't like spicy food.

"Tell me what you've been doing," Chris said. "Anything good coming up?" He really wanted her to do well, but he also wanted her to be doing well because that would make him feel better about being away so much.

"Not too much," Liz said. "The usual. Two auditions yesterday, one the day before."

"Well, I really admire the way you hang in there," Chris said. "I know how hard you've worked—I can remember when you'd have three or four calls a day, and you'd run in and out, showering and changing and back out again. You sure deserve a big break."

Liz didn't say anything.

"Do you need money?" Chris asked.

"No, I'm fine," she said. "I really thought that by this time I'd be able to support myself."

"Hey, no problem," Chris said. "I know it's important for you to keep on with the singing lessons, and the acting, and all that jazz."

He smiled at his little wordplay, but Liz just looked wistful.

"I've been wondering just how important it is, anymore," she said. "I've been thinking—maybe it's time for us to have a baby."

"But I thought—you always wanted a career," Chris said.

"I know," Liz said, "But I've been thinking—I wouldn't have to give it up completely. I think I could handle both. I don't mean going out on the road with industrials or anything, but I could still do some modeling, a few things like that."

Chris didn't say anything. He didn't know what to say.

"Maybe it's because I miss you," Liz continued quietly. "You're gone so much. All the time."

"Well, that's a big decision," Chris said. "That's something to really think about."

"I'm thirty years old," Liz said. "And I love the amplifier, by the way. I use it all the time."

"Well, thirty," Chris said. "You've got a lot of time yet."

Back home, Liz brought out a set of proofs. She needed new publicity photos, she said, and she wanted him to pick out the ones he liked. "As long as you're paying for them, you ought to have some say," she said lightly. Chris thought the cost of the photos was exorbitant—nearly five hundred dollars—but he also thought that, under the circumstances, it was the least he could do.

He did some paperwork in the den for about an hour, then they walked out again, to the Baskin-Robbins on the corner, for ice cream cones.

"Why are you wearing your sunglasses?" Liz asked.

"Oh, I don't know—my eyes hurt a little," Chris said. "Just eyestrain, I guess. Nothing wrong."

It was a trivial, meaningless lie. It was nothing. But it bothered him. He wasn't sure whether it was getting easier or harder to lie to Liz, and he wasn't sure which was worse.

8

"Do me a favor," John said to Chris one Sunday after dinner. "I have to go into the city tomorrow. Will you drive me in?"

"Sure, no problem," Chris said.

He tried to act normally the rest of the evening, but he was a nervous wreck. He couldn't imagine why John had suddenly asked this. Actually, he could think of a handful of reasons, none of them appealing. One: He wants to know more about me. Two: He wants to know my intentions toward his daughter. Three: He's going to tell me to keep away from his daughter. Four: He already knows about me.

At daylight, Chris was still wide awake, lying in bed with his eyes open, talking to himself. Will Marty be there? No, Marty won't be there. She'll be at work already. Anna will be there, won't she? What about Anna? Will Anna be there? Where else would Anna be at nine o'clock in the morning? What if Anna doesn't answer the door? Why don't you just pick up the phone and call him and say you can't make it? Why not just call and say you're tied up? Because you gave him your word. Because the only way you don't show up, if you gave him your word, is if you are dead.

"Good morning," Anna said, with a smile that had never seemed so warm or so welcome. She kissed him lightly as he came in and stood at the door. It occurred to him that Anna always made the first move to kiss him, whether in greeting or good-bye.

"He'll be ready in a minute," Anna said. "Would you like some coffee?"

"No thank you," Chris said.

John came into the foyer and took his hat from the rack. "I remembered you said you had to go into the city today," he said. Chris knew he hadn't said any such thing, but he wasn't going to argue about it.

Anna kissed her husband and then kissed Chris on the cheek again. "Drive carefully," she said. She stood in the doorway and watched as they got into John's car and drove away, Chris at the wheel.

"Nice car," Chris said, as they pulled out of the driveway. John said nothing. For most of the drive in, John just looked out the window, although once in a while, Chris could feel John looking over at him. Chris said something about the weather, and John just grunted, so Chris figured the old man didn't want to talk. Chris stopped talking, too.

In Manhattan, John directed him downtown. "Pull over here," John said. "I'll be out in ten minutes." When John went inside the place, Chris quickly tossed the car. He looked in the glove box, under the seat, between the cushions. If he'd found a gun, he'd have just left it where it was, but he'd have felt better knowing its location. There was no gun in the car.

They made three more stops before noon. Chris noticed the precision of John's timing: When John said, "I'll be back in ten minutes," he was back in ten minutes, on the dot. He didn't explain anything, and Chris didn't ask. He knew that when this report went in, somebody at Intel was going to bitch about it. "Why the hell didn't Jason *ask* him what he was doing?" Chris couldn't do that. John may have been testing him, trying to find out how nosy Chris was, whether Chris would try to pump him, whether Chris could be trusted. Chris knew Harry would understand and would get the brass to understand, too.

"That's it," John said, shortly after noon. "I'm finished. I don't have to do anything else. You have to do anything?"

"No, I don't have to do anything," Chris said.

"You want to stop at a diner?" John asked. "You want to stop, we'll stop." From the way he said it, Chris figured that John didn't want to stop, so he didn't want to, either. "No, that's okay, I'll eat later," Chris said.

On the drive back, John still said almost nothing. As they turned off the parkway, he spoke, still looking out the side window. "Are you and Marty going out tonight?"

"Uh, yeah, yes, I'm seeing her tonight," Chris said.

When John said nothing, Chris felt compelled to say something more. "You have a wonderful family," he said.

John grunted. "I know that," he said. "I've been married to the woman for thirty years, and I'm lucky to have the daughter I got."

"Oh, yes," Chris agreed. "You're very lucky. And I'm lucky too." He realized how hideously wrong that sounded, so he continued quickly. "She's very, very nice. Very bright. Very intelligent."

John did not respond. Chris pulled in the driveway and parked in front of the house. John got out; Chris got out, to go over to his own car. As they stood between the two cars, John pointed his finger at Chris and spoke sternly. "You treat her gently," John said. "You treat her with respect."

"Oh, I do," Chris said. "I always do."

Chris waited until John had entered the house and closed the door before he drove away. He felt relieved that the morning had gone so smoothly, that John hadn't yelled at him or threatened him, ordering him to leave his daughter alone. But in a way, the very fact that John hadn't yelled, and seemed to accept the relationship, worried him a little. Chris had the feeling that John hadn't asked questions because he already had some answers. Or why would John have allowed him to come into his daughter's life?

Chris felt he'd made a good impression, all along. He didn't hold Marty's hand when they left the house together; it would have been a natural thing to do, but to avoid Marty reaching for his hand, he always shoved his hands in his pockets. He'd never put his arm around her or kissed her in her house. He knew that if he had a daughter, he wouldn't want to see some guy doing that in the house.

Maybe John even liked him. John wouldn't have said so; Chris doubted that the phrase was in the old man's vocabulary. But he knew one thing: if John *didn't* like him, Chris would surely know.

True, John was no longer a shooter. Nor did he give anyone such a direct order, as far as Chris knew. But he could have been the person to authorize a hit; or one of the persons: OC leaders had learned to put differences aside and work together for a common cause, which made it easier for a job to be carried out and harder for the law to pinpoint the responsibility. John had the power to make decisions, and power created fear, just as it did on Wall Street, say, or in any corporation. Chris could almost smell the fear, sometimes, on Sunday afternoons.

John had a way of looking at people, with his mouth stretched in a tight line and a flat look in his eyes, that sometimes made Chris want to get out of the house in the worst way, even though he wasn't looking at Chris that way. Chris saw the effect it had on other people. One Sunday before dinner at John's table, one man was sweating so heavily that he actually couldn't pick up his glass of wine. When he tried, he would get it only an inch or so above the table when it would start to slip through his grasp, so he would carefully set it back down.

Driving John into the city, one or two days a week, and spending Sundays at the house became routine for Chris. He always brought Anna a bunch of mums, because he wanted to. Sometimes on Sundays he would leave early, making some excuse to get out of the house before any of the other men left; if any new men were there, Chris wanted to get their plate numbers. But as time went on, he stopped leaving early. He felt it was rude to Anna, who had arranged for him to be invited to that first Sunday dinner. And he didn't want to give up the rest of the evening with Marty. What am I leaving for? he asked himself one time, when he left early. I was invited here for dinner, and I'd like to stay. So mostly, from then on, he stayed.

He kept hoping that John and the men who came to see John would speak in Italian. Chris knew enough Italian, from his mother, to keep up, and John didn't know he knew. Both John and Anna were born in this country, but their parents were immigrants, and they'd grown up in homes where Italian was the first language. From the few times Chris heard Anna speak in Italian, he judged her Italian to be quite good. But when John tried it, once in a while, he spoke poorly. Chris thought John must have been too busy doing other things to pay attention to language skills.

Even in English, John didn't say much that was clear or definite. Like other OC people, he relied on clichés. If somebody said, "This guy has to be taken care of," John might say, "Do what you have to do," or, if he wanted to be specific, "Give it to the short guy." Professionals didn't say, "I'm going down to the Ravenite Social Club to discuss this problem with Neil Dellacroce." They said, "I'm gonna see the right guy." Not, "I made ten grand on the airport job," but "I scored big on this one." Someone who'd been around would know what was being talked about, and sometimes Chris did know, or could make a reasonable guess.

Not all the discussions involved business. Domestic issues sometimes came up—a problem with somebody's kid. Even a grown son or daughter was a kid.

"Did you know that Sal's kid Carmela is going out with a cop?" a man asked John one day. "And he's a fucking *foot* cop."

"Yeah, but it's okay," John said. "He's Italian, that's the main thing."

Chris looked closely at John to see whether he was joking, but the man seemed perfectly serious. Not that you could readily tell when John was joking. Chris estimated he'd heard the man laugh less than a half dozen times in two years, and then it wasn't much of a laugh, sort of a semicough that came up from deep in his throat and got stuck somewhere along the line.

Sometimes, when there was a financial dispute, John didn't negotiate. He just settled it. "Okay, Sal's paid enough. He doesn't owe you any more money." That was the last word, then. The chairman of the board always had the final word.

Not all disputes could be settled, though, not by John or anybody. Screwing somebody's wife could not be worked out. Stealing money from the pot could not be worked out. If you mess up a lucrative scheme—perhaps by selling narcotics to an undercover—it won't get worked out. When a guy burglarized an apartment on Mulberry Street, it couldn't be worked out because within twenty-four hours he fell off the roof. Talking to the law could not be worked out: If you are an informer, you are *gone*.

Nearly a dozen men whom Chris knew well were assassinated during his time undercover. Chris made sure he always had his weapon with him when he drove with John. It was a sensible precaution, like wearing a seat belt.

Chris tried to gauge the old man's feelings. He thought that if John sensed danger, he would tell Chris to drive another way to their destinations. But John never changed the route. When Chris, on his own, occasionally varied the route, John never questioned him. Chris thought John must have had the cop's attitude: Be smart, stay alert, and nothing bad will ever happen to you. Cops had to have that attitude, or they'd never rush into the dangerous situations they often had to rush into. Drivers had to have that attitude, because when an OC figure was hit, in or around his car, he took his chauffeur with him.

As the Sunday dinners and the weekday drives became a habit, Chris came to feel reasonably comfortable with John. John always acted formally—every time they met, they shook hands—but he no longer spoke so sharply. In his own impenetrable way, John seemed to feel comfortable with Chris.

Sometimes, Chris thought, they looked like a pair of salesmen, making calls.

John was neither a flashy dresser, nor three-piece gray flannel. He was in between, leaning toward the dull side: white shirt, solid-color tie, navy-blue suit. Once in a while he wore white-on-white, but not in a garish way that screamed MOB! At Sunday dinner, he didn't wear his jacket, but he kept his tie on, without loosening it. At the christening party, Chris remembered, John had worn suit and tie, not the way some OC guys dressed when they wanted to be dressed up: no tie, with the collar of the shirt worn over the collar of the jacket. John didn't wear a big diamond ring, but a black onyx in a gold setting—18 karat, Chris assessed. It was big, but the man had big hands, with thick fingers, so the ring looked good on him. It reminded Chris of the big ruby ring Julie Podell at the Copa used to wear.

When Chris was sizing up a guy, in the OC world or anywhere, he looked at the shoes and the tie and the wrist-watch. If a guy wore polyester ties, forget him. Cheap shoes, forget him. A huge watch that looks like a compass, the guy thinks he's flying a plane, forget him too.

John wore silk ties—he showed Chris the shop on Hester Street where he bought them—and Bruno Magli shoes. A couple of times, he asked Chris to drive down to Allen Street, where he bought three or four pairs of Bruno Maglis at a time. John could have paid uptown prices without noticing any dent in his wallet, but like other OC people he always wanted to make a deal, get the edge.

John's watch was big and expensive, with a leather strap. It looked like a Timex but it wasn't. Chris was particularly good at analyzing watches, since he'd bought a couple of watches from a guy in East Harlem, early in this job. Cartier watches, the guy had said, fifty bucks. "On my mother's eyes," the hustler vowed, rolling his own eyes, "these are the real thing."

Then Chris and Frankie took a couple of girls to a birthday dinner at Patsy's, on 117th Street.

"Hey, happy birthday," Chris said. "Here's something from Cartier for you."

He reached into his pocket and made a grand gesture of bringing out the watch and handing it to her across the table. She smiled in delight at the beautiful, rectangular watch with a gold band. Her hand reached out as Chris's went out, but their hands didn't quite meet. The watch dropped onto the tablecloth and fell apart. All the insides scattered over the cloth.

"What the hell," Chris mumbled. "I gotta take this back to Cartier."

He gathered up the tiny bits and wrapped them in a napkin. At home, he painstakingly put it back together, using a tweezers and Krazy Glue—after all, fifty bucks was fifty bucks. He gave it to the girl next time he saw her, but this time he'd wrapped it and put it in a box.

Other than driving him, the only work Chris did for John was to pick up envelopes, from time to time. Chris didn't try to look inside the sealed envelopes, but he assumed they were thick with cash. Chris thought that John's keeping him uninvolved was the man's way of protecting his daughter. He wouldn't want her boyfriend to get into serious trouble. Although Chris knew, from conversations he overheard, and from Harry's information, that John was involved in some risky ventures, Chris never felt threatened. Sometimes he even felt like an insider, especially when John met Solly to talk about what got delivered, what got slowed down, and what was left to sit around, rotting.

Chris came close to violence just once. At a pizza place where John told him to stop, the old man said, "Wait for me." Minutes after John had gone inside, Chris heard shouts and yells. A chair, then a table came crashing through the plate-glass window. Some pots and pans came flying out onto the sidewalk. John stormed out, then turned back toward the building, his arms raised.

Chris jumped out of the car, but John waved him away. "Stay in the car!" John called. Chris obeyed, as John picked up a pot from the sidewalk and hurled it back through the broken window.

"Now *nobody* has a job!" John yelled.

John got back in the car. "Let's go," he said.

"I thought you might need me," Chris ventured, as he pulled away from the curb. "If something happened in there."

"Zips!" John said angrily. "A bunch of zips! Greenhorns from the other side! They're only here a couple weeks and already they want more money."

The episode reminded Chris that guys like John were not as ordinary as they seemed. As Joe Valachi had put it, philosophically, "You live by the gun and the knife, you die by the gun and the knife." In fact, though, more mobsters died in bed—their own, the hospital's, the prison's—than were mowed down in the street or in a barber's chair. In one ten-year span, five well-known OC men—Frank Costello, Vito Genovese, Three-Finger Brown, Lucky Luciano, and Joe Valachi himself—had died normal deaths, all because of their bad hearts. And so Chris found he was becoming less edgy with John, as the old man loosened up, too.

"You like baseball?" he asked Chris one day, in the car.

"Baseball, sure," Chris said. "I don't get to many games, though."

"The Redbirds," John said. "Now that's a team. Maybe not like the old days, but good." Chris listened in surprise as John reminisced about the St. Louis Cardinals and their players: Joe Garagiola, Stan Musial. "Stan the Man," John said heartily. "A powerhouse."

Chris parked the car near a restaurant in the Corona section of Queens and leaned back, to wait for John as usual. But John laughed in his gravelly, semicoughing way. "C'mon in, have some lunch," he said.

Chris followed John into the restaurant. It was a fairly big place, but it had a cozy feeling, with red-checked tablecloths. A plump woman came forward to greet John, wiping her floury hands on her apron. A man approached John with outstretched arms, smiling broadly.

John sat at a table in the back, facing the door, and motioned Chris to sit at his right. "Good people," John said briefly. "Mama and I always came here."

There was no menu. The plump woman brought a platter of antipasto, with lots of red peppers, and a bowl of bocconcini, little balls of mozzarella marinated and dusted with spices. The man who had greeted John brought a jug of red wine and sat with them for a while.

It was a long lunch, over two hours, and as far as Chris could tell, it was just a lunch for John. Even a homecoming of sorts: People kept coming over to the table, sometimes just to shake hands with John, sometimes to sit and chat. Chris said almost nothing. He had spaghetti with clam sauce and a salad and enjoyed it, although a bouncy young waitress made him uneasy. She seemed to be trying to catch his eye, flirting, and Chris wondered, am I being eyeballed? Is this some kind of test? Did John bring me here so somebody can look me over? Nobody asked Chris anything, though, so when someone came to speak to John, Chris just nodded and kept eating. Only once, when two men came to the table, and one man put his hand on John's shoulder, John motioned toward Chris.

"This is Chris. He's with me now," John said.

They had coffee and sambuca and cannoli. "All fresh, I made this morning," the plump woman said. Finally John gave a satisfied grunt, patted his stomach, leaned back in his chair, and motioned for the check. Chris reached down toward his pocket, as John lurched toward him and clenched his arm.

"Never put your hand in your pocket when you're with me," John said.

"Well, okay, thanks," Chris said, a little shakily. "Thanks for the lunch."

Chris drove John home, then went on his way, with two new things to think about. "Never put your hand in your pocket when you're with me." That was clear enough. It didn't take an Einstein to figure that out.

"He's with me now" was harder to decode. On the surface, the statement was clear enough, too. John had turned away questions about Chris by vouching for him, and vouching for someone, in John's world, was a kind of sinister blessing. But why John had done that was puzzling. Chris thought it was probably John's way of saying to him, watch your step, I'm keeping tabs on you.

Chris didn't know whether to be pleased by that, or worried. In a way, it was good, because it helped his image, improved his status and credibility. But in another way, it seemed a handicap, because it indicated that John expected a certain loyalty from Chris. It put John in a supervisory position that, in a way, summarized for Chris the dimensions of their relationship, an eerie version of *Father Knows Best.*

Women never came to the Sunday dinners, which didn't surprise Chris. In the world of organized crime, women knew their place, and it was not at the conference table, nor at the corner table at the Kew. When the girlfriend of a man Chris was sitting with there had come over to the table, the man had screamed at her. "This is business, don't you EVER come over while I'm doing business, you go wait for me at the bar and stay there till I tell you to move." Women never crossed the threshold of a social club; sometimes when Chris left the Prince Street Club, he saw a woman sitting in a car, waiting for a man who was inside drinking, playing cards, taking his own sweet time.

John treated his wife and his daughter with respect, but with a clear sense of authority. Neither Marty nor Anna was a mouse, and they expressed their opinions on general topics. But they seemed detached from John's activities, as mobsters' women usually were. You hardly ever saw a mob wife hauled into court. A girlfriend, maybe, but not the wife.

Anna and John would have been married sometime in the 1940s. Maybe she didn't know what he was doing, then. Maybe she didn't want to know. She wasn't a stereotypical Italian housewife in the sense that she didn't stand in the kitchen all day, stirring the sauce, but Chris felt she was typical in her hear-no-evil, see-no-evil attitude. She was clearly devoted to her husband. Sometimes she stood by his chair, with her hand on his shoulder, waiting to see if he wanted something. Chris saw John soften then, almost imperceptibly, and sometimes he put his own hand up, laid it on hers, and left it there for a moment. Anna always stood in the doorway when John left the house to drive with Chris, and watched as they drove off. Wives of men like John could never be sure when or if their husbands would be getting home from work.

Chris came to feel that maybe Marty didn't have the big picture about her father. Or maybe she'd blocked it out, which a person could easily do. As he had done with his father's death. Chris had been to Maple Grove Cemetery just once, in the limousine on the day of the funeral. Katrina and his sisters went often, but Chris had never gone back to visit the grave.

When Marty fell back on the phrase, "As long as I can remember," Chris felt she was being truthful. She was born in 1952; assuming that she would have noticed things about her father and remembered from, say, the age of ten, she would not have remembered anything violent or flagrantly criminal. She called many of the men who came to the house "Uncle," when Chris knew for a fact they were not her uncles. When he quizzed her about that, she just said she'd known them since she was little, they'd been coming around and she'd been calling them Uncle "as long as I can remember." Chris thought maybe she really didn't know what was going on.

Or maybe he just wanted to think that. Maybe he didn't want to know what she knew. His goal had been to get her to trust him, so that she would then talk about her father. Now that she trusted him, he didn't want her to talk about her father. That would have been a betrayal of her trust.

In fact, Marty didn't seem to want to know much about what was going on.

"Where did you and Daddy go today?" she asked him one evening.

Chris just shrugged. "Oh, here and there, no big deal," he said. "What do you want to know for?"

"Oh nothing, I just wondered," she said.

Chris thought maybe John had put her up to it, and had asked her to ask Chris that question, to see whether Chris was a talker. Then he dismissed that thought as unworthy—not of him, not of John, but of her.

Chris could tell that Anna was pleased when he stayed on Sundays until all the others had gone. Marty must have thought so, too.

"Let's not go out tonight," she said, one Sunday after dinner. "Let's play cards."

She and Anna cleared the dishes, then Marty brought cards and they took places on opposite sides of the dining table. John stayed seated at the head of the table, skimming through the Sunday *News*, while Anna sat at the other end, watching. Chris and Marty played War, just throwing down cards and high card takes them, a game that goes on forever. John was watching as he read through the paper, talking to Anna, nothing much, regular husband-and-wife small talk. Then he interrupted.

"You play gin rummy?" he asked Chris.

"Yes, I do," Chris said.

"I'll play you, penny a point," John said.

Chris was a very good player because of his splendid memory, but John was better. John won every time, one hundred points. He seemed to enjoy winning.

It was a very pleasant evening. Although Anna wasn't doing any mending, Chris was reminded of his mother, on Sunday evenings when he was a kid. People didn't watch TV then; they played cards and checkers at the table. Finally, reluctantly, Chris looked at his watch.

"I'd better be going," he said.

But Marty stopped him. "Oh no you don't," she said. "This is family night. Do you play pool?"

"Sure I play pool," Chris said. "I used to cut school and go to a poolhall at Sixty-third and Third. But not very often," he added hastily, glancing at Anna, who laughed.

"You mean you want to go play pool?" Chris asked. "Now?"

"Not far," Marty said. "Just downstairs."

When Chris looked doubtful, Anna spoke.

"We'd like for you to stay, Chris, if you can."

"Oh yes, I can stay," Chris said.

He followed Marty down the stairs to a huge recreation room that looked like a clubhouse, with a pool table, a player piano, a croquet set, and stacks of games in boxes. The minute Marty picked up the cue, Chris knew he was in trouble, from the way she handled it and from the way she grinned at him. "You're a poolshark," he moaned. She proceeded to run the rack; she didn't miss a shot.

When they got upstairs, John wasn't around. But Anna was sitting in the living room, reading. With the lights on, and with Anna in the room, the living room didn't seem so stiff and formal. Chris walked over to her to say goodnight. She reached up and drew him near her, with her hands on the sides of his face.

"I'm very glad you stayed," she said softly. "We like having you with us. I hope you had a good time."

"I sure did," Chris said. "Thank you."

As he drove away, Chris felt great, for a minute or two. Then, as he pulled out onto the road, he tensed. He looked into his rearview mirror. Was anybody behind him? What about the van? He'd seen a van parked in the neighborhood, a long job with grayish windows that you couldn't see into. The lettering said GREENTHUMB LAWNKEEPERS, but Chris knew a police van when he saw one. He knew there were cameras behind those windows, maybe forty thousand dollars' worth of surveillance equipment.

He didn't want to think about the van. He just wanted to feel the way he'd felt briefly, that first night, that he was just a regular guy having dinner at his girl's house.

Now it was a full-blown feeling.

He didn't feel like a wiseguy when he was with Marty and her parents, and he didn't feel like an undercover cop, either.

He felt like himself. Anna was a wonderful lady. She was devoted to her husband; she'd been married to the man for thirty years. If John got hurt, Anna would be hurt too. Chris didn't want to be the one to hurt her. He didn't want her name, or Marty's name, in the Intel files; he didn't want their house targeted.

Chris had already begun to edit his reports. He never lied to the department, and he always gave his location, but he didn't give the address anymore; he would say he was "in the vicinity of . . ." Harry seemed satisfied just knowing where Chris was driving John, during the week, knowing who he was meeting and where, and how he was greeted. Chris described that as best he could; if John was greeted with a lot of respect, that guy was a nothing guy.

Other than that, Chris didn't want to send in more detailed reports that might involve Anna and Marty. He just wanted to feel the way he felt tonight, relaxed and at ease, happy to have just spent a perfectly normal evening, with people he liked to be with, in a perfectly normal way. It was an illusion, of course. But undercover work, by its very nature, was an illusion of one kind or another. This one was just more comforting, and it was beginning to seem more real.

Solly told Chris The Daily Planet was closing. Somebody would stay around to manage the pross part, which was still flourishing, with plenty of customers from about four to seven P.M. But the gambling part had died out. "We shot our load there," Solly said. "We'll look around and open someplace fresh." Chris hoped Solly wouldn't find a new job for him right away. He wanted to spend as much time with Marty as he could.

On his own, he'd cut back his games at Waterside, from once a week to once a month. He was getting edgier about the men who were coming. Not because of their numbers—he was averaging eight to ten men a night, now that the games had settled into expert affairs—but because of their backgrounds. These were professionals, men who were more likely to spot one of the electronic devices and finger him as an informer. He had to watch carefully who sat where, and what that guy might be watching—was he going to use the phone and quickly unscrew the mouthpiece? Did that guy really have to go to the bathroom? and if he did, why was he staying in there so long? One man who came to Waterside regularly was a close associate of a Luchese capo who was involved with the Purple Gang, a network for narcotics distribution. The young members of the Purple Gang had been errand boys in East Harlem for the established OC chiefs there, the men whom George had despised. "I spit on them!" George had said. Then the errand boys had grown up. They continued to work for some of the bosses, including that Luchese capo, but they also liked doing things on their own initiative. They especially liked fingering informers. One informer whom they found was left in pieces—his lacerated torso on a side street in Queens, his head on the 97th Street entrance to the Grand Central Parkway, eastbound.

Sometimes Chris and Marty got out of the city, when she left work on Friday, and drove upstate.

Even with the heavy Friday evening traffic, they liked to leave then, so that when they woke up on Saturday, they'd be in the country. Chris had another new car—he got a new car from Harry about every year to keep up appearances. After the Buick he'd had an Oldsmobile, then had moved up to a white Lincoln. The car was so flashy it almost hurt your eyes, so big you could have put a bathtub in it. Chris had a lot of fun driving that car, and he loved going to the country in upstate New York. The only thing that bothered him was a pain he was beginning to feel in his groin. Well, considering his life-style, all the running around, not sleeping much, why wouldn't his body rebel in some way? He took a lot of aspirin, and tried not to think about it.

Marty knew a little inn, a hideaway, where they always stayed. Their room had a fireplace; one chilly night, Chris made a fire. "Where did a musician who grew up in New York City learn to make such a good fire?" Marty asked. She was teasing, but he could tell that she really was interested, and a bit puzzled. Chris mumbled something vague and changed the subject quickly.

With less to do in Manhattan, at least temporarily, Chris went back to Astoria more often to keep his hand in. By now, he knew everybody who came in to the club. He knew Rudy well. Since the early days when Rudy saw him as a cigarette hustler, Chris's reputation had soared, thanks to his association with Solly, mostly. Chris thought that buying the guns from Rudy had probably helped, too. Chris had seen Rudy from time to time, off and on, usually in Astoria, and Rudy had always been agreeable. He didn't look all that agreeable—Rudy was a big guy, about six one, two hundred and fifty pounds—but Chris had no reason to think otherwise, when Rudy came in around two A.M. and sat at the bar with a scotch.

"I used to do undercover work," Rudy said.

Chris just looked at him. Everything in his head was going BOING! BOING! BOING! as he tried to think how he should react. Do I look straight ahead? Do I look away? Do I look surprised? Do I look nonchalant? Do I look interested?

Chris figured he probably reacted in all those ways. "Oh, yeah?" he said.

"Yeah," Rudy said. "I used to work for the CIA. So I know what it's like to work undercover."

Rudy said something about the CIA and Cuba, but Chris wasn't paying close attention. What is he getting at? Chris was thinking. "C,mon, Rudy, you're bullshitting me, aren't you?" he asked.

"No, no," Rudy said. "I was with the CIA, and I know all about working undercover."

"So what are you telling me for, Rudy?" Chris asked.

Rudy gave him a long, level look. "I just felt like telling you," he said.

When Rudy left, Chris was relieved. As bizarre as it seemed, maybe the guy *had* worked for the CIA. Chris had reached the point where he could believe almost anything. On the other hand, he doubted that a guy who had worked for the CIA was going to come right out and say so. He was still mulling it over when Rudy returned. He sat at the bar and had another scotch.

"I have to go over and see a guy on Roosevelt Avenue," Rudy said. "I want you to come with me."

"Hey, sorry," Chris said, "I got a place to run here, I can't leave."

"Sure you can," Rudy said. "Gene is here. C'mon, do me a favor, go with me to see this guy. It won't take long, maybe an hour."

Something told Chris not to go. It would be a mistake to go. But something else said, go with him, see what he's up to. Chris thought that if he didn't go, it might reinforce whatever ideas Rudy had about him. Then Rudy would just come back another time. Better to see it through now. If I don't go, and he doesn't come back, I'll always wonder what this was all about.

He remembered clearly what Big Lou had said: "Rudy's good with a gun." But Chris thought that as long as he stayed alert, remained aware, he'd be okay. You had to be aware on the streets of New York, anyway; everybody did. If you weren't aware, on the street, you might get hit by a bus, or somebody would bump into you and pick your pocket.

"Okay," Chris said, "gimme a minute."

Chris went into the bathroom. He made sure his gun was loaded. He chambered one round, so he wouldn't have to cock it. All he would have to do was pull the trigger.

"Okay, let's go," he said to Rudy, as he took his overcoat from the office. "But I gotta be back in an hour." He swung the coat around and transferred the gun to its pocket, making a small production of putting it on as Rudy got up.

"Yeah, an hour," Rudy said. "Don't worry about it."

Rudy drove a red Cadillac with a white leather interior. The car was immaculate, gleaming, which didn't surprise Chris. When wiseguys parked their cars on Mulberry Street, or out by the Bergin club, it was like pulling into a service station, with half a dozen guys swarming all over the vehicle—washing, waxing, buffing.

Chris had spent more than twenty years in Queens, both in the outside world and in the OC world. He could have found his way around these streets blindfolded. As they drove east on the Grand Central Parkway, he knew the exit for Roosevelt Avenue was the exit for 111th Street and Shea Stadium, then a right, under the El.

Rudy drove past the exit.

"What are you doing, Rudy?" Chris said. "That was the exit."

"I'm going on a little farther," Rudy said. "There's another exit."

That's right, Chris thought. There *is* another exit, for the Long Island Expressway. It's a little out of the way, but Rudy could turn off there and double back.

Rudy passed that exit, too.

"What are you doing, Rudy?" Chris asked again.

"Don't worry about it," Rudy said. "I'll take the next one."

Rudy took the next exit. But instead of turning back, he continued to drive east on Parsons Boulevard.

"Hey, you're going the wrong way, Rudy," Chris said. "Roosevelt Avenue is back there, the other way."

Rudy laughed. "Maybe we'll just take a little ride," he said.

"Hey, I gotta be back in an hour," Chris said. "I got some people to see, back at my place." He tried to keep his voice low and growly, sort of aggravated, rather than shaky.

Rudy laughed again. "What's the matter? You worried about something?" He turned off Parsons onto a side street. He was still driving fast, over fifty. The minute he slows down, Chris told himself, the very minute, I have to shoot.

Chris reached into his overcoat pocket. He gripped the little automatic, held it for an instant, then eased it up out of his pocket. Keeping his left arm bent and slightly raised, as a shield, he slid the gun noiselessly up his right side and across his chest, under his coat. He aimed the gun directly at Rudy's head.

Chris could feel his heart thumping, right under the gun.

He'd never shot anyone. He'd pulled it often, but in all these years, in all these situations, he'd come close to using it only once or twice. The first time was way back, when he was a rookie, on his first post in Rockaway. It was a summer evening, just getting dark. He was standing on a street corner, feeling bored, when a big guy in a T-shirt and shorts came running toward him. The man was yelling, and as he got closer, Chris could understand the words. "I'm going to KILL you!"

The guy was huge—like Hercules, Chris thought, all muscle. Chris was strong, but in a taut, wiry way. He felt he was no match for this monster.

"You talking to me?" Chris called.

The man was growling and snarling, making animal sounds. He was flailing his arms in the air. Chris began to back up, even as he was remembering what he'd just been told at the Academy: Never back up. Never retreat.

"Listen, pal," Chris shouted. "Stay where you are! Stop right there! I don't want to hurt you!"

The man kept coming. About ten feet in front of Chris, he stopped. He began moving very slowly forward, inching toward Chris, as though in a horror movie. He was still growling, his arms raised liked enormous clubs. Chris could feel the smash of those arms on his head.

Chris had been holding his nightstick in his right hand. He switched it to his left and put his right hand on his gun in its holster.

"I don't understand, do you have a problem?" Chris asked. He realized how ludicrous that sounded, but he didn't know what else to say.

The man stopped for a moment, glaring. Small globs of thin, whitish foam dripped from the sides of his mouth. Oh God, why me, why me, why me? Chris thought wildly.

"I'm warning you!" he yelled. "Take one more step and I'll kill you! I'll put one in your head! I'm telling you right now, STOP!"

He pulled his gun and pointed it at the man's chest. Bits

and pieces of the firearms lectures at the Academy were spiraling through his head. The toughest decision you will ever have to make. Split-second. Must be necessary. Must be certain . . . your life in danger. Someone else's life. Must be necessary. Absolutely. No choice. Then shoot. To protect yourself and public. Shoot!

Chris had backed up as far as he could go. He was bumping against the building. He was afraid that the guy would wrest the gun from him and shoot him with it, or run with it and shoot somebody else. He was just saying to himself, "Shoot! You have to shoot this guy!" when he heard frantic yells.

"Don't shoot! Don't shoot, Officer!"

Two men came racing up behind the hulking fellow and pushed him away.

The men were his brothers.

"Listen, he just goes off the handle once in a while," one of them told Chris. "Sorry."

Rudy wasn't slowing down. He was still driving fast on these dark, deserted streets, making conversation.

"How's the piece you got from me?" Rudy asked.

"It's good. It's okay," Chris said.

"You got it with you?" Rudy asked casually.

"No, I keep it at my house," Chris said.

He thought it worked to his advantage to say he was unarmed. If Rudy thought he was armed he might not hesitate, just shoot. Boom! That was the edge the bad guys had; they knew what they had in mind. The good guy—the cop—couldn't be sure when it was time to shoot, but the other guy always was. If Rudy thought Chris was unarmed, he might not be in a hurry to shoot. He could take his time, wait for the perfect spot, the right moment.

Rudy made a sharp turn. Chris thought he couldn't wait, then, for him to slow down, or to make some obvious move. He would have to shoot now. He would have to shoot first. Shoot to kill. He could feel the index finger of his hand on the trigger. The finger felt detached and isolated, as though it didn't belong to the rest of his hand. For the first time in his life, Chris was prepared to shoot someone just on the basis of what he was thinking.

"The hell with it," Rudy said suddenly. "Let's go back to your place. Where's the fucking parkway?"

He braked sharply. The tires shrieked. He made a U-turn on the empty street and got back on the parkway. They were back within the hour.

"Surprise," Marty said. "My parents have gone out. I'm making dinner for just the two of us."

"Well, okay, fine," Chris said, as he came inside. He was indeed surprised; he'd never been in the house without Anna and John around. When Marty had asked him out for dinner, he'd had no reason to think it was anything but a normal night.

"You look wonderful," he said. "But how can you cook in that outfit?" Marty was wearing a long white dress in some thin, silky material that he could see right through.

Marty laughed. "You'd be surprised what I can do," she said.

She took him into the living room, where there was a small table set up, with candles and wine glasses and one rose in the center of the table. A bottle of champagne was nestled in an ice bucket. Marty opened it with only a slight pop! skillfully, and poured for them both.

"There's another surprise," she said, as they sat down. "You probably think I'm making Italian food, but I'm not. I'm cooking Chinese."

"Well, hey, that's great," Chris said. He'd hated Chinese food since the night at The Golden Slipper, and he wasn't fond of champagne, for that matter, but what the heck? He would just enjoy it, in this dramatic setting, with Marty sitting there in the candlelight in that see-through dress. To keep his mind from going fuzzy, he asked something about her father.

"Let's don't talk about my father," Marty said.

"Well, then, how about your mother?" Chris said. "I really like your mother. She's a wonderful person."

"She thinks a lot of you," Marty said. "I don't know if you realize that."

"Well, gee, that's nice," Chris said. He knew he sounded like some schleppy kid, but he didn't know what to say. "I'm really glad, because I sure do like your mother. She's really nice."

Marty took another sip of champagne, keeping her eyes on him. "My mother wants to know if we're getting serious."

"Well," Chris said. "Well, what did you tell her?"

"I didn't tell her anything," Marty said. "I don't discuss things like that with my mother."

"Hey, you should," Chris said. "She's a very understanding woman. You should talk about things like that with her."

Marty stood up. "I'm going to make dinner now," she said. "Come watch."

In the kitchen, she put on a plaid apron and poured oil into a wok. "Everything's ready," she said, motioning to little dishes with chopped-up things in them—vegetables, walnuts, green beans, slices of chicken. Chris watched with interest as she poured things into the wok and stirred it so quickly that dinner was ready almost immediately.

Chris had made up his mind to eat the Chinese food, no matter what, and was pleased to find that it was really very good. Marty brought another bottle of champagne from the kitchen, and he found he was enjoying that, too.

Marty carried in the dishes. "Stay where you are," she commanded. "I'll be right back."

When she returned, she crossed the room and put a record on the stereo.

"Where did you and Daddy go yesterday?" she asked, not looking around.

"Oh, here and there," Chris said, as he'd said once before. "No big deal."

"Here and there, here and there," Marty said in a mocking

tone. She stood looking down at the stereo. "Why do you want to be a tough guy, Christy?"

"Who, me?" Chris said. "I'm not a tough guy. I'm a nice guy. You know that by now, don't you?"

She turned, and held her right hand out, her index finger pointed at him, as though she had a gun.

"The cemeteries are full of tough guys," she said in a tough, growly voice.

"Why—where did you hear that?" Chris stammered. "That doesn't sound like you. What makes you say that?"

Marty came back to where he was sitting and poured the last of the champagne. But she didn't sit down. She stood looking at him.

"Have you thought any more about opening a music store?" she asked, in her regular voice. "You've got the money, haven't you?"

"Well, yeah," Chris mumbled. "But right now I'm—I'm doing a couple other things. Maybe someday. A music store or—or a club."

"Maybe someday," she mimicked. "When is someday?"

"I don't know," Chris said.

Marty set her glass down and held out her arms. The music was soft and slow. Her filmy dress swirled as she came toward him. "Hey, I don't dance," Chris said. "You know I don't dance."

Marty just held her arms out, swaying and smiling. He got up and stepped into her arms.

"See, you can dance," Marty murmured, her cheek pressed against his. "I never believed you when you said you couldn't dance. You're a bad liar."

"This isn't dancing," Chris said. "This is just moving."

"Well, whatever it is, it's nice, isn't it?" Marty whispered.

"Oh yes," Chris said.

Marty took her arm from around his neck and took him by the hand. She led him through the foyer and up the stairs. Chris went in a happy daze, willingly, knowing it was a mistake.

Her bedroom seemed to belong to another house. In contrast to the heavy, dark furniture downstairs, hers was white wicker. An amber light from a small porcelain table lamp gave the room a soft glow. There was a four-poster bed with a canopy in some misty color.

"What color do you call that?" Chris murmured, as they moved toward the bed.

"Champagne," Marty said. "Hey, you want to talk interior decorating? Or you want to make love?"

Because he felt like a schoolboy doing something bad—very, very bad—when his parents weren't home, Chris thought they'd never had such a marvelous time in bed. And he'd never felt so tense, afterward, as he strained to hear the sound of the front door.

"Don't worry," Marty said. "They won't be home till very late, I know."

Chris sat on the edge of the bed and ran his fingers through his hair. "I believe you, but still, I better go now."

Marty pulled her dress back over her head and walked down the stairs with him. She seemed subdued, then.

"What's the matter?" Chris asked, as they stood in the foyer. He put his arms around her and looked into her eyes. "Didn't you like it?"

"Of course I liked it," Marty said. "I always do. I just wish—oh Christy, I wish you didn't have to leave."

"I wish I didn't, either," Chris said. "I'll call you tomorrow."

She laughed, lightly. "So what should I tell my mother? *Are* we getting serious?"

Chris mumbled something that was unintelligible, even to himself.

"We've known each other over two years, Christy," Marty said quietly. "Is there going to be something more to this?"

"What do you mean?" Chris asked, stalling.

"You know what I mean," she said softly. "I mean getting married. Us. Married. That's what I mean."

"Married," Chris said. "But didn't you—I thought you wanted a career."

Marty smiled. "I think I could handle both."

* * *

If only he'd met Marty in another situation. If only he wasn't married. If only he wasn't a cop. If only her father wasn't her father.

It was pointless to keep thinking "if only." But as he drove away, he couldn't stop. She was the right woman. At the wrong time, in the wrong place, in all the wrong circumstances. But he knew she was the right woman for him. And obviously she thought he was the right man for her. She was everything he'd ever wanted in a woman. Warm and earthy. Intelligent and sophisticated, but not in a cool way. Not in Liz's way.

It was stupid and wrong to compare them, but if he'd met Marty first, he'd have picked her. No, not "picked." You didn't pick a woman as though she were a piece of merchandise in a shop. And a woman didn't pick a man that way. The right man and the right woman just found each other. Even in the most bizarre circumstances, they found each other, when they finally realized what they were looking for, and what they needed.

At the dinner table, Chris could hardly swallow. The food was perfect, as usual. The chicken cacciatore was thick and gleaming in its sauce, the potato salad chunky and delicious, as usual. But Chris wasn't eating as usual, Anna noticed. "Is something the matter?" she asked, sounding concerned.

"Oh no, nothing's wrong," Chris said. "Everything is wonderful."

He picked up a forkful of potato salad and smiled, while still trying to keep his eyes on the man across the table. It was Angelo. Chris had met Angelo the first time he came to the house for Sunday dinner.

Angelo was an informer.

He'd been staring at Angelo ever since he arrived, trying to figure out if the guy was wired. He looked for suspicious bumps. He thought the guy must be wired, because before dinner, when Chris had tried to maneuver close to him, Angelo had moved swiftly aside.

Chris had talked a lot before dinner, much more than usual. He kept hoping that Angelo wouldn't stay long. But Angelo was staying. Angelo wasn't going to give up easily.

There was no business talk at dinner. But when Marty and Anna took the dishes into the kitchen, Angelo turned to John.

"You know what's going on downtown, don't you?" Angelo asked.

John grunted. "Why can't they settle it without me? What do they need me for?"

"Well, because you're the guy, aren't you?" Angelo asked. "Didn't you . . ."

Chris broke in. "Hey, I was at a great new place the other day," he said loudly. "Great food! I mean, scampi like you wouldn't believe."

Angelo glared at him, then turned to John again.

"You know what's going on, don't you?" Angelo continued.

"We could all go down together," Chris continued enthusiastically. "Take the family, have a good time." He rambled on, knowing that he sounded noisy and garrulous, not knowing what he was saying, knowing only that he musn't let John commit himself.

Finally Angelo gave up. He left, then Chris left too. He had to get out of the house.

When he kissed Marty goodnight, he felt like Judas. Even worse. Judas had betrayed one man one time. Chris was caught up in multiple betrayals.

9

"Who's that loudmouth at the bar?" Lou asked. "Anybody know that jerk?"

He gestured toward a man at the bar who was drinking too fast, talking too loud, laughing, making himself conspicuous. Chris was sitting at the Kew's corner table, with Lou and Nick and Solly. He turned to take a look.

It was Harry.

Harry swiveled around on the bar stool. He looked toward their table and grinned. When he saw Chris staring at him, he lifted his glass in their direction. "Give those people over there a drink! Give everybody in the place a drink!"

"Aw, who cares?" Chris mumbled. "Some stupid out-of-towner. Who the hell cares?"

His mind was a jumble. This was Harry. This was worse than the night at the Lakeville Manor. The idea of Harry turning up at the Kew was so improbable, so totally unbelievable that Chris even wondered for a moment whether it was just a guy who looked exactly like Harry. It *couldn't* be Harry.

Harry had a woman with him whom Chris recognized as a policewoman from Intel. From time to time, Harry leaned toward her, said something, then turned to look at the corner table.

Chris was trying to think of an excuse to leave when Harry stood up, dropped a handful of bills on the bar, and walked out. On his way out, he looked once again at the corner table, with a wide grin. The policewoman went with him.

"Let's go," Nick said to Lou. They got up swiftly and went out. Chris sat there for a few minutes, dazed. Then he finished his drink, said goodnight to Solly, and left.

He drove to Astoria. He was anticipating what he would say when he talked to Harry the next day. He was going to yell at him so loud he'd pierce Harry's eardrum over the phone. It would serve him right. What in God's name was he doing at the Kew? Chris was so unnerved that he just wanted to get back to his own place, relax, have some drinks.

He parked across the street and walked into the downstairs bar. He hadn't had anything to eat, at the Kew; maybe a sandwich would help the sinking feeling in his stomach. The place downstairs didn't serve real food, no dinners, but behind the bar there was a small grill for heating sandwiches wrapped in foil.

He opened the door and stepped in. Loud music from the jukebox hit him in the face. He walked along the edge of the tiny dance floor, just a circle in the middle of the room, heading for the end of the bar. As he walked along, he glanced around.

Harry was dancing. Dancing! Harry was having a marvelous time, jumping around in the middle of the floor, waving his arms, snapping his fingers, as he danced with the policewoman.

Chris turned away quickly, but not quickly enough. Harry reached over and grabbed him by the arm.

"Hey, buddy, what are you doing?" Chris said angrily. Harry grinned at him and winked. Just then, at that precise moment, from the corner of his eye, Chris saw Nick and Lou. Maybe he didn't actually see them; maybe he just sensed their presence. But he knew they were there. They couldn't hear what Chris was saying, but they could see Harry holding him by the arm, smiling and winking.

Chris shook loose. He just wanted out of the place. But as he got near the door, Lou called to him. "Hey Chrissie, c'mon over, we wanna talk to you."

This is trouble, Chris thought dully. This is major trouble.

"Here's a question for you," Lou said, in a quiet voice. "How did that guy get from the Kew to your place?"

Chris shrugged. "How the hell do I know?"

Nick was frowning. "Who told him about this place?" Nick demanded. "How did he get from there to here?"

"Hey, Nicky, how do I know?" Chris said. "Look, I gave the girl at the Kew a lot of my cards—fifty, maybe a hundred—maybe she gave him one."

"Yeah, maybe that's it," Nick said slowly. "Maybe you're right. Maybe that's what happened." He frowned again. "When did you give her the cards?"

"Hey, what are you questioning me for?" Chris said angrily. "What's the matter with you, anyway?"

Nick laid a hand on Chris's arm. "C'mon, let's go outside," he said.

Chris followed him out onto the sidewalk, then across the street, where Nick stopped behind a parked car.

"We'll wait for him here," Nick said. "Lemme tell you, if this guy's somebody, I'm gonna get him."

He reached into his pocket. Chris heard a snap. He saw the flash of Nick's knife with the eight-inch blade.

"Are you nuts?" Chris yelled. "What's the matter with you, anyway? The guy's a fucking harmless out-of-towner."

Nick pushed him slightly. "You calling me nuts?" he demanded. "Nobody calls me nuts!" He flexed his hand, turning the knife from side to side.

"Hey, Nicky, take it easy," Chris said. "I'm just saying, why bother with this guy? Some dumb tourist—why get so upset about him?"

"He's not harmless," Nick insisted. "Why did he go from there to here?"

Chris was suddenly very, very tired. All the energy seemed to drain right out of him, through his body and down his legs, out his feet. He thought he was going to collapse. All the trust he had built up with these guys, all the work he'd done, down the tubes. Part of his mind didn't believe this was happening. Part of his mind knew it was happening, and knew he couldn't deal with it.

"I don't know," Chris said. "I don't know why he went from there to here, Nicky."

"Well, we're gonna find out," Nick said. He laughed shortly. "Lou's watching him in there. When he comes out, we're gonna tail him. And if he's somebody, we're gonna get him."

Chris had to sit down or he would fall down. "I gotta go now," he told Nick. "Do what you have to do. I don't give a shit."

He went up to his club, using the street entrance. He couldn't stand to see Harry again. He sat down on a barstool and just stayed there, without seeing or hearing anything. He felt as though he were in a trance. This is it. This is how it ends. Right here in Astoria, where it started.

He had no idea how long he'd been sitting there when Lou and Nick burst in. Chris just looked at them.

"The guy's a cop!" Lou told him. "He's a fucking cop! We followed him, and he went over to the precinct and got gas for his car."

Nick put his hand on Chris's shoulder. "Yeah, a fucking cop," Nick repeated. "So why did he come here, Chrissie?"

"Maybe he's talking to the weasel downstairs," Chris said. "I heard the weasel was talking. Or maybe"—he looked Nick straight in the eye—"maybe he just wanted to see what I was doing."

"I just wanted to see what you were doing," Harry said, when Chris called him from Waterside. He yawned into the phone. "Hey, it's four o'clock in the morning. You woke me up."

"I *know* I woke you up!" Chris yelled. "Man, are you *crazy*? You gotta be crazy, Harry! You put me in the jackpot! You were followed!" Chris was sputtering with fury; he could hardly talk.

"Naw, I wasn't followed," Harry said sleepily.

"I am telling you, man, you were followed!" Chris shouted. "You are an idiot, Harry! You almost got whacked out, and me with you."

"Naw, I wasn't followed," Harry repeated. "Calm down. Get some sleep. Talk to you tomorrow." Harry hung up the phone.

Chris poured some bourbon over ice and sat in the dark living room.

He was overwhelmed with shame.

Of course Harry had to check on him. His reports had gotten so thin that the people at Intel who saw them must have questioned Harry. Maybe they thought Chris had crossed the line, gone over to the other side, a double agent. As stupidly as Harry had acted—he shouldn't have had so much to drink—Chris knew that Harry was just trying to protect him. He must have tried to mollify the brass: "Jason's okay. I'll just run out, take a look, see what he's doing."

Chris had been able to string everybody along, including himself, until the dinner with Angelo. Once he'd sabotaged that conversation, it was out of control. He'd reported simply that Angelo had been there, and that nothing important had been said. His report said, basically, that there was nothing to report. It occurred to him that Angelo's report probably said the same thing.

What a joke! What a terrible black joke! He felt so good, so right with Marty and her parents that the real Chris—the Code of Conduct officer, the boy whose father had taught him never to lie or cheat or steal—was coming through.

But was that the real Chris? He'd been successful in this job because he was so believable. He had immersed himself so deeply in his character that he had become that person.

Had he *always been* that person? It was a terrifying thought. But look at the evidence. Look at how he'd slipped into his wiseguy role as though it were a second skin. Look at the way he'd always liked to live—drinking, spending money. His father's money. He used to take guys to his father's restaurant late at night and sign the check. George never forbade that, but said to him once, "I don't mind if you bring your friends. Just be sure these people *are* your friends, because it takes me a long time to earn forty dollars." His friends had always been half wiseguys, at least. True, he'd straightened out, when he was in the army, but that was only a temporary rehabilitation. He'd gone back to drifting and drinking and bouncing around, until he'd joined the NYPD as a way of redeeming himself.

Maybe, of all the illusions he'd been involved in, the expectation of redemption was the most deceptive of all.

"We're both doing God's work," Father Conlin had said to him, years ago. And Chris had always thought so. But everybody knows that the devil doesn't look ugly or disgusting. The devil disguises himself in very attractive ways, and influences you in ways that make wrong things look right.

At the beginning of this job, Chris had thought he was doing the wrong things for the right reasons. He had manipulated people. Undercover work meant manipulating people; that's what it was all about. But he had gone beyond the point where manipulation was necessary. He was frightened when he realized that he'd passed that point easily, without even noticing.

He still wasn't exactly sure of that point. Of course it had been wrong to manipulate Liz, and Marty, and Anna, and Harry, beyond a certain point. But what about Solly? The old guy liked him. He'd looked out for him. "Go down and put it in the car," Solly had told him, not wanting him to be nabbed for carrying a gun. Solly had kept him clean when Chris had tried to buy drugs. "You're not gonna do babania, Chris." Chris even thought Solly hadn't had all that much to do with drugs. Or maybe he just wanted to think that. What about John? "No matter what you've heard about him, he's still my father," Marty had said. If Chris himself had a daughter, he knew how he'd feel if somebody deceived her, and his wife, in such a way.

Had John become a father figure to him? Chris didn't want to think so, but he had to admit the possibility. He just didn't know. Certainly he felt that Anna could be his mother. Anna was a wonderful lady, devoted to her husband. She loved her husband very much. Katrina had loved George very much. He just didn't know.

He was totally confused. He wasn't crazy. He knew he wasn't losing his mind. But the thoughts tumbled through his head as he sat in the living room. This is not my home. I have a home. I have a wife. I have a job. What am I doing? How am I going to get out of this?

He didn't know where to turn. He knew the department said it would help a guy in trouble. But he felt that what the department said and what it did were two different things. He knew a guy who'd gone for help with a drinking problem—on his own, just turned himself in. They sent him for treatment, but then they sent him to some hellhole in Brooklyn where somebody told him, off the record, never to bother applying for a transfer, he was lucky that Brooklyn had agreed to take him on, and he was stuck there forever. As for the department's psychiatrist, cops joked you'd have to be crazy to go there. Sure, he'd talk to you, but they'd take your gun away, mark you "unstable" or worse, in your file, and God knows what they'd do with you then. Cops weren't supposed to need psychiatrists. Cops were invulnerable. Cops could handle anything. Which is why cops hit the bottle, or jumped off a bridge, or went home and belted the wife across the mouth. Anyway, what would Chris tell a shrink? "Well, doc, my problem is, I'm two different people . . ."

He'd stopped going to church. He'd always gone to church when he was a kid. He was an altar boy at St. Gerosimus, on 105th Street, every Sunday. One morning he'd sneaked a sip of the altar wine, and when the priest saw him, he'd grabbed Chris and twisted the boy's ear so hard that Chris thought it would tear off. His ear had stayed red and painful all day.

He prayed a lot, when he was a kid. He had a bad fall in the playground one day, and when he walked home, everything was blurry. He prayed hard, then—please God, please don't let me be blind. When Katrina took him to the doctor, the doctor pressed against Chris's head and asked, "Does it hurt back here?" When Chris said it didn't, the doctor said his eyes would be all right. Chris even remembered to pray then, to thank God that he wasn't blind. In fact, Chris had prayed so hard when he was a kid, that he thought probably nobody prayed as much as he did, not even the Dali Lama.

He was always careful how he prayed to God, though, because he was afraid of God. You had to be, because that's what kept you from doing wrong. If you weren't what they called a God-fearing person, you would run around doing all kinds of bad things. So Chris was afraid of God, but not Jesus. Every year at Eastertime, Katrina took Chris and the girls to see *King of Kings,* the silent movie, with H. B. Warner as Jesus. Whenever Chris was in church, and the priest said the name "Jesus," Chris immediately saw the face of H. B. Warner, so he was never afraid of him. He thought Jesus was a nicer man than the priest at St. Gerosimus.

When he worked at the 4-oh, he couldn't get to church regularly because of the hours, but he stopped by when he could. Sometimes, after they made an arrest, Phil would say, "Butch, let's stop by church and say thanks that we didn't hurt anybody, and they didn't hurt us, and we made a good arrest." When they couldn't find a Greek church in the South Bronx, they would hit a Catholic church; St. Rita of Cascia, or St. Jerome's, right across the street from the station. Chris especially liked St. Ann's on 140th Street, a lovely little stone church with windows and doors trimmed in red brick, and a tiny cemetery with graves going back to the early 1800s. Even when he found out that St. Ann's was Episcopal, not Roman Catholic, Chris didn't mind, and he was pretty sure God didn't, either. The only thing that bothered Chris about churches was when they started locking their doors, except when it was time for services, because the neighborhood had gotten so bad. After that, he rarely got to church. He met a priest on the street one day and complained about it; the priest invited him to the rectory for lunch. Chris was impressed by the big, dim, baronial dining room, where his voice echoed as he talked from his end of the long table to the priest at the other end. He felt like Henry VIII, and he drank like Henry, as the housekeeper shuffled from one end of the table to the other, back and forth, pouring more wine. Chris always thought priests and cops had a lot in common: They started out thinking they were going to save the world, they saw people at their worst, and when they realized they weren't going to save the world, and turned to the bottle, they were sent to drying-out farms in Jersey.

Even after he was working more regular hours at the 4-oh, Chris didn't go to church. Liz didn't go to any church, and sleeping late on Sunday was very nice. When he went under, he didn't think about it. He and Marty went to St. Patrick's once, but as visitors, just wandering around, part of a day in Manhattan, with brunch afterward. They'd gone uptown to St. John the Divine because it was such a historic landmark. When Chris had had his appendix out, when he was a kid, he'd been at St. Luke's Hospital, and he told Marty he'd been able to see the steeple and part of St. John's from his hospital room.

Marty's father didn't go to church on Sunday. Anna went to Mass on Saturday evening, which took care of the Sunday rule, as far as the church was concerned. He was pretty sure Marty had been in the habit of going with her mother on Saturday, until he and Marty began going out on Saturdays most of the time. He hadn't thought about any of this for a long time, but now he admitted he felt uncomfortable going to church. How could he go to church with somebody he was deceiving so? Even on the visit to St. Patrick's, when he was just there as a tourist, he'd felt uncomfortable when he looked at the crucifix.

He'd stopped going to church, and he'd stopped praying

because he felt uneasy about trying to talk to God. It seemed unlikely that God would care to listen. Now he felt he had to go to church. He felt he had, literally, no place else to go.

He found a church at the edge of Little Italy, Our Lady of Pompeii. It became a sanctuary. The church was locked during the day, but it was open very early in the morning, for Mass. When he was out all night, he would head over to the church and wait on the opposite corner until he saw lights go on. Then the church would be unlocked in a few minutes.

When he went in, he was too sick at heart to kneel and look at the altar. He lay flat on his back in a side pew and stared at the ceiling.

Thou shalt not lie.

Thou shalt not steal.

Thou shalt not commit adultery.

It wasn't that simple, though. It wasn't just guilt, though God knows he felt guilty. But guilt was relatively simple. Ordinary adultery would not be so difficult, in itself, to handle, to explain and possibly atone for. He thought that if Liz had been unfaithful, had an affair, he'd have tried to understand. He wouldn't have jumped up and yelled, "I'm leaving you, you tramp!" He could have found a million excuses for her.

But he could find no excuse for himself. This was much more complicated. His entire identity was in question here: his heart and mind and soul. This went to the basic question of who he was and who he had been and who he was going to be. "Remember who you are," Harry had warned. Whoever that was.

"I'm not feeling so hot," he told Frankie. "Do you know a doctor I could go to?" Besides the emotional distress, he was in physical pain; he could feel a lump in his groin. Frankie sent him to a doctor who wrote a prescription for Valium, no questions asked.

Between the Valium and the Jack Daniel's, Chris was able to get along reasonably well. He was glad he wasn't as busy as he had been, now that The Daily Planet was closed, Zero's was about to close, and the C&G Club was winding down. He was able to visit his mother about once a month, usually in midevening, around eight o'clock. He didn't call first, because Katrina was always home in the evening. She was always happy to see him, never questioning his silences or his absence. "I'm working," Chris told her briefly, and that was the end of it. He sat at the kitchen table and drank coffee as she told him what was going on in the family. Katrina always tried to give him supper, but he wouldn't eat, because he was squeezing in these visits before beginning his nighttime rounds, when there would be more than enough to eat and drink. He stayed about an hour, and when he left, he circled the block to make sure he wasn't being tailed. Even a visit to his mother wasn't entirely safe. Nothing was entirely safe, of course, but some things were more unthinkable than others, such as the thought of Katrina having an unexpected visitor, after Chris was gone.

He went with Frankie one night to a restaurant on the Grand Central Parkway, a big place, a supper club with a good vocalist. They were eating when a guy came in, followed by two guys, all making a kind of grand entrance. The guy in the lead was smoking a fat cigar. The three men were at a table when a couple of other men surrounded them; there was loud cursing, arguing. Two of the men at the table stood up; then there was pushing and shoving. Then all three men were escorted, emphatically, out the door. The guy with the cigar was very mad, waving his cigar and yelling as he was being thrown out.

"Who's that?" Chris asked Frankie.

"Oh, that's Carmine G," Frankie said casually.

Chris was surprised. The newspapers made Carmine Galante, the Bonnanno chief, sound like a godfather, but Chris thought he seemed like a fat slob, if not a deadbeat: He heard that the commotion involved a large unpaid tab.

When he wasn't immersed in thinking about his own situation, Chris felt steady as a rock. He was able to pay attention, when it was a clear-cut job, just a matter of intelligence. He was at the bar at the Plaza with a couple of bad guys, one weekday evening. He didn't like going to the Plaza on business, anymore, because Marty liked the place and he liked going there with her. But Chris had run across a guy—a big fellow, German, something of a wacko—who was scoping the place for burglaries. When Chris heard about it, he arranged to meet the guy there. The German was tall and weird; he had a car with a sunroof, and he would stick his head up out of the sunroof when he was driving.

They were drinking at the bar when two girls approached. The German started talking to one girl, and the other girl started talking to Chris. She wouldn't tell him her name. "You can call me Sugar," she said. "Are you in New York on business?"

"I'm from New York," Chris said. "Astoria."

"Oh, Astoria, then you must know my boyfriend," Sugar said.

"Well, who's your boyfriend?" Chris asked.

"He's Pete," she said. "Pete the Greek."

Bingo! "Yeah, I know Pete," Chris said. "I always liked Pete, but you know what he did? He whacked out a good friend of mine." He spoke slowly, picking his words carefully. "I could never figure out why Pete did that, because I always liked Pete."

"Who told you about that?" Sugar asked.

"I don't remember," Chris said. "What difference does it make? I'm just sorry he killed my friend, that's all."

Sugar lifted her glass shakily.

"Yeah, and they killed him in my house, too," she moaned. "Oh my God, do you know what they did? Do you know what Pete did? Pete cut him up in the bathtub in my house. There was hair and pieces of scalp stuck in my bathtub drain."

Her hands shook, and some of her drink spilled.

"I can't believe Pete did that," Chris said. "What did he do that for?"

"I don't know," Sugar said, "but he did. And Pete's crazy. I found a finger under my radiator, oh God." She began to cry.

Chris took her outside.

"Oh, I shouldn't have told you," Sugar moaned. "I don't know who you are. Pete's going to be mad at me. You're not going to tell Pete I was here hooking, are you?"

"No, no, I'm not going to tell Pete," Chris told her.

"Promise! Promise me you won't tell Pete! Pete's crazy. Pete would kill me."

"I won't tell Pete, I promise," Chris said. "You give me your phone number so I can call you and make sure you're okay. Here, take this." He fished in his pocket for a twenty. "Take a cab, go home and get some sleep."

He called Harry. "You're always waking me up," Harry complained. "Can't it wait?"

"Listen, Harry," Chris said. "Remember that guy they found in the river, that torso? . . ." Harry remembered, and he agreed it couldn't wait.

Harry got in touch with Homicide. Chris got in touch with Sugar and asked her to meet him at Mumbles, on Second Avenue. Chris was wired with two recorders—one personal, one that Harry could pick up in his car, where he was parked around the corner on 33rd Street. It felt odd to be wired again. He'd stopped wearing the wire except for selected situations, such as this meeting with Sugar. Otherwise, he left it at home or in the trunk of the car. Once he'd become intimate with Marty, the wire had become an impossibility. What was he going to say to her, "Don't come any closer—don't touch me!"

Sugar came in swaying and smiling. She was stoned, bombed out of her mind. When Chris brought up the subject, she looked at him as though she were trying to bring him into focus.

"I don't know what you're talking about," she said.

"About Pete killing the guy in your bathroom," Chris said. "I just can't believe Pete would do a thing like that."

"Hey, I thought you were going to forget about that," Sugar said. "Hey, you promised."

"You told me . . ." Chris began, when Sugar spotted someone down along the bar.

"Doctor Maxwell, Doctor Maxwell, hi! It's me! Remember me, you did my abortion for me, remember?" She was leaning across Chris, trying to talk to the doctor on the other side.

Chris gave up. "Listen, I gotta run," he told her. He fished a twenty from his pocket. "Here, take a cab, go home and get some sleep."

Through the conversation they picked up on the tape, they traced the doctor, who came up with Sugar's name and address. Then she couldn't be found. When Pete the Greek couldn't be located, either, Chris worried about her. Eventually, Homicide tracked them down at a motel near the airport. When that unit took over the investigation, Chris was no longer involved. Still, he felt good about it. He hadn't been wearing a trenchcoat, not waving a cigar, but he'd come close to fulfilling his old dream: "I'm Detective Anastos. I'm here to solve the homicide for you."

As often as he could, Chris just slipped away and went down to Waterside. He listened to his radio a lot. He'd grown up with radio. George had bought a big Philco, with all kinds of dials; you could even pick up foreign stations on shortwave, though there was a lot of static. The Philco had doors in front, opening to a record player. You stacked records on the metal pole, and the records fell, one at a time, with a thump. On Saturdays, Chris had listened faithfully to a children's program, with Little Sparky and Big John. Big John had a deep, strong voice. "Hello, little guys, I can see you out there. I can see you brushing your teeth. Have you brushed your teeth today, Billy? How about you, Mary? Have you brushed your teeth today?" Big John called out just about every name you could think of, but he never called out, "Chris."

Waterside was just a handful of blocks from the Police Academy. Chris began walking around the neighborhood nearly every day, going past the Academy, up and down that block. He was standing at the corner of Second Avenue and 22nd Street one day, waiting for the light to change, when a radio car pulled over to the curb. A cop got out and looked at the front tire, bending over to peer at it closely.

The light changed, but Chris didn't cross the street. He just stood there staring at the car. A wave of remorse and nostalgia and sorrow swept over him so strongly he felt shaken. He looked at the two uniformed cops and was suddenly, irrationally, furious. You guys have got the greatest job in the world and you don't appreciate it! You don't care! All you want to do is to get out of that car and into plainclothes—well, you are stupid! You are fucking crazy!

The light had been changing, as Chris just stood there. He was staring so fixedly that the cop who was inspecting the tire was now staring at him. Chris recovered, and walked over to the car.

"Hi, where's the subway, Officer?" he asked.

The cop looked blank.

Chris leaned down and spoke to the cop in the driver's seat.

"Where's the subway, Officer?" he repeated. He didn't look at the cop; he just looked at the inside of the car, smelling it, remembering it. He just wanted to fling open the door, get in, lean back and just sit in that car, safely, forever.

"Three blocks over," the cop said, pointing. "Twenty-third and Park."

"Thanks. Thanks a lot," Chris said. He looked at the cop then. "God bless you," he said. The cop blinked. Chris crossed the street, but he stood on the opposite corner and watched the radio car until it pulled away and was out of sight.

He walked back to Waterside and sat in the plaza. He couldn't think of anything but that radio car. He wished he had his memo books; they were stored at his mother's house. Everything a cop did had to be recorded in the little book he carried in his pocket, every minute of the tour accounted for, including "personals"—a lunch break, a trip to the bathroom. "The memo book either saves you or hangs you," Chris was told, early on, and he'd been scrupulous, in the beginning, about writing down not only the time of his lunch break but the exact spot: Hal's Confectionery, Sam's, the Bow-Wow Restaurant on Cross Bay Boulevard. He made note of the weather: "Clear/Cold. Man on lawn face down, possible stroke." At Rockaway, he'd had time to write at some length that he'd "warned and admonished" a bunch of surfers attempting to surf off a restricted beach. When he got busier, his memos got terser. At the 4-oh, he'd just scribbled "Homocide," not bothering to check his spelling.

He'd liked the routine of the memo book, the structure of the day at the 4-oh. When the weather was good and there wasn't a problem with demonstrators or snipers, morning roll call was held outside. All the guys were in spanking clean blue; you put your arm out and touched the other guy's shoulder, Dress Right! and then snapped to, while the sergeant came around to inspect. As careless as he may have been about some things, Chris was always careful about his appearance. He always made sure his buttons were sewn on tight, his uniform crisply pressed, his gun cleaned, his shoes shined. Actually, his mother looked after the buttons, the shirt, and the uniform-pressing. Chris took care of the gun, and he used the machine at the precinct to shine his shoes. All you had to do was apply the polish, then turn on the switch; the machine did the work. Each cop who used the gadget kicked in five dollars a month.

He couldn't remember now why he'd wanted to get out of uniform. Why, in God's name, had he ever wanted to? Being in the blue uniform of the New York Police Department was the greatest feeling in the world. When you wore that uniform, the world knew who you were. You knew who you were. The old Jewish man at his tiny button-and-thread shop always gave him tea with lemon and a piece of cheese sandwich on dark rye bread. "I made half for you and half for me," the old man would say. He had a concentration-camp number on his arm.

When you were in uniform, you felt you could handle anything. Even in those days, with no bulletproof vests, he and Phil knew they could handle anything. They were working midnight to eight when they had a call, a woman reporting shots fired into her window. They went up, found an elderly Irish woman, lived alone, scared to death. She showed them three holes in her bedroom window.

"Those are bullet holes, no doubt about it," Phil said.

They could tell by the angles of the cracks in the glass where the bullets had come from; it looked like a straight-on shot, from someplace exactly opposite, on the same level. The building was U-shaped; there was an apartment across the courtyard, facing hers. They went over to that apartment, knocked; they had their guns out. Nobody answered; there were no sounds. Three o'clock in the morning. They holstered their guns and turned away. The door opened. They turned back. A man was standing in the doorway, pointing an automatic. If they went for their guns, he would shoot. They talked as they inched forward. Phil grabbed the guy's gun hand as Chris pulled his gun and put it to the guy's head. Phil was trying to push the guy's arm down, get the gun pointed to the floor, as the door gave way and they all fell into the apartment. The door slammed shut. It was pitch black. Three men with two guns, grappling.

The guy was yelling, "I'll kill you!"

Chris was yelling, "Drop the gun! Drop the gun or I'll shoot!"

Phil was thinking, "I wonder if Chris knows where my head is."

Finger by finger, Phil pried the guy's gun from his hand. The gun dropped. Chris found the light. The whole thing took ninety seconds, start to finish.

When you were in uniform, you knew exactly what you were supposed to do. You had to check the glass: At the beginning and end of your tour, you walked around and made sure no windows of the stores on your post were broken. When you were in uniform, you knew where you belonged. Where did Chris belong now? Not at Andy Glover's funeral. Too many cops there. Policemen in white gloves had lined two blocks along 145th Street, a hushed blue sea, as Andy's coffin, covered with the white, green, and blue NYPD flag, was borne into the Convent Avenue Baptist Church. Where did Chris belong now? Not at Carlo Gambino's funeral, when the old don had a Mass of the Resurrection. Same reason: too many cops there.

The lights in the plaza had come on; there were no people around. A security guard making rounds came over to Chris. "I live here," Chris said.

"Okay, have a good evening," the guard said.

Chris went up to his apartment. He stood at the window, looking down at the black water. He had talked down suicides. You had to be careful, if they were on a roof, not to get too close, or they might take you over the edge with them. You talked them down, then you called a priest. It didn't matter whether they were Catholic or not, you called a priest anyway. The longer you talked, the less chance they'd jump. "Nothing can be that bad," Chris would say. "No matter what's the matter, it can't be that bad." When he'd gone on a domestic-dispute call, the woman was standing there with a black eye, then she begged him not to lock the guy up. So Chris had let him off with a lecture. "Listen! I don't want to have to come back here again. If I get another call, I am going to come back and beat the living shit out of you." Cops were allowed to talk like that, in those days. "Settle down, now! You have a wonderful wife and family. You have your health and a place to live. Enjoy your life—it's simple."

Now Chris knew it wasn't simple. Something *could* be that bad—so bad that there seemed no other way out. Judas had thought so.

He didn't seriously consider it for himself, though. That was an ultimate law he couldn't break. He just walked over to the kitchen and poured himself a drink. He'd been drinking, all along, because it was part of the life-style. Now he was drinking because it eased the pain and because he just felt like drinking.

Against all the rules, he met Phil.

They'd talked on the phone often, since Phil had been

back in New York, but getting together had been out of the question, too risky for both of them. As an FBI agent, Phil didn't wear a uniform, but Chris thought Phil looked as though he were always in uniform. It wasn't just the dark suit and the tie; it was his whole bearing, his straight-arrow look. He looked so much like a lawman that some people thought he never laughed. Chris knew better, and he'd missed Phil a lot. The last thing Chris needed was for somebody to see him talking to a fed. Hanging around with a wiseguy wouldn't have been a good career move for Phil, either.

Chris phoned Phil at his office.

"How are you doing? How's it going?" Phil asked.

"Fine," Chris said. "I've got to see you."

They met at the safest place Chris could think of, a tiny, out-of-the-way beach in Queens. It wasn't much of a beach, just a strip of dark-brown sand on an inlet off Jamaica Bay. Planes taking off and landing at Kennedy Airport, less than a mile way, made a racket, and the smell of jet fuel hung in the air. Chris had been going to Rockaway for thirty years, so he knew about the little beach. He used to drag-race on Cross Bay Boulevard, in a souped-up Chevy, starting at the Bow-Wow restaurant and ending at the channel bridge, a quarter of a mile with no traffic lights. You could see the channel bridge from the beach. Partly because it was so small and secluded and basically unappealing, Chris and Phil were the only people there.

"Hey, you look great," Chris said. "How's it going?"

"You look terrible," Phil said. "What's the matter with you? What's wrong?"

"Oh, nothing," Chris said. "I just wanted to see you, keep in touch, you know? How's the family?"

"Fine," Phil said. "Everybody's fine." He was appalled at the way Chris looked. He saw that Chris had gained weight, yet his face had a strained, tight look, and he looked as though he were drinking a lot. He had a bleak expression in his eyes that Phil had never seen.

"Come on, sit down," Chris said. He motioned to a piece

of broken log, embedded in the dirty sand. "This is my beach chair. I found this place a long time ago. It's a good place to sit and talk."

"Great, let's talk," Phil said.

Chris sat at one end of the log, Phil at the other. Chris was wearing blue jeans and a T-shirt, but Phil was in his suit and tie. Phil figured he must look ridiculous, sitting there like that, but he was never comfortable taking off his jacket or loosening his tie. He opened a paper bag he'd brought and took out two cans of diet cola.

Chris took the can. "Hey, can I keep it this time, Dad?"

Phil laughed. "But I never said it was corruption to take the can of soda. I just said it was better . . ."

Chris chimed in. "Better not to take anything at all, that isn't paid for."

Chris took a swig of his soda.

"You were a better cop than I was," he said.

"What are you talking about?" Phil demanded. "You were a terrific cop. At least, my mother said so."

Chris brightened a little. They'd always said their mothers were stereotypes of Greek mothers, who lived only for their children, and they'd made up a joke. "What's a Greek mother? A Greek mother is a mother who, if her son cuts her heart out one day because he needs money and he's going to take it out and sell it, she calls to him as he's running out the door, 'Be careful, don't trip and fall!' "

"How's your mother?" Chris asked.

"She's fine," Phil said. "She's still down in south Jersey, that little place with the big garden. How's yours?"

"She's fine, I think," Chris said. "I haven't seen her for a while."

Phil knew in general what Chris was doing, and he knew from looking at him, and hearing what Chris was saying, and what Chris wasn't saying, that something was very wrong. But he didn't want to press. Better to let him say whatever he's got to say when he's ready, he thought. So Phil talked about his family—his son, who was a Scout, all excited about going to summer camp; his wife, Judy, who'd gone back to nursing, part-time.

"How's your wife?" Phil asked.

"She's fine, I think," Chris said.

Chris stared out at the murky water. Two stray seagulls were skimming near the edge of the water.

"I wish we could go back," Chris said. "I wish we were back in the radio car again. I've been thinking about those days, a lot, and about the Academy."

"Well, those were the good old days," Phil said. Looking at Chris, he thought maybe it would help to reminisce. So he talked about old times. As a cadet at the Academy, Phil had been sent out for a couple of days to direct traffic. He'd been sent to what he thought must have been the busiest intersection in the world, Times Square, where Broadway and Seventh Avenue intersect. He was petrified. He was just standing there shaking, traffic whizzing all around him, when a cop approached.

"What are you doing here?" the cop asked.

"I'm supposed to be here, sir," Phil said.

"Don't call me 'sir,' " the cop said. "I'm not your superior; my badge is the same color as yours." He pointed to the traffic signal. "See that light? That is a traffic light. It turns red and it turns green. Now, this may come as a shock to you, but that light is going to turn red, then green, then red again, all day, whether you're standing here or not. And people are going to stop and go and stop and go whether you're standing here or not. So take it easy. Relax."

"Yes sir, I will," Phil said.

Chris laughed. "They sent me to Eighth Avenue and Forty-second Street," he said. "A terrible corner. Sink or swim. I'll never forget it. I didn't know how to talk with the whistle in my mouth, and a truck was coming through the intersection, and I hollered at him, and the whistle went flying out of my mouth and the truck ran right over it.

"Then a woman comes running up to me, and she's hollering, 'Officer, Officer, there's a building collapsed over on

Ninth Avenue!' I just looked at her, because my sergeant had said to me, 'Don't get involved in anything, kid. Just do traffic and don't get involved.' So I said to her, 'You better call the police.' She says, 'But you're a policeman, aren't you?' And I said, 'Yes, I'm a policeman, but please, lady, call *another* policeman.' And I gave her my dime, from my memo book."

Chris laughed again, then stopped abruptly. He squeezed the empty soda can between his hands, making crackling sounds.

"How long have you been under, Butch?" Phil asked.

"Four years and two months," Chris said. "They call me 'Curley.' "

"Well, my God, that's too long," Phil said. "That's way too long! A couple of years, okay, but after that it takes too much of a toll. I can see it's taking a toll. It's time to bow out, Butch. Pull the plug."

"No, not yet," Chris said. "I've almost got one guy right where I want him. I have to stay in a while longer, because it's taken me a long time to get to this point, and nobody else could get to this point."

"Look, if you got hit by a car tomorrow, there'd be somebody to take your place," Phil said bluntly. "There are other cops. There are even other Greek cops!"

"You don't understand," Chris said wearily.

"I understand that you have been in this job about twice as long as you ought to be," Phil said. "You look god-awful. You can't keep on like this, Butch."

Chris laughed shortly. "The word 'can't' isn't in my vocabulary," he said. "At least, somebody once told me that."

"Look, you've done your duty," Phil argued. "You've fulfilled your obligation, whatever that was. You can only live the way you're living, always on guard, for just so long. And frankly, Butch, I doubt you'll accomplish much more, at this point. It'll just be more of the same."

"You don't understand," Chris said. "There's another situation that I—that I have to deal with. I have to stay in a while longer."

"Well, how much longer?" Phil demanded. "How long is this going to take?"

"I don't know," Chris said.

After their meeting, Chris felt bad that he hadn't leveled with Phil. He'd always felt he could tell Phil anything. Phil had always felt he could tell Chris anything, too, even something that maybe, for some reason, he couldn't tell his wife. At the 4-oh, other cops had been puzzled by their friendship. "What do you guys have to talk about so much?" one cop had asked. Chris didn't know what to answer; he knew only that if he and Phil were locked in a room together for six months, they'd never run out of things to talk about.

But Chris felt that this whole mess was his burden, his responsibility. It was too much to dump on Phil. He'd gotten himself into it, and he'd have to find his way out. Besides, if he told Phil the whole story, Phil would tell him what to do, and whatever he told him would be right. Chris wasn't ready for that. But it was so good to see Phil, such a relief just to be with him for a little while, that they continued to meet once, sometimes twice a week, on the little strip of beach. Chris wanted to talk, hoping Phil wouldn't hear.

When he told Phil about the pain in his groin, Phil insisted he see a doctor. When Chris hemmed and hawed, Phil drove him to Astoria General one night, to the Emergency Room. He waited while Chris was examined.

Chris came out smiling. "He doesn't think it's serious," Chris told Phil. "He says it's a water seal, or a groin sprain, something like that, and it's not serious. He says if it doesn't go away in a couple of weeks, I should see a specialist. But it's nothing urgent."

The doctor gave him Tylenol with codeine, which made him feel better. He felt better when he was at Our Lady of Pompeii. He'd confessed to God. Now the time had come to confess to Marty.

10

A German shepherd named Duke kept watch at the Ravenite in the predawn hours, from three to six A.M., when nobody was there. At other times, the dog was locked in a back room. Chris was annoyed by the animal's frequent barking. He'd never been fond of dogs, anyway. When the family moved to Queens, they got a dog because it seemed like the thing to do, now that they had a backyard. Chris was supposed to take care of Lady, but it usually ended up with Katrina doing the feeding and the washing. Chris knew that boys were supposed to like dogs, but he would have preferred a couple of cats.

Harry told Chris that things were happening around the Ravenite, though he was careful not to tell him too much. He didn't tell him about the observation post that had been set up, with a camera, in an apartment across the street, with a Chinese guy as tenant of record. Harry didn't want Chris to look up at that window, automatically, when he stepped out onto the sidewalk. Chris could tell that the guys at the club were getting edgy. They were especially suspicious of a strange car that remained parked on the street, and they talked of setting it on fire. Then they settled on hooking up a hose to a fire hydrant and flooding the vehicle. That would take care of any eavesdropping equipment.

What Harry did tell Chris was that the NYPD's black-bag team was ready to break in and plant bugs. Getting in was not the problem. There wasn't a lock made that the black baggers couldn't handle, no piece of equipment they didn't find a use for. But to get in and wire the place, they needed a court order, illegal bugging having gone out of style after Watergate. To get the order, they needed proof of criminal activity. Informers had been talking about lots of criminal activity, but a judge wasn't going to sign an order just based on what an informer said. Chris guessed the judges must have felt as he did, that an informer might bullshit you and tell you anything he thought you wanted to hear. A judge would authorize it on the word of an undercover, though. An undercover cop was dependable. So Harry wanted Chris to get in, one more time, wearing his wire, and get that proof.

Chris didn't want to do it. For one thing, he felt that with so many people running around, wires could get crossed, and they might start shooting the wrong people. In a way, the longer Chris was in this world, the safer he felt, because he was accepted. But in another way, the longer he was in, the riskier. Sooner or later, by the law of averages, something was going to happen. A guy's luck would run out.

His nerves were shot. Around eleven o'clock one night, he went down from his apartment to the Waterside garage, where he kept his car. He'd caught a few hours sleep and was off to make his rounds. When he unlocked the door and got in, he smelled something odd, like a mixture of booze and garlic.

He hurled himself out of the car. He pulled the automatic and held it straight-arm, using both hands, in the classic police stance: *STAY!*

Stiff with tension, holding the gun in his outstretched arms, pointed at the back seat, he inched toward the car and peered in. No one was there.

He got back in the car, then just sat there, unable to bring himself to start the car. Come on, come on, turn the key, start the car, he told himself. But he couldn't. He got back out, lifted the hood and looked for wires. He got down on the greasy concrete floor and squirmed underneath the car, on his back, and looked for wires. Finally he just forced himself to get in the car, turn the key and *go*.

Another night he was driving out Queens Boulevard, heading for the Kew. It was a warm night; he had the window open. He stopped at a red light. The driver in the car in the lane beside him took his hand off the steering wheel, reached down to the front seat and picked up something. Chris could just see, from the corner of his eye, the shank of a long object. It was a shotgun!

Chris yanked at the steering wheel and rammed his car crossways in front of the other car. With his right hand, he grabbed his gun, while he threw open his car door with his left. He ran to the driver's side of the blocked car and stuck his gun in the guy's face. As the man stared at him, his eyes popping, face ashen, speechless, Chris saw the long-handled object on the seat. It was a tennis racket.

"I'm sorry, I'm sorry," Chris mumbled. He ran back to his car and took off.

He began to carry his service revolver instead of the little automatic. It made him feel safer. It was a bigger-caliber weapon, more reliable. He didn't holster it; that looked too professional, a giveaway. He just stuck it in his waistband, with tape around it so it wouldn't slip through. He took the handles off before he wound the tape around the frame so that it wouldn't look like the "detective special," but like some homemade piece of crap. He had a hundred excuses ready, in case somebody got nosy—"I was carrying a lot of money today, I needed a bigger piece"—but nobody ever asked. He began sleeping with the lights on.

He would confess to Marty when they were at the beach. He always felt better when he was near the water. Marty asked for a week's vacation, and they headed south.

They stopped at Colonial Williamsburg, and at Gettysburg, but Chris couldn't enjoy it. As much as he loved history, he wanted to get on down to Virginia Beach. He didn't even want to stop at Monticello, which surprised Marty, because he'd always said he wanted to see Monticello. He'd talked about Thomas Jefferson on one of their very first dates, she reminded him. Chris said he'd make it to Monticello another time. Anyway, he knew exactly what Monticello looked like, from pictures. There were columns in front of the house, and seven steps leading up to the front door. Seven steps didn't sound like many, but these were long, stretching almost the width of the house, so that you knew, as you walked up the steps, that you were about to enter someplace special.

At Virginia Beach, they checked into a place right on the ocean. There was a little balcony with two chairs facing the ocean, but Chris didn't want to talk there; there was another little balcony right next to theirs. All the rooms had these little balconies facing the ocean. A beehive, Chris thought. It looks like a damned beehive!

"What's the matter, Christy?" Marty asked. He'd said nothing, but he was frowning.

He looked at her. "Nothing. I'm just tired from all the driving."

"Why don't you take a nap?" Marty suggested. "I'll go down to the gift shop, get some postcards and walk around."

Chris took a shower and stretched out on the bed. He couldn't sleep, but it felt good to lie there, sorting out his thoughts, planning on how he would tell her. But it wasn't easy to sort out his thoughts, as the sudden recollection struck him—a Gambino soldier was known to be operating a chain of pizza shops around Virginia Beach. That man's father had been pinpointed by Intel as an international heroin trafficker who was wanted in Italy for the murder of seven police officers. A cop-killer, seven times over. And his son was running around Virginia Beach! Would he recognize Chris? Would Chris recognize him? Could Chris chance eating in a restaurant tonight? Was he being paranoid? Would somebody be lying in wait for him in the parking lot? At least then he wouldn't have to tell Marty.

He had to tell her. He couldn't go on without telling her. And she would understand. She had to understand. She lived in two worlds, too. At home she was a dutiful daughter who knew her place. A Mafia daughter. Away from home, she was her own person, freer. She would understand because she loved him.

But which Chris did she love? Would she still love him when he told her? "Guess what I do for a living. I'm a cop! Isn't that great?" Maybe she would hate him. Maybe she would tell her father. Maybe she would throw her arms around him and say it was all right. Maybe she would tell her mother. When he thought of Anna, he felt so bad that he rolled over in the bed and just stuck his face in the pillow.

When Marty returned, she showered and dressed and they went to dinner at a steakhouse next door to the hotel. Chris had three bourbons and most of a bottle of wine. He thought drinking would make it easier to talk, because drinking and talking went hand in hand, as he knew from spending time with the Penguin.

They took towels from the room and walked out onto the beach. They spread the towels on the fine, white sand and sat in the moonlight. It wasn't a full moon, but very bright, about three-quarters. If he was ever going to tell her, there would never be a better time, never a better place than tonight, on this beach in the moonlight.

And he *was* going to tell her. But he had to work up to it, first.

"I always did like going to the beach," he said. "When we started going down to Sandy Hook, I remember I had raspberry ice cream for the first time. I never even knew there was such a thing as raspberry ice cream. I tried to find it in New York, but I never could.

"We had a bungalow at Sandy Hook. It was just a rented place, but we went there for a month every summer. Not when I was real little, but later on, when my pop had more money. He didn't get down much, though. He used to come on Saturday night and go back to the city on Sunday night. Sometimes he worked on Sundays and sometimes he didn't.

"I really liked going down, because I always did like the beach. I loved to smell the water. The only reason I didn't like it at Sandy Hook was because my sister's godmother had a bungalow down there, too. She never liked me at all. In fact, I think she hated me. One day, I remember, I wanted to get back at her for hitting me, so I set fire to her clothesline. She had a clothesline in the yard and I put a match to it, and when it started to burn, I ran back in my house and hid under the bed. I think I really wanted to burn her house down, and maybe her, too. The thing about it was . . ."

He stopped talking suddenly. This was ridiculous. He was going nowhere. Marty was just sitting, listening. She must think he was crazy, rambling on like this. Better to just blurt it out.

"There's something you have to know," he said.

Marty waited. Chris said nothing.

"What is it, Christy?" she asked. She sounded concerned. "What is it I have to know?"

He couldn't answer. The words stuck in his throat.

"Christy, what's the matter?" Marty asked.

"Nothing," he said. "I'm just thinking."

"Oh, Christy, what do you think about so much?" Marty said wistfully. "You're always thinking. I thought that when you got out of New York, you would be the way you were in Boston. You were wonderful in Boston. You seemed so happy and relaxed, and now you're all tense again."

Chris stared at the waves breaking on the beach. The crash of the waves seemed to get louder and louder, echoing in his brain so that he couldn't think. He couldn't get it straight in his head.

"You just have to know that people are complicated," he said wearily. "People are not always what they seem."

Back in New York, it was worse than ever. Except for running to Our Lady of Pompeii, he could find no refuge.

Once, being with Marty had been an escape. Now it seemed like escaping into a trap. Marty talked of marriage almost every time they were together. Every time he saw her, he knew that, sooner or later, the subject would come up, and he would be taut with anticipation. What will I say this time?

She didn't nag him or pressure him. It was a sense of her expectations, her quiet question: "Have you thought any more about when we can get engaged, Christy?"

"No, I haven't had a chance to think about it yet," he would say. "Soon, though. If not at Christmas, then maybe Valentine's Day, or Easter."

She didn't pursue it when he said that, but she looked so disappointed that he actually thought of becoming engaged. After all, engagements could be broken. He wasn't really leading her on, he told himself. She was the one who'd brought it up in the first place.

Thinking about becoming engaged to this girl was so unreal that it was easy to think about. Everything seemed unreal, now. The fact that he was married and had a wife somewhere seemed unreal. The only thing that seemed real was a given moment, a certain situation. So he just got through the moment, or the situation, as best he could, in any way he could. It was a way of buying time. If he could buy some time, maybe whatever the problem was would go away. Or if it didn't go away, if it came back, by then he would surely have figured out how to handle it. In the meantime, he would just say whatever had to be said to anybody to satisfy them, for the time being. That seemed the only way to handle it. Anyway, he didn't think he had much longer.

When Marty reminded him of the wedding of her school friend, he had to go. He'd promised he would. He'd forgotten about it; she'd asked him so long ago that he must have thought then that the day would never come. But it came, and Marty was a bridesmaid.

He told her he wouldn't go with her to the church. "You'll have a partner there," he told her. "Somebody will escort you down the aisle, and I'd just be in the way." He joined her at the reception, at Leonard's of Great Neck. She was stunningly beautiful in a pale-blue dress—more beautiful than the bride, he thought, though that girl was very pretty, too. And Chris was right: Marty did have a partner, a tall, good-looking guy who seemed to think that being in the wedding party gave him some kind of claim on her. The guy kept asking her to dance, and Marty kept saying yes. She explained to Chris that the guy was the bride's cousin, from Chicago, so of course she had to be nice to him. It seemed to Chris that she was being nicer than she really had to be, though. As he sat at the table, drinking bourbon, watching her dancing with the guy, looking at him and laughing happily, Chris realized he was jealous.

When Marty came back to the table, there was another guy right behind her. Marty sat down quickly beside Chris and leaned against him, cocking her head. "Smile," she told him. "Say cheese." The wedding photographer snapped the picture so quickly that Chris didn't have time to duck his head or turn away. He just sat there and had his picture taken.

He wanted to do the laundry. When he was first married, he'd found, to his surprise, that he enjoyed domestic chores. Doing the laundry, folding heaps of clean towels, was a satisfying thing to do, for some reason. So he went to Forest Hills, late one afternoon. Liz wasn't home, but there was plenty of laundry around. Some of her things were hanging on the backs of chairs; there were towels all over the floor.

He straightened up the place, stuffed the laundry into big plastic bags, and went down to the basement. He did four loads, but he didn't fold the things downstairs. He brought the bags up and spilled everything out onto the bed. He was sitting on the edge of the bed, folding towels, when Liz came home.

"A friend of mine said he saw you in a nightclub with a woman," Liz said. Her voice wasn't accusing, just conversational.

Chris tried to keep his voice level, too.

"It's possible," he said. "It's very possible. Because of the work I'm doing. Somebody could see me with a woman, or two women, or half a dozen women." He paused. "Who told you?"

"I can't tell you," Liz said.

"When did your friend see me?" Chris asked. "Was it last night?"

"Yes, last night," Liz said.

Chris felt worse, in a way, than if someone had actually seen him with Marty. He hadn't been at a nightclub the night before. Why was Liz lying? Was she trying to trap him into some sort of confession? Did she suspect something? Of course she must suspect something. It wasn't bad enough that he was such a liar and deceiver. Now he'd turned his wife into a liar, too.

"Where did he see me?" Chris demanded. "I go to thousands of places. Where was this place?"

"He didn't tell me that," Liz said.

Chris knew he should drop it, let it go. But he couldn't.

"Well, why is it his business to tell you what I'm doing?" he said angrily. "And why is it your business to tell him all about me?"

Liz just looked at him. "I didn't tell him all about you," she said quietly. "I've known him for a long time, and he says he knows you, and he knows you're a policeman."

"Well, who is this guy, anyway?" Chris demanded.

Liz laughed. "Why is that any of *your* business?" she asked.

She walked out of the room. Chris finished folding the towels and put them in the hall closet. Then he went into the den and closed the door. There was no point in trying to talk to Liz now. He thought she probably hadn't wanted him to be a policeman, anyway.

Sundays at Marty's house were becoming unbearable. Anna had always seemed fond of him, but now she smiled at him in a special way. "When you have a place of your own, I hope it will be near us," she said, one day. "I'd like to watch my grandchildren growing up."

Chris kept thinking of the Sunday afternoons when he was

a kid, when people came to ask George for favors, paying their respects, asking George to vouch for a family member who wished to come to America. Chris remembered how, on their careful budget, his parents had served good wine in Katrina's precious cordial glasses. When he thought of his father's life of thrift and hard work, with no time to enjoy himself, then looked at John at his abundant table, he saw John as sleek and greedy and evil, and he longed to "get him good." Then he looked to the other end of the table, and he saw Anna. He saw Marty. Then he saw John as Anna's husband, Marty's father. The thought crossed his mind that maybe John knew he was a cop, and was accepting it, because he knew his daughter loved him.

He sometimes wondered whether maybe it would work out. He would explain everything to everybody, and everybody would understand, and he and Marty would ride off into the sunset, just like in a movie. But the movies never showed what happened, after they rode off into the sunset. Of course it would never work. He would have to resign from the department. Even if he resigned, how could he explain that he was going to marry a mob guy's daughter, after working undercover for almost five years? He would be charged with breaching confidentiality; he would almost surely be prosecuted.

Apart from all that, how could he expect Marty's parents to believe him? "I'm a cop, and I've been spying on you, but I've changed my mind." Even if he didn't explain anything to anybody, and just ran away with Marty—assuming that she'd be willing to run—where would they go? There was no place in the world that would be far enough.

Of course it wouldn't work out. He knew that, and because he knew that, he didn't want to end it. He wanted to prolong it as long as he possibly could.

He had a few more things to do, anyway. He got some more pieces of jewelry for Solly's son-in-law, who had the antiques shop on Third Avenue. He even did some mediating, having been around so long, and being so well-respected.

A guy named Irving, who had a tennis club in Howard Beach, had complained that a wiseguy had come into the tennis club and demanded money. When Irving refused, the hood had begun throwing things around, making a mess of the place. Chris could understand Irving's problem; nobody liked to see fights going on, on the sidelines, when they were trying to play tennis.

When Irving went to Frankie for help, Frankie brought Chris into it. Frankie and Chris met the wiseguy at a booth at the Lindenwood Diner. Chris knew the guy was a bad, bad apple; he'd heard that he'd killed some women. His M.O. was to shoot them, then put them in a car, drive it someplace and burn it. Chris thought the fellow a psycho. Chris had met him at J.J.'s, a joint in Queens, and he wasn't thrilled to be sitting with the guy in a close situation, in a booth at the diner. The wiseguy was quick with a gun; he had a special gun, Irving told them, with a red barrel.

So Chris let Frankie do most of the talking. He just listened as the hood told them he'd loaned money to Irv, to open the tennis club, so Irv owed him, now. Frankie told the guy that he and Chris would talk to Irving to get his side of the story. Irving told them that he had never borrowed that money, though Irv admitted he'd been involved in an airport job with the guy, taking down an armored car. He said the other guy had used the gun with the red barrel.

Chris called the Penguin.

"You wanna buy some TV sets?" Chris asked. "I got some nice new ones."

The Penguin was ready to deal. Chris loaded a van with thirty thirteen-inch RCA color sets and drove down to Mulberry Street. The Penguin told Chris to take them to another club nearby, not the Ravenite. Chris was pleased, because he hadn't even known about the other place. In a back room, one of the Penguin's crew had the money ready, wrapped in brown butcher paper.

Chris didn't hang around then. One quick drink; he was

edgy, being wired. The merchandise didn't have to be actually stolen, under the law. As long as the customers thought they were buying swag, it showed probable cause. The TV sets weren't even confiscated. When the property clerk couldn't come up with thirty new TV sets, Chris had bought them at Alexander's. He paid a discount price, but then he lowballed them for the Penguin, to make the offer too good to refuse, so in the short run, the NYPD lost money on the deal.

For the last few months of his assignment, Chris just drifted through the days and weeks, thinking, floundering, hurting. The lump in his groin was growing; Marty had noticed it, when they were in bed.

"It's nothing," Chris assured her. "Just an old hernia."

He was so entangled in his own problems that he scarcely noticed what was going on in the world, though he couldn't help hearing. When Carmine Galante was assassinated, he heard about it from both sides. Nobody seemed surprised at the disrespectful way the guy had been hit—eating lunch at a Brooklyn restaurant—and Chris wasn't surprised, either, considering how Galante had been booted out of the restaurant in Queens. From his side of the law, Chris heard that when detectives reached the scene, one of them stuck a cigar in Galante's mouth. "He looks better that way," the detective said. The photos of the dead man showed him lying on his back, in his short-sleeved shirt and summer slacks, his head tilted to one side and a cigar in his mouth.

Chris heard the Pope was coming to town.

"Is there any way I can meet the Pope, Harry?" Chris asked. Intel handled diplomatic escorts, visiting dignitaries, that kind of thing. "Not to be part of it, but just to meet the man, you know?"

"Are you crazy?" Harry said. "There'll be pictures, cameras, TV, the works. Of course you can't meet the Pope!"

"Think about it, Harry," Chris persisted. "I just want to get his blessing. I'll make it quick: in and out. I could wear a disguise."

Harry grumbled and said he'd think about it. Chris was fairly optimistic. Maybe Harry could arrange it. They both knew this assignment was winding down. And after the night at the Kew, Harry owed him one.

Harry called back to say it wouldn't work. "I ran it by the inspector and he said he didn't see how we could do it. He said if there was a way to do it, okay, but he had his doubts."

"Keep trying," Chris urged. "It would be a real honor, Harry. I wouldn't make a big deal about it, I promise. In and out. Pull some strings, Harry."

Harry called back. "Cardinal Hayes High School," he said. The Pope would be making a stop there to use the facilities, take a short nap, maybe; have a bite with some church bigwigs. It was a small segment of the Pope's day, very private, closed to the press and almost everyone else. Very few people. Harry would be stationed at one of the entrances; Chris was to use that entrance. "I can't guarantee you'll see him," Harry said, "But I can get you in. And no disguise, for Chrissake. Just a nice suit."

The hot Brioni was the nicest suit Chris owned, but that didn't seem right, somehow. He found a three-piece gray suit and had his best silk tie cleaned. It occurred to him he might run into some people he knew. If the mob could penetrate the White House, why not Cardinal Hayes High School?

At the door, Harry looked at him, nodded curtly and handed him a round button to wear, to show that he was authorized. Inside, "very few people" turned out to be swarms of guys with walkie-talkies, some uniformed cops, but mostly men in dark suits—Secret Service, FBI, State Department, you name it. One of them buttonholed Chris the minute he stepped across the threshold.

"Who are you?" he demanded.

Chris fingered his ID button and looked the guy straight in the eye. "I'm with catering," he said. "Where's the dining room?"

"Upstairs," the man said.

The upstairs hall wasn't as crowded. A few more guys with walkie-talkies, some uniformed cops stationed at points along the wall. Nobody said anything to him, so he wandered around, inspecting the dining room with interest—Harry had said they were even bringing in food tasters.

He wandered out into the hall and was just standing there by the elevator when suddenly the elevator door opened and the Pope stepped out.

Chris looked at the Pope. The Pope looked at Chris. After that frozen milli-second, Chris lunged forward, grabbed the Pope's hand, and bent his head. The Pope laid his hand on Chris's curly mop and murmured a blessing.

As the Pope moved past, with his entourage behind him, Chris straightened up. He stepped into the elevator the Pope had just come out of, and rode down.

In and out.

Marty told Chris that Anna had been preparing for days for Christmas Eve dinner. Both Anna's parents and John's parents had been raised in villages in Italy where seven fish dishes were traditionally served on Christmas Eve, in honor of the seven sacraments: Baptism, Confirmation, Holy Eucharist, Penance, Holy Orders, Anointing of the Sick.

And Matrimony.

Chris was so immobilized by the thought that Marty was expecting an engagement ring at Christmas that he didn't buy anything for anybody. In midafternoon on Christmas Eve he ducked into a department store to buy something for Anna. He stood at the perfume counter, feeling dazed. "I want the best perfume you've got," he told the clerk. She began naming perfumes, when a name Chris had heard somewhere stuck in his head. "Chanel Number Five," he said. When she gave him the cellophane-wrapped box, he looked at her doubtfully. "Are you sure this is the best you've got?" he asked. The woman told him he was making an excellent choice.

Marty's house was a swirl of lights and laughter and music. Chris put the package for Anna under the Christmas tree. "I don't have a present for you right now," he told Marty.

She smiled brightly at him. "Valentine's Day, then," she said. "Right now you're my Christmas present. You're all I want for Christmas." She pulled him into the archway between the foyer and the dining room, where a thick bunch of mistletoe was pinned up, and kissed him.

The table was laden with more fish dishes than Chris thought existed. Some of them were familiar to him—the stuffed clams, and the mussels marinara—but some were new. When Marty told him that one fish had been marinated in olive oil and white wine, then baked in a paper bag, he said he'd never heard of such a thing. The linguine was served with a thick lobster-and-tomato sauce.

Chris counted twenty-two people, including wives. Christmas was a family holiday in OC; the gummares got New Year's Eve.

After dinner, they sang "Silent Night" around the tree. Then some people got ready to go to Midnight Mass. Anna asked Chris to join them at Mass, but Chris said he was sorry, he couldn't.

He told Marty he'd call her. He shook hands with John. He reached out to Anna and kissed her, for once, before she could kiss him. He held on to her hand and looked at her for a long moment.

"I'm sorry," he said again.

Liz was asleep. Chris tried to be very quiet as he made a pot of coffee. He sat at the kitchen table with coffee and cigarettes. He was watching the sky lighten when he heard the alarm clock, and Liz moving around.

She came into the kitchen, fully dressed. Two shopping bags brimming with gifts stood by the door.

She opened the closet and got her coat. She took a woolly blue hat from the closet shelf, and her warm gloves from the coat pocket.

"Are you coming?" she said.

"No," Chris said. "I'm not coming."

When he heard the door slam, he jumped at the sound.

He looked around, startled. Then he folded his arms and put his head down.

He cried and cried. "Oh, Pop," he mumbled. "Hey, Pop, help me. Please, Pop."

He made another pot of coffee and watched the clock. When he thought Liz would have reached her house, he telephoned. "I'm coming," he said. "I'm leaving now."

"Don't bother," Liz said. "I don't want you to come. I want a divorce."

All that Christmas Day Chris sat in the apartment. Several times he picked up the phone to call somebody, then put it down again. He couldn't speak to his mother or to his sisters. He couldn't speak to Marty. He couldn't speak to Phil. He had nothing to say to anyone, including himself.

In late afternoon, when it was already dark, he went out. He walked up and down Austin Street, his feet stiff with cold.

He thought he never could have imagined a time when he would be glad his father wasn't around. He thought it was a blessing that George had not lived to see how deeply he had disgraced himself, and the family name.

He thought it was incredible that anyone could ever rationalize loving two different women in two different ways because he was two different men. He thought that anyone who could think that way was a rotten person, a liar and deceiver and cheat.

He thought it was as simple as that.

"You've had it, kid," Harry told him. "You're coming up."

"Give me a couple more weeks," Chris pleaded. "I've got some things to do."

"Look, you're going nowhere," Harry said. "You did enough. You've had enough. What else do you have to do, for Chrissake?"

"I just have to figure some things out," Chris said.

"What's the matter?" Harry asked. "What do you have to figure out?"

"Just some things," Chris said desperately. "I just need a little more time, Harry. Please."

"Okay," Harry said in a surprisingly soft voice. "Two weeks, but then I've got to yank you. Two weeks, then you're coming up, that's it, period."

Chris felt he had to prepare Marty—he couldn't just vanish. So he told her he was going out to the Coast. A friend of his was opening a health club in L.A. It was going to be a knockout place, with entertainment—that's how they did things in L.A.—and his friend wanted him to come out and set up the music. Chris told her he didn't know how long he'd be gone—a few weeks, maybe a month, maybe longer.

Once he'd done that, he didn't know what else he had to do. He didn't go back down to Mulberry Street. He'd gone back a couple of times, after the TV deal, because he didn't want to just disappear. He'd played some cards, hung around a while, engaged in some conversations. Everybody was talking about the dog. When the caretaker had come by at six o'clock to take Duke out, the dog had lifted its leg against a hydrant and keeled over. Duke went out like a light and had to be dragged back inside. "The fucking dog was drunk!" they kept saying. "He was stupified!"

There wasn't a lock made that the black baggers couldn't handle, no piece of equipment they didn't find a use for, including tranquilizing guns.

He went to see his mother. When he found that Katrina had turned part of his room into a storeroom, with boxes stacked along the wall, some old toys, a tricycle that his nephew had outgrown, he resented it a little. That had always been his room, with his books—the set of encyclopedias Katrina had bought, when he was in fourth or fifth grade—and the drums packed away in the closet. There was a framed newspaper article on the wall: HERO COPS TIP SCALES OF JUSTICE FOR A SLUM CHILD

He went over to the Grotto and had a drink with Kostos. He had lunch at Stani Sistaria, with its plaintive Greek music and sentimental oil paintings of Mediterranean scenes on the walls. He walked past the building on 23rd Road. The weasel's place downstairs looked busy, but the C&G club was closed. Gene's wife had refused to take him back; Gene had gone to Florida. The place had served its purpose: Like many clubs, it had allowed him to do some social climbing.

He went to the urologist. He thought it was funny that, for all of today's high-tech equipment and sophisticated medical procedures, the doctor still used just a flashlight in a darkened room.

"How long have you had this?" the doctor demanded.

"About a year, year and a half," Chris said.

The doctor stared at him. "Why didn't you come to me sooner?"

"I was busy," Chris said.

"Are you *crazy?*" the doctor said. "I should take your own gun and beat you over the head with it. This has to come out."

"I know," Chris said. "I'll have to have that done sometime, I guess."

"*Now,*" the doctor said. "It has to come out *now.*" He pointed his finger at Chris sternly, but his voice was gentle. "Do you know what this could be?" he asked.

"Yes, I know," Chris said.

Marty insisted on driving him to the airport. He was going to L.A., and when he got there, he was going to turn around and come back. He knew he could have handled it more simply, without flying all the way out to L.A. for nothing, but it seemed important that Marty see him leave, knowing he was going far away. He showed her his ticket.

"Just drop me off," Chris said. "You don't have to bother parking."

"I know I don't *have* to," Marty said. "I want to. I want to be with you till the last minute."

They walked to the ticket counter, where he got his boarding pass. They went through security and down to the gate. Thank God the plane was already boarding.

"Here's your Christmas present," Marty said. She handed

him a small package wrapped in plain white tissue paper. "Don't open it now, there's no time. Open it later."

He slipped the package into his pocket.

Marty began to cry.

He wanted to cheer her up. He wanted to take her in his arms and comfort her, tell her everything would be all right. But he had lied long enough. So he just held her face between his hands and said what he'd always found so difficult to say. He told her the truth.

"I love you," he said.

EPILOGUE

In January, 1980, Chris had surgery for testicular cancer. He was given a 65 percent chance of surviving. He thought those were good odds, considering.

On February 13, 1980, a Gambino soldier from Brooklyn met with Sicilians in Palermo to arrange for the shipment of 40.6 kilograms of heroin, worth one hundred million dollars, to New York via Milan.

When Chris left the hospital, he moved into a studio apartment near the little beach where he and Phil had met. He kept a portable police radio near him at all times, because Harry thought that Chris should be able to communicate with the department instantly, if he needed to. Chris thought so too. He continued to sleep with the lights on.

In July, 1980 and in December, 1980, armored-car robberies took place in Queens and in Brooklyn. One robber used a gun with a red barrel.

Chris was in and out of the hospital all year, taking massive doses of chemotherapy. His curly hair fell out in chunks. He vomited so severely that he tied a robe around his stomach to keep his insides in place. Phil came to see him every day. Chris lost fifty pounds. Phil lost twenty.

In the summer of 1980, Chris met Nick Gregoris outside the McDonald's on Cross Bay Boulevard. Chris told Nick he'd been on the West Coast. Nick smiled and said that's what he'd heard.

In 1980, electronic listening devices at the Ravenite Social Club recorded conversations about the murder of Carmine Galante.

In November, 1980, Chris had a second operation. He was cut open, breastbone to groin, in a procedure that took ten hours. The surgeon told Chris that the purpose of the operation was not to prolong Chris's life, but to save it. The surgery took place on Election Day, so Chris didn't vote that year, either.

In February, 1981, the gunman with the red-barreled weapon was sentenced for the armored-car robberies.

In March, 1981, Chris returned to full-time duty with the New York Police Department. Phil thought Chris hadn't wanted to return until all his hair grew back. When Chris was assigned to diplomatic escort, Katrina made him a tuxedo of wool and rayon.

It was suggested to Chris that he return to John's house and borrow $50,000, so that John could be charged with usury. Chris declined. It was suggested that he change his identity, leave New York, and live under a protection program. He declined.

On January 26, 1982, the men who had met in Palermo were among several dozen men indicted in Italy for drug trafficking and conspiracy.

At 4:30 A.M. on May 8, 1982, Nick Gregoris and three other men were gunned down at the corner of 156th Avenue and Cross Bay Boulevard. Nick died instantly, with four bullets in his upper chest, and a shotgun blast.

On September 3, 1982, an undercover cop with the NYPD, a woman, was stabbed while attempting a "buy and bust" with a drug dealer on the street.

In June, 1983, the Italian court convicted the defendants of heroin trafficking. More arrests and convictions followed, in Italy and in the United States, in cases involving the FBI, the DEA, and other agencies, as well as the NYPD. Organized crime figures in this country were shown to have worked often through some Sicilian immigrants, nicknamed "zips."

In February, 1985, Aniello Dellacroce and Paul Castellano were among several men indicted on charges of operating a "Mafia Commission." Dellacroce, his son Armond, and John Gotti were indicted on RICO charges of conspiracy and racketeering.

In November, 1985, Chris was transferred from diplomatic escort and reassigned to undercover work.

On December 2, 1985, Aniello Dellacroce died of cancer at Mary Immaculate Hospital in Queens, where he had been admitted as "Timothy O'Neil."

On December 6, 1985, Armond Dellacroce pleaded guilty. He disappeared before trial.

On December 16, 1985, Paul Castellano was shot six times in the head and chest as he got out of a car in front of Sparks Steak House in Manhattan. He took his driver with him.

On November 19, 1986, eight organized crime figures were convicted of operating a "Mafia Commission." One of them was Anthony Corallo, head of the Luchese crime family.

On January 13, 1987, seven of the eight men were sentenced to one hundred years in prison. Apiece. In court, a prosecutor called it a "never-before day." Law enforcement officials gave credit for the convictions to a series of successful undercover operations, involving the use of "probable cause" to allow the placing of listening devices and hidden cameras. A detective who was part of the operations on Mulberry Street says that Chris appears in a surveillance photo, but Chris has never seen it. He never saw the photograph of him and Marty, either.

In June, 1987, Chris went down to Little Italy. He didn't see the Penguin, but he saw Solly standing in front of a pizza place on Prince Street, smoking a cigarette. Chris was wearing jeans, a leather jacket, and a cap, while at the Kew he'd always been impeccably dressed. Still, Chris turned back. Why take the chance?

In April, 1988, Armond Dellacroce died in Pennsylvania, where he had been living as a fugitive.

Since the Mafia Commission verdict, more OC figures have been tried under RICO. John Gotti has been acquitted. Among those convicted was Frankie's uncle. More trials are expected.

Chris still lives in the little apartment near the beach, with his books and records and his favorite Hopper print, "Early Sunday Morning." There are no people in that picture, just a persistent sense of loneliness.

Liz came to see Chris when he was in the hospital the first time. He has not seen her since. Bing came then too, bringing a pair of slippers. Chris reminded Bing he'd told him it was going to be all right.

He has stopped drinking. His regular checkups show no recurrence of cancer. He doesn't go to the opera anymore, or to museums. He chooses restaurants carefully, and does a grid search. He wears dark glasses. At the racetrack he saw both Kostos and Frankie. Neither man saw him. He goes to the movies often. He saw *An Officer and a Gentleman* as soon as it came out. "Piece of cake," he said.

He sees his mother nearly every Sunday. Katrina has been offered half a million dollars for the house in Queens that George bought for sixteen thousand dollars cash, but she will not sell. Why would a person want to leave home? Chris has not yet gone back to Maple Grove Cemetery, but he intends to go, someday. At some point, atonement has been made, or what is redemption all about?

He still reads a lot, including *Bulfinch's Mythology*. There's always a lesson there. Bulfinch seems uncertain about the lesson of Jason, though. He suggests that perhaps, in the end, golden prizes may not be worth it. Bulfinch just relates in a straightforward way what Jason did—some heroic things, some things unworthy of a hero. He makes clear that Jason did what he was sent out to do. Jason accomplished his mission. Beyond that, Bulfinch doesn't analyze or assess the blame. Maybe he thought it wasn't as simple as that.

Chris never saw Marty again. When he thought he might die, he considered calling her. But he didn't know what to say, except he'd always wanted to tell her he'd met the Pope. On his flight to Los Angeles, he opened her present. It was the Florentine cross—blue enamel, with a thin overlay of gold. He keeps it in a safe-deposit box to give to his niece when she gets married.

When he was sick, Chris got a letter from Chief Bouza, who had taken an interest in him early on. "I always wanted to be a cop just like you," the chief wrote. But Chris can never be a cop in the way he was. His undercover experience has made him too valuable to be sent back to the 4-oh. He's still with the Intelligence Division, on undercover jobs. But now he's not living it; he's just doing it. He has been a hospital porter, a construction worker, an electrician, and an elevator starter. As a member of the team investigating corruption in the Health Department, he worked in a coffee shop.

The bad-cop story has been deleted from his file. But because he's still undercover, his name didn't go back on the roster. Anyone calling for him will be told there's no one by that name in the New York Police Department. His name is "off the wheel." No such person exists.

He belongs, though. He can even attend meetings of the Honor Legion again. He always carries his gold shield, which Harry brought to him in the hospital. Harry had been keeping it in his locker downtown. It shows the emblem of the City of New York on blue enamel, with gold around the edges.